BUCKLING-RESTRAINED BRACES
AND APPLICATIONS

Edited by

Toru Takeuchi and Akira Wada

The Japan Society of Seismic Isolation

Editing members

Akira Wada   Advisory editor, President JSSI, Prof. Emeritus Tokyo Institute of Technology
Toru Takeuchi   Chief editor, Prof. Tokyo Institute of Technology, Japan
Ryota Matsui   Assoc. Prof. Hokkaido University, Japan
Ben Sitler   Tokyo Institute of Technology, Former Structural Engineer, Arup
Pao-Chun Lin   Assis. Prof. National Cheng Kung University, Taiwan
Fatih Sutcu   Assis. Prof. Istanbul Technical University, Turkey
Hiroyasu Sakata   Prof. Tokyo Institute of Technology, Japan
Zhe Qu   Prof. Institute of Engineering Mechanics, CEA, China

Notice

The copyright of this book belongs to Toru Takeuchi, Akira Wada and JSSI (The Japan Society of Seismic Isolation). All rights reserved. No part of this publication may be reproduced, stored in a retrieval system, or transmitted, in any form or by any means, electronic, mechanical, photocopying, recording, or other, without the prior written permission of the publishers.

Disclaimer

Neither JSSI, nor its committees, editing members, or individuals who have contributed to this document provide any warranty or assume any legal liability or responsibility for the use, and/or application of the contents of this document. Individuals who use this document in any way assume all risk and accept total responsibility for the application and use of this information.

This book is written in English by the above editing members for JSSI in 2017.

JSSI was established in 1993 with the primary aim of promoting seismic isolation, thereby contributing to the construction of safer and higher quality buildings, resulting in a more prosperous society.
Objectives:
· Promotion of investigation and research on seismic isolation for buildings.
· Dissemination of information on the proper usage of seismic isolation and improvement of seismic isolation technology.
· Exchanging information about seismic isolation in partnership with organizations of other countries.
· Contribution to the development and improvement of reliable seismic-resistant technology.
· Contribution to a safer living environment and broadening of the interests of society.
JSSI Members:
· Construction Companies
· Architectural and Structural Design Offices
· Device Manufacturers
· Academics
ISBN978-4-909458-01-8

Contents

Preface

Chapter 1: Composition and history of buckling-restrained braces   1

     1.1 Composition of buckling-restrained braces   2

     1.2 History of development   3

     1.3 Types of BRBs   6

Chapter 2: Restrainer design and clearances   11

     2.1 Restrainer design   12

     2.2 Debonding gap   17

     2.3 Core material and overstrength   18

     2.4 Hysteretic models for analysis   20

     2.5 Quality requirement for stable hysteresis   23

Chapter 3: Local bulging failure   25

     3.1 Failure caused by local buckling   26

     3.2 Estimation of outward force demand   28

     3.3 Local buckling wavelength estimation   28

     3.4 Estimation of steel tube capacity   30

     3.5 Test results and evaluations   33

     3.6 Required mortar strength   43

     3.7 Local bulging criterion for circular restrainer   44

     3.8 Summary   45

Chapter 4: Connection design and global stability   47

     4.1 Typical connection details and design forces   48

     4.2 Global instability including connections   49

     4.3 Stability condition with one-way configuration   57

     4.4 Stability condition with chevron configuration   70

     4.5 Evaluation for key parameters   78

     4.6 Connection design against in-plane deformation   81

Chapter 5: Cumulative deformation capacity 87

5.1 Low-cycle fatigue induced fracture 88

5.2 Effect of the debonding clearance 101

5.3 Effect of the plastic core length 108

Chapter 6: Performance test specification for BRB 111

6.1 Test configurations 112

6.2 Test resume and loading protocol 114

6.3 Qualification requirements 118

6.4 Post-earthquake inspection 118

Chapter 7: BRBF Applications 123

7.1 Damage tolerant concept 124

7.2 Response evaluation of BRBF 133

7.3 Seismic retrofit with BRBs 147

7.4 Response evaluation of BRBs retrofit for RC frames 157

7.5 Direct connections to RC frames 172

7.6 Applications for truss and spatial structures 190

7.7 Spine frame concepts 205

Appendix 223

A.1 Typical BRB details 224

A.2 Rotational spring at connections 228

A.3 BRB buckling capacity 232

A.4 Pδ moment distribution at connection zone 237

Index 238

Preface

As we live on Earth, it is necessary to build structures that can resist gravity, as well as the demands imposed by natural phenomena such as earthquakes, strong winds and heavy snowfall. Structural engineers are charged with designing efficient and elegant buildings or bridges, while ensuring that the structure can safely withstand these demands. It takes great ingenuity to achieve these competing objectives.

Although major structures are composed of timber, reinforced concrete or steel, all of which are economic materials with good structural properties, steel has proved to be uniquely useful. The unit weights of timber, reinforced concrete and steel are 0.5, 2.4 and 7.85 t/m^3, respectively. However, timber has low stiffness and is relatively weak, particularly at the connections. While concrete has proven to be economic, the compressive strength is only 10~30% of steel, and the tensile strength is almost negligible. To overcome these limitations, steel is used in the connections or to provide the tensile capacity. Steel is an elegant resource, providing 10 times the stiffness of concrete, equal tensile and compressive strengths, and large ductility.

For timber or reinforced concrete structures, solid sections such as rectangular or circular shapes are generally required. However, steel members can be easily fabricated in all types of shapes including I/H sections, angles, channels, pipes, and boxes. This results in a more efficient use of material and produces lighter structures.

To take full advantage of steel as a structural material, it is necessary to consider several important design criteria, summarized as follows.

1. Details
Steel is first produced as plates or hot rolled section in steel mills, and then cut, spliced and bent by fabricators to achieve the desired member geometry. Modern frames are assembled either by bolting or welding, which leads to short construction periods, particularly relative to concrete structures. Therefore, a well detailed structure and due consideration of the construction process is necessary to achieve a good design.

2. Deflection
Although the material properties of steel, such as stiffness and strength are relatively large, the required area and moment of inertia are generally smaller compared to timber or reinforced concrete structures. Therefore, steel members are often slender, with performance determined by member deflection, overall structural deformations or vibration. Additionally, flexural and lateral torsional buckling are critical issues, and attention must be paid to local buckling when a plate is thin relative to its width.

3. Stress
Introductory structural engineering classes frequently focus on the stress distribution due to axial force or bending moments. Although strength is essential, many other checks are required to avoid instabilities or unexpected large deflections.

Buckling of slender steel members subject to compression has intrigued engineers since at least 1799 when the Iron Bridge was completed in England. One of the most famous theories of buckling behavior is the Shanley model, considering the inelastic buckling capacity of column members.

Pure axial compression imposes uniform stresses, but to ensure lateral stability, flexural stiffness is also required. However, members of moderate slenderness ratios will buckle below the Euler's elastic buckling strength. This is due to destabilizing $P\delta$ moments introduced by geometric imperfections, as well as early yielding due to compressive residual stresses at the cross section extremities. As a result, the compressive resistance of non-compact members deteriorates prior to the nominal axial yield force.

The buckling behavior of structural members is complicated even under monotonic uniaxial loading. Braces used to resist seismic forces are subjected to cyclic loads, which further complicates the buckling behavior. Plastic ductility demands can be limited by enlarging or shortening the braces to increase the buckling load, but this imposes larger demands on the columns, beams and foundations. Particularly in chevron configurations, the unbalanced tension and compression strengths create large demands on the beams.

The coupled relationship between the axial capacity and lateral stiffness complicates the brace performance. When these two functions are isolated, the hysteretic behavior is greatly simplified and repeatable stable behavior can be obtained. This is the fundamental concept of the buckling restrained brace. An important distinction is that buckling is restrained, but not completely eliminated. A small debonding gap is still required to accommodate transverse Poisson expansion of the core member, permitting small amplitude higher mode buckling waves to form.

Buckling-restrained braces provide uniquely efficient hysteretic behavior and have a wide range of uses, limited only by the engineer's ingenuity. Modern buckling restrained braces are used not only for buildings, but also for long span bridges and other spatial structures. While buckling-restrained braces were developed in Japan, they are now widely used throughout the world. To use the buckling-restrained brace properly, I truly expect structural engineers and researchers to read and study the contents of this book deeply.

Akira Wada
Professor Emeritus
Tokyo Institute of Technology

Notations

Page

a_c	initial deflection at midspan in restrained part	13
a_{eq}	acceleration response of SDOF model constituted by frame and damper	135
a_f	acceleration response of SDOF model consituted by frame	135
a_r	initial imperfection at restrainer end	57
c_r	restrainer end modal Pδ moment distribution factor	58
e	axial force eccentricity	14
h_0	initial damping ratio	134
h_B	depth of beams	172
h_d	damping ratio of BRB	161
h_{eq}	average equivalent damping ratio for random amplitude	134
h_{eq}'	equivalent damping ratio for constant amplitude	134
h_f	damping ratio of RC frame	161
i_c	radius of gyration at connection zone	56
l_B	restrained zone length	13
l_p	half lengths of local buckling wavelength	102
$l_{p,s}$	in-plane buckling wavelength	28
$l_{p,w}$	out-of-plane buckling wavelength	28
n_i	number of cycles for strain range $\Delta\varepsilon_i$	90
m_i	mass of each story	137
p	ratio of secant stiffness of frame at a given story to initial stiffness	159
s_r	clearance between core and restrainer (per face)	14
s_{rw}	clearance between core and restrainer in the weak axis (per face)	26
s_{rs}	clearance between core and restrainer in the strong axis (per face)	26
t_c	thickness of core plate	26
t_m	mortar thickness between core and steel tube wall inner face	42
t_r	thickness of restrainer	31
u_d	axial deformation of BRB	22
y_r	total out-of-plane deformation at restrainer end	60
y_{re}	restrainer end out-of-plane deformation due to connection flexure	61
y_{rs}	restrainer end out-of-plane deformation due to gusset spring rotation	61
y_{r1}	total restrainer end out-of-plane deformation at column connection end (chevron configuration)	71
y_{r2}	total restrainer end out-of-plane deformation at beam connection	

	end (chevron configuration)	71
y_{re1}	restrainer end out-of-plane deformation due to connection flexure at the column connection end (chevron configuration)	71
y_{re2}	restrainer end out-of-plane deformation due to connection flexure at the beam connection end (chevron configuration)	71
y_{rs1}	restrainer end deformation due to gusset spring rotation at the column connection end (chevron configuration)	71
y_{rs2}	restrainer end deformation due to gusset spring rotation at the beam connection end (chevron configuration)	71
A_c	cross section area of the core (plastic zone)	20
A_e	cross section area of the neck (core elastic zone)	20
A_i	story shear coefficient	137
B_c	core plate width	26
B_i	shear force ratio	137
B_n	core plate width at restrainer-end zone	53
B_r	Restrainer width (rectangular)	26
C_B	base shear ratio	137
C_d	damping factor of damper	133
D_r	Restrainer depth (rectangular and circular)	26
E	modulus of elasticity of steel	13
E_t	tangent modulus of steel	29
F_h	response reduction ratio by damping	135
H_i	height of i-th story from ground	158
H_{eq}	equivalent height of SDOF model	158
I_B	moment of inertia of restrainer (restraint tube)	13
K_{ai}	combined stiffness of both damper and connection of each story	133
K_b	connection stiffness	133
K_{bi}	connection stiffness at i-th story	133
K_d	horizontal stiffness of damper (BRB)	128
K_{di}	horizontal stiffness of damper at i-th story	133
$K_{d\mu}$	secant stiffness of damper at a given deformation	160
K_{eq}	equivalent horizontal stiffness of SDOF model	134
K_f	horizontal stiffness of main frame	128
K_{fi}	horizontal stiffness of main frame at i-th story	133
K_{fy}	secant stiffness of frame at yield	158
$K_{f\mu}$	secant stiffness of frame at a given ductility	158
K_{Rg}	gusset rotational stiffness	51

K_{Rg1}	gusset rotational stiffness at the column connection (chevron configuration)	71
K'_{Rg2}	gusset rotational stiffness at the beam connection (chevron configuration)	71
K_{Rg2}	gusset rotational stiffness at the beam connection, reduced to account for the stiffness of the attached beam (chevron configuration)	71
K_{SF}	initial stiffness of steel frame	160
$K_{\Sigma\mu}$	total secant stiffness	161
L_0	total length of BRB including connections	19
L_p	plastic zone length of core plate	19
L_{in}	insert zone length at restrainer end	53
$M_0{}^r$	imposed bending moment at restrainer end due to out-of-plane drift	60
M_{eq}	equivalent mass of SDOF model	137
$M_y{}^B$	bending strength of restrainer	14
$M_p{}^g$	plastic bending strength of gusset plate including axial force effect	63
$M_p{}^r$	restrainer moment transfer capacity	60
$M_p{}^{r-neck}$	restrainer moment transfer capacity determined by cruciform core plate at neck	63
$M_p{}^{r-rest}$	restrainer moment transfer capacity determined by restrainer section at rib-end	63
N	axial force	13
N_{cu}	maximum axial strength of core plate	18
$N_{cr}{}^B$	global elastic buckling strength of BRB including effect of gusset plate rotational stiffness	79
$N_{cr}{}^E$	elastic buckling strength of BRB restrainer	14
$N_{cr}{}^r$	elasto-plastic buckling strength with pin conditions at restrainer ends	56
$N_{cr}{}^R$	elastic buckling strength with pin conditions at restrainer ends	56
$N_{cr}{}^P$	elastic buckling capacity for mode shape considering yield at gusset and restrainer end	60
N_{lim1}	expected failure force assuming elastic gusset plates	62
N_{lim2}	expected failure force assuming plastic hinges at gusset plates	63
$N_u{}^c$	ultimate axial strength of cruciform core plate at neck	63
$N_{wy}{}^c$	yield axial force of cruciform core plate at web zone	63
N_y	yield axial force of core plate	18
Q_B	base shear	137
Q_{fc}	cracking shear of RC frame	158
$Q_{FS\mu}$	horizontal strength of steel frame	160

Q_{fy}	yield base shear of RC frame	158
Q_i	story shear	137
T_0	initial natural period	134
T_{eq}	equivalent natural period of SDOF model	134
Z_{cp}	plastic section modulus at neck	63
Z_{rp}	plastic section modulus of restrainer tube	64
α_c	strain concentration ratio	105
$_d\alpha$	overstrength strain hardening factor (not defined in p.14)	14
$_e\alpha$	overall safety factor for BRB	15
β	compressive-to-tension overstrength factor	18
$\beta_{(g,r)}$	moment shift factor due to locked in axial force considering yield at gusset and restrainer end $(=(1-N_{cr}^P/N_{cr}^B)/c_{(g,r)})$	60
γ_s	stiffness ratio of steel frame to damper	160
$\gamma_J, (\gamma)$	bending stiffness ratio of connection zone	51
$\delta_{(y)}$	axial (yield) deformation	20
δ_{dy}	story drift at damper yield	160
δ_{eq}	displacement response of SDOF model constituted by frame and damper	135
δ_f	displacement response of SDOF model constituted by frame	135
δ_{fc}	craking displacement of SDOF model of RC frame	158
δ_{fy}	yield displacement of SDOF model of main frame	158
ε_y	axial yield strain of core plate $(=N_y/EA_c)$	20
ε_{max}	maximum core plate strain	17
$\varepsilon_n, \varepsilon_{eq}$	normalized axial deformation $(=\delta/L_p)$	76
ΔH_i	height of i-th story	142
$\Delta\varepsilon_h$	local strain range	105
$\Delta\varepsilon_{eq}$	normalized axial deformation range	101
ε_{eqtm}	maximum value of the normalized axial deformation in tensile side	102
$\Delta\varepsilon_p$	plastic strain range $(=\Delta\varepsilon_{eq}-2\varepsilon_y)$	88
$\overline{\Delta\varepsilon_p}$	average plastic strain range $(\sum\Delta\varepsilon_p/2N_f)$	108
$\overline{\Delta\varepsilon_{ph}}$	average plastic strain amplitude (half plastic strain range, $=\overline{\Delta\varepsilon_p}/2$)	88
$\sum\Delta\varepsilon_p$	cumulative plastic strain	108
η_d	loss factor	133
ν_p	plastic Poisson ratio	17
χ	cumulative strain	94
χ_w	normalized cumulative absorbed energy $(=E_p^d/\sigma_{cy}A_c)$	98

$_\xi K_{Rg}$	normalized rotational stiffness for gusset plate ··	57
$_L K_{Rg}$	normalized rotational stiffness for gusset plate by total length ·············	79
$_\xi K_{Rg1}$	normalized rotational stiffness for column-side gusset plate $(=K_{Rg1}\xi_1 L_0/\gamma_J E I_B)$ ··	71
$_\xi K_{Rg2}$	normalized rotational stiffness for beam-side gusset plate $(=K_{Rg2}\xi_2 L_0/\gamma_J E I_B)$ ··	71
λ_r	equivalent slenderness ratio for global elastic buckling strength with pin conditions at restrainer ends ··	73
θ_0	initial imperfection angle of connection zone ·································	57
$\theta_{(i)}$	target drift angle of each story (at i-th story) ·································	142
θ_{dy}	damper yield drift ··	133
θ_{dyi}	damper yield drift of each story ···	133
θ_{fu}	maximum story drift angle before retrofit ···	162
$\theta_{\Sigma tar}$	story drift at target ···	162
σ_{cy}	yield strength of core plate material ··	29
σ_{ry}	yield strength of restrainer tube material ··	31
σ_n, σ_{eq}	normalized strength of BRB $(= N/A_c)$ ···	76
μ	ductility ratio ···	20
μ_c	ductility ratio of RC frame at cracking ··	158
μ_d	ductility ratio of damper ··	160
μ_f	ductility ratio of main frame ··	163
μ_{tar}	target ductility of retrofitting project ···	160
ξ	connection zone length ratio ···	51
ξ'	length between gusset plate end and rib end ratio$(= \xi + L_{in} / L_0)$ ···········	58
ξ_1	connection zone length at column-side ratio (chevron configuration) ······	71
ξ_2	connection zone length at beam-side ratio (chevron configuration) ········	71

Chapter 1

COMPOSITION AND HISTORY OF BUCKLING-RESTRAINED BRACES

CHAPTER CONTENTS

1.1 COMPOSITION OF BUCKLING-RESTRAINED BRACES

1.2 HISTORY OF DEVELOPMENT

1.3 TYPES OF BRBS

1.1 COMPOSITION OF BUCKLING-RESTRAINED BRACES

The buckling-restrained brace (BRB) is a seismic device consisting of an axially yielding core and axially-decoupled restraining mechanism, which supresses overall buckling. As shown in Figure 1.1.1, the buckling restrainer is often composed of an outer steel hollow section with in-filled mortar and a debonding layer surrounding the core. However, a number of other restrainer shapes and material combinations are currently in use, as shown in Figures 1.1.2 and 1.1.3. The thin debonding layer or gap provided between the core and the restrainer is an essential feature of modern BRBs, limiting axial load transfer to the restrainer by providing a low friction interface and accommodating lateral expansion of the core resulting from Poisson effects. Under compressive demands and prior to yielding, the core will start to buckle with progressively higher mode shapes developing due to the presence of the restrainer as shown in Figure 1.1.4. As buckling is constrained rather than completely eliminated, yielding is not purely axial. As a result, BRBs do not achieve the same cumulative fatigue capacity as a uniaxial coupon test. Never-the-less, the energy dissipation characteristics are excellent and compare favourably against other fully ductile

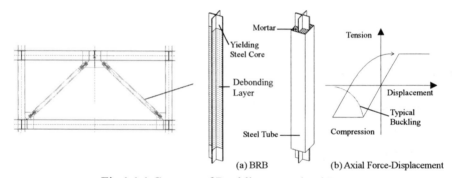

Fig 1.1.1 Concept of Buckling-restrained Brace

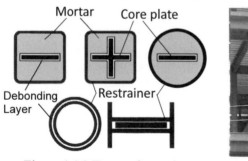

Figure 1.1.2 Types of restrainers

Figure 1.1.3 Typical BRB application

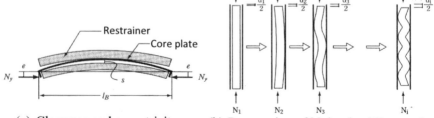

(a) Clearance and eccentricity (b) Progression of higher buckling mode
Figure 1.1.4 Buckling modes within the restrainer

systems. For the reason, BRBs can be employed as hysteretic dampers.

The hysteretic characteristics are stable and nearly symmetric once the full cross section has yielded, differing only slightly from the base material hysteresis, as shown in Figure 1.1.5. Since buckling is restrained, no associated degradation should be visible during the compression cycles. However, the normal force associated with the higher mode buckling results in friction and some load transfer to the restrainer, slightly increasing the apparent compressive force. Despite this unique overstrength behavior, BRBs can be modelled using truss elements and uniaxial material hysteresis rules, assuming strain is spread along the full plastic core length.

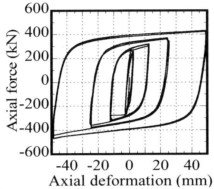

Figure 1.1.5 Hysteresis of well-designed BRB

1.2 HISTORY OF DEVELOPMENT

The basic concepts of buckling-restrained braces date from the 1970's, when limited successes were reported by several researchers in Japan and India. Takeda et al. [1.1] in 1972 tried to improve the post-buckling behaviour of H-section braces by encasing the steel section in reinforced concrete, and confirmed an improvement in performance. However, because no debonding mechanism was provided between the core and concrete restrainer, the restrainer received a significant portion of the compressive force, cracked and ultimately experienced overall buckling. Kimura et al. [1.2] reported the performance of braces consisting of a conventional brace encased in a mortar-filled square steel pipe. While a few stable plastic cycles were achieved, it was found that the transverse deformation of the mortar resulted in a permanent void space sufficiently large to allow local buckling. In 1973, Wakabayashi et al. [1.3] proposed a precast concrete wall with encased steel plate braces separately by a debonding layer. This wall showed stable hysteresis up to 2.5% story drift angle, and then failed due to local buckling. In 1979, Mochizuki et al. [1.4] proposed a brace with an unbonded core plate and reinforced concrete restrainer. This proved successful in decoupling the restrainer and the hysteretic properties were similar to that of the core plate. However, the system tended to buckle at the unrestrained core extension, and would consequently become unstable after several cycles due to cracking and deterioration of the concrete restrainer.

The first practical buckling-restrained brace was achieved by Saeki, Wada, et al. [1.5], [1.6] (Figure 1.2.1) in 1988. They employed rectangular steel tubes with in-filled mortar for the restrainer, and determined the optimal debonding material specifications to obtain stable and symmetric hysteresis behaviour. In addition, the basic theory to design the restrainer was established and the first project application soon followed. In 1989, these BRBs (Unbonded Braces) were applied to the 10 and

15-story steel frame office buildings shown in Figure 1.2.1 as the first project worldwide to use BRBs (Fujimoto et al., 1990) [1.7]. BRBs soon increased in popularity and other configurations soon followed, notably the all steel tube-in-tube type shown in the bottom left of Figure 1.1.2. Through the 1990's, BRBs were used in around 160 buildings in Japan. Some of these were up to 20m in length, as shown in Figure 1.2.2. In July 1995, the "Damage Tolerant Structure" was proposed by Wada, Iwata, et al. [1.8] (Figure 1.2.3), which uses BRBs as energy dissipating elasto-plastic dampers within an elastic main frame and is now commonly used in Japan. The AIJ design recommendations first included BRBs design guidelines in 1996 [1.9].

(a) Cyclic loading experiments in 1987

(b) The first BRB structure (Nippon Steel Second HQ. 1989)
Figure 1.2.1 First practical BRBs in application

Figure 1.2.2 Jumbo BRBs for Osaka International Convention Center (1997)

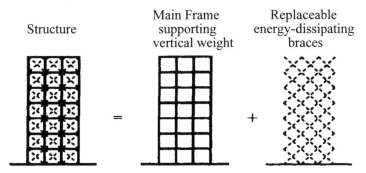

Figure 1.2.3 Damage Tolerant Concept [1.6]

Collaboration with US colleagues soon led to the first international application with the construction of the Plant & Environmental Sciences Building at UC Davis in 1998, followed by an experiment at UC Berkeley in 2000 [1.10] (Figure 1.2.4(a)). Numerous other buildings with BRBs were soon constructed throughout California, including in seismic retrofit applications as shown in Figure 1.2.4(b). In 2002, design guidance for buckling-restrained braced frame (BRBF) was included in the Seismic Provisions for Structural Steel Buildings (ANSI/AISC 341-05) [1.11].

During these early years of technology transfer to international markets, a series of symposiums on passively-controlled structures were held at Tokyo Institute of Technology, sharing code developments, BRB design and novel applications [1.12]. Through the following decade, BRBs increased in popularity in numerous countries, from Taiwan in the early 2000's [1.13] to the recent implementations in New Zealand as part of the Christchurch rebuild. BRBs are now widely known in seismic areas throughout the world, with research ongoing in countries including Japan, Taiwan, China, U.S., Canada, Turkey, Iran, Italy, Romania, New Zealand and Chile, among others.

(a) Plant & Environmental Sciences, UC Davis   (b) Bennett Federal Building Retrofit/ Salt Lake City

Figure 1.2.4 Early US applications in 2000's

1.3 TYPES OF BRBS

While several suppliers export internationally, a remarkable range of unique BRB designs are used locally in various countries, distinguished by restrainer shape and/or core material, debonding material, core shape and connection type. Representative types are shown in Figure 1.3.1.

The most popular BRB composition features a rectangular or cruciform steel core restrained by a mortar-filled rectangular or circular hollow section, as shown in Figure 1.3.1(a) [1.14-16]. While the fabrication time, cost and weight can be higher than some other designs, this type of BRB offers the best performance, assuming that the design criteria specified in Chapters 3 to 5 is followed. Numerous variations of this design have been proposed using alternative restrainers or in-fill materials, though the specific material used for the debonding layer is typically not published. End connections can be categorized as bolted, welded or pin-ended and suppliers typically have patented details featuring various advantages. Regardless of the specific combination, performance of the BRB is sensitive to the tolerances and fabrication quality. Therefore, it is important that each new system or manufacturer be validated with full-scale testing as described in Chapter 6.

Figure 1.3.1 (b) shows the tube-in-tube type BRB [1.16]. The yielding core member is a circular hollow section, with buckling restraint provided by a second circular tube positioned either inside or outside. Although the restrainer is effective in preventing overall buckling, local buckling can still occur, leading to friction and a tendency for plastic strains to concentrate near the ends.

Figure 1.3.1 (c) shows an all-steel configuration with a longitudinally welded restrainer. This type of BRB is lightweight as infill mortar is not required, although the restrainer plates tend to be thicker to satisfy the bending stiffness requirement. Furthermore, preventing local bulging as discussed in Chapter 3 is more difficult, as the out-of-plane forces caused by local buckling of the core member directly apply concentrated demands on the restrainer walls.

Figure 1.3.1 (d) presents another all-steel configuration where the restrainer can be bolted on site. While this composition has advantages in assembly and inspection, the bolted joints must be carefully designed for the local out-of-plane forces due to higher mode buckling. Also, it is difficult to achieve significant moment-transfer at the restrainer ends, which is beneficial for satisfying the stability requirements discussed in Chapter 4.

Even in these all-steel BRBs, the tolerance of the clearances is depending on the fabrication process, which has effects on the performance. Therefore, performance of these types of BRBs also have to be confirmed with the real-size mock-up tests defined in Chapter 6.

Chapter 1. Composition and history of Buckling-restrained Braces   7

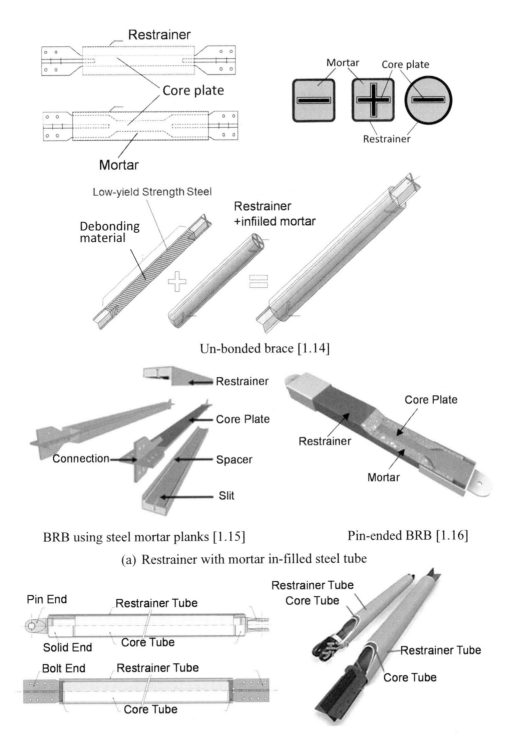

Figure 1.3.1 Representative types of BRB compositions-1

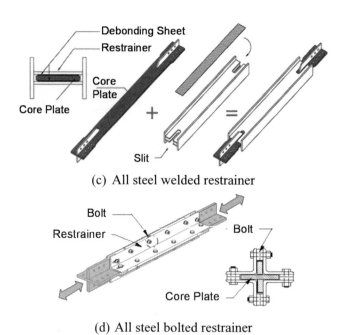

(c) All steel welded restrainer

(d) All steel bolted restrainer

Figure 1.3.1 Representative types of BRB compositions-2

References

[1.1] Takeda T, Takemoto Y, Furuya Y: An experimental study on moment frame with steel braces Part 3, *Summaries of technical papers of Annual Meeting Architectural Institute of Japan*, 1972; **47**:1389-1390. (*in Japanese*)

[1.2] Kimura K, Takeda Y, Yoshioka K, Furuya N, and Takemoto Y: An experimental study on braces encased in steel tube and mortar, *Summaries of technical papers of Annual Meeting Architectural Institute of Japan*, 1976; **51**:1041-1042. (*in Japanese*)

[1.3] Wakabayashi M, Nakamura T, Kashihara A, Morisono T, Yokoyama H: Experimental studies on Precast concrete wall including un-bonded braces under cyclic loading Part 1, *Summaries of technical papers of Annual Meeting Architectural Institute of Japan*, 1973; **48**:1041-1042. (*in Japanese*)

[1.4] Mochizuki S, Murata Y, Ando S, Takahashi S: An experimental study on the buckling behaviour of steel braces with concentric axial forces Part 1, *Summaries of technical papers of Annual Meeting Architectural Institute of Japan*, 1979; **54**:1623-1624. (*in Japanese*)

[1.5] Fujimoto M, Wada A, Saeki E, Watanabe A, Hitomi Y: A study on the unbounded brace encased in buckling-restraining concrete and steel tube, *Journal of Structural Engineering*, 1988; **34B**:249-258. (*in Japanese*)

[1.6] Watanabe A, Hitomi Y, Saeki E, Wada A, Fujimoto M: Properties of brace encased in buckling-restraining concrete and steel tube, *Proc. of 9th World Conference on Earthquake Engineering*, 1988; **IV**:719-724.

[1.7] Fujimoto M, Wada A, Saeki E, Takeuchi T, Watanabe A: Development of unbonded brace, *Querterly Column*, 1990; (115):91-96.

[1.8] Wada A, Iwata M, Huang YH: Seismic Design Trend of Tall building after the Kobe Earthquake, *Proc. Int. Post-SMiRT Conf. Seminar on Seismic Isolation, Passive Energy Dissipation, and Control of Vibrations of Structures, Taormina, Italy*; 1997:25-27

[1.9] Architectural Institute of Japan: *Recommendations for Stability Design of Steel Structures*, 1996

[1.10] Clark P, Aiken I, Kasai K, Ko E, Kimura I: Design Procedure for buildings incorporating hysteretic damping devices, *68th annual convention SEAOC, CA*; 1999:355-371.

[1.11] AISC: *Seismic Provisions for Structural Steel Buildings* (ANSI/AISC 341-05), 2002.

[1.12] Tokyo Institute of Technology: *Proceedings of Passively controlled structure symposium*; 2000, 2001, 2002, 2004.

[1.13] Tsai KC, Lai JW, Hwang YC , Lin SL, Weng CH: Research and application of double-core Buckling-restrained Braces in Taiwan, *13th World Conference on Earthquake Engineering*, 2004:Paper No. 2179.

[1.14] Nippon Steel Sumikin Engineering: Unbonded brace, http://www.unbondedbrace.com/

[1.15] Iwata M, Murai M: Buckling‐restrained brace using steel mortar planks; performance evaluation as a hysteretic damper, *Earthquake Engineering and Structural Dynamics*, 2006; **35**(14):1807–1826.

[1.16] Star Seismic: Star Seismic, http://www.starseismic.net/

[1.17] Core Brace: Core Brace, http://www.corebrace.com/

[1.18] JFE Steel engineering: Double tube braces, https://www.jfe-civil.com /system/device/products2/

Chapter 2

RESTRAINER DESIGN AND CLEARANCES

CHAPTER CONTENTS

2.1 RESTRAINER DESIGN

2.2 DEBONDING GAP

2.3 CORE MATERIAL AND OVERSTRENGTH

2.4 HYSTERETIC MODELS FOR ANALYSIS

2.5 QUALITY REQUIREMENT FOR STABLE HYSTERESIS

2.1 RESTRAINER DESIGN

Generally, BRBs are a reasonably well tested system that can achieve superior performance when the system is carefully designed and detailed by informed engineers and reputable suppliers. However, the unique characteristics of these braces can produce several undesirable failure mechanisms, which are directly influenced by decisions made for the adjacent framing, connections and restrainer. A good system-level design therefore requires the engineering consultant to understand the nuances of the brace itself.

Detailed studies in recent years have demonstrated particular mechanisms which can occur at loads and displacements significantly less than anticipated by conventional design checks. In general, the BRB must be designed for strength and stability, considering both the local and global behaviour, as shown in Figure 2.1.1.

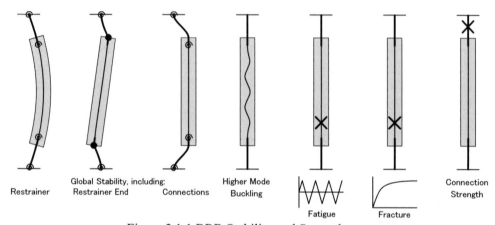

Figure 2.1.1 BRB Stability and Strength

This chapter is primarily concerned with BRBs consisting of a steel yielding core restrained by a mortar-filled steel tube and connected to a frame with gusset connections. To achieve stable hysteresis, the following design conditions shall be satisfied [2.1].

1. *Restrainer* successfully suppresses first-mode flexural buckling of the core *(Chapter 2)*
2. *Debonding mechanism* decouples axial demands and allows for Poisson effects of the core *(Chapter 2)*
3. *Restrainer wall bulging* due to higher mode buckling is suppressed *(Chapter 3)*
4. *Global out-of-plane stability* is ensured, including connections *(Chapter 4)*
5. *Low-cycle fatigue capacity* is sufficient for expected demands *(Chapter 5)*

Other restrainer, the core or debonding materials may require consideration of additional design criteria. For instance, some all-steel BRBs are limited by the effects of local buckling on stability and low cycle fatigue capacity, while early reinforced concrete restrainers tended to crack and undergo cyclic degradation. Likewise, softer materials in lieu of the restrainer mortar infill may compromise global stability by reducing restrainer end continuity, in addition to increasing the potential for restrainer wall bulging. However, these supplier-specific aspects are beyond the scope of this book.

Restrainer design is foremost a problem of providing sufficient flexural stiffness and strength, while limiting the overall dimensions and doing so in an economic manner. Conceptually, as the flexible core yields under compression the buckling amplitude is restricted to the debonding gap, and with a sufficiently stiff restrainer will gradually snap into higher modes (rippling). Note that it is because of the corresponding curvature demands that BRBs have a lower low cycle fatigue capacity than a coupon test of the base material, but never-the-less, the energy dissipation efficiency is far superior to a conventional buckling brace. As indicated by Wada et al. [2.2], the required stiffness to promote this higher-mode buckling mechanism can be derived as follows.

As shown in Figure 2.1.2, the first mode buckling wavelength is estimated by the restrainer length, with some initial deflection at midspan denoted as a_c. This initial deflection is caused by the initial core buckling inside the clearance between the core and the restrainer, imperfection of the restrainer, and the eccentricity of axial loads. The deformation curve $a(x)$ is idealized as a sine wave, as shown by:

$$a(x) = a_c \sin(\pi x / l_B) \tag{2.1.1}$$

As compressive load is applied, the core will continue to deflect laterally, with the additional buckling displacements $y(x)$ given by:

$$y(x) = y_c \sin(\pi x / l_B) \tag{2.1.2}$$

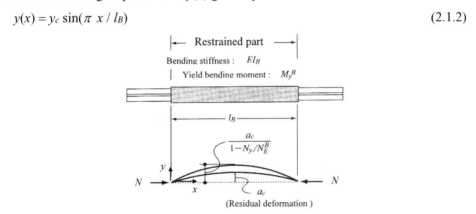

Figure 2.1.2 Buckling restrain conditions

The presence of the compressive load N introduces Pδ moments, subjecting the restrainer to a corresponding bending moment demand $M_e(x)$ determined from the total displacement:

$$M_e(x) = N(a(x) + y(x)) = N(a_c + y_c)\sin(\pi x / l_B) \tag{2.1.3}$$

However, the internal resisting moment $M_i(x)$ can also be determined:

$$\begin{aligned} M_i(x) &= -EI_B \phi(x) \\ &= -EI_B \frac{d^2}{dx^2} y_c \sin(\pi x / l_B) = \frac{\pi^2 EI_B}{l_B^2} y_c \sin(\pi x / l_B) \end{aligned} \tag{2.1.4}$$

From equilibrium, with $M_e(x)$ equal to $M_i(x)$, the following relationship is derived:

$$N(a_c + y_c)\sin(\pi x / l_B) = \frac{\pi^2 EI_B}{l_B^2} y_c \sin(\pi x / l_B) \tag{2.1.5}$$

Introducing the elastic buckling load $N_{cr}^E = \dfrac{\pi^2 EI_B}{l_B^{\,2}}$, Equation (2.1.5) is simplified to:

$$N(a_c + y_c) = N_{cr}^E y_c \tag{2.1.6}$$

Equation (2.1.6) can of course be rearranged to express the total midspan displacement $a_c + y_c$ in terms of the initial imperfection a_c and standard amplification factor:

$$a_c + y_c = \frac{N_{cr}^E \cdot a_c}{N_{cr}^E - N} \tag{2.1.7}$$

Once again noting that the Pδ moment is a function of compressive load and total displacement, the minimum restrainer flexural capacity can be determined. Considering the maximum compressive force N_{cu} that the core can transfer, the maximum restrainer flexural demand M^B is expressed as:

$$M^B = N_{cu}(a_c + y_c) = \frac{N_{cu} N_{cr}^B a_c}{N_{cr}^B - N_{cu}} = \frac{N_{cu} a_c}{1 - N_{cu}/N_{cr}^B} \tag{2.1.8}$$

Therefore, the restrainer flexural yield strength M^B_y should satisfy:

$$M^B = \frac{N_{cu} a_c}{1 - N_{cu}/N_{cr}^E} = \frac{N_{cu}\left(a + 2s_r + e\right)}{1 - N_{cu}/N_{cr}^E} \leq M_y^B \tag{2.1.9}$$

Where,

a : fabrication imperfection of core and/or brace

s_r : clearance or thickness of debonding material (per face)

e : eccentricity of the axial force

M^B_y : flexural strength of the restrainer

$N_{cu} = {}_d\alpha\, N_y$: core yield strength amplified by overstrength and strain hardening

N^E_{cr} : Euler buckling strength of the restrainer, given by:

$$N_{cr}^E = \frac{\pi^2 EI_B}{l_B^{\,2}} \tag{2.1.10}$$

Initial imperfections are dependent on the supplier-specific fabrication method and quality. Some suppliers longitudinally weld the restrainer in two halves or otherwise directly attach it around the core, and so fabrication tolerances (a) are related to the initial restrainer bow. In other cases the tube is stood upright and the mortar placed from above, such that fabrication tolerance is related to how well the core is kept vertical. The method of controlling the debonding gap (s_r) is also supplier specific, whether through the use of a compressible wrap of a given thickness, or by some direct means. In many cases the eccentricity (e) can be taken as zero, but various eccentric connections or framing tolerances may merit.

It is conservative to exclude contribution of mortar to the restrainer stiffness EI_B, avoiding the need to assess the cracked state or degree of composite action. The effective buckling length l_B depends on the connection type and stability concept, but it should be taken as not less than the restrainer length. For pin connections buckling in-plane the distance between pins should be adopted. The elastic effective length is a complex subject and discussed in greater detail in Chapter 4.

The core yield strength N_{cu} is discussed in Section 2.3, which shall be computed by strain hardening, the actual yield stress, and material variability. The strain hardening coefficient is approximately $_{d}\alpha=1.4\sim1.5$ for normal steels grades such as LY225, SN400, and SN490, but much higher at $_{d}\alpha=2.0$ for low yield strength steels such as LY100.

An alternative formulation is to express the flexural yield strength M^B_y as $2(I_B/D_r)\sigma^B_y$, where D_r is the depth of the restrainer and σ^B_y the nominal restrainer yield strength. Equation (2.1.8) can then be expressed as follows:

$$\sigma_{ry}\frac{2I_B}{D_r} > \frac{N_{cu}N^B_{cr}a_c}{N^B_{cr}-N_{cu}} = \frac{N_{cu}a_c}{N^B_{cr}-N_{cu}}\frac{\pi^2 E I_B}{l_B^2} \qquad (2.1.11)$$

$$\frac{N^B_{cr}}{N_{cu}} > 1+\left(\frac{\pi^2 E}{2\sigma_{ry}}\cdot\frac{a_c}{l_B}\right)\Big/\left(\frac{l_B}{D_r}\right) \qquad (2.1.12)$$

Equation (2.1.12) is graphically depicted in Figure 2.1.3, with the safety factor against elastic buckling N^B_{cr}/N_{cu} on the Y-axis and the effective length by restrainer depth l_B/D_r on the X-axis. Initial imperfections of 1/100, 1/200, 1/500, 1/1000 and zero are plotted for $\sigma_{ry} = 330$ MPa. It is apparent that Equation (2.1.9) can be simplified to Equation (2.1.13) for the case of initial imperfections $a_c/l_B \leq 1/500$, a relatively slender restrainer with $l_B/D_r > 20$ and with an overall safety factor of $_e\alpha \geq 1.5$.

$$N^B_{cr} = \frac{\pi^2 E I_B}{l_B^2} > {_e\alpha} N_{cu} \qquad (2.1.13)$$

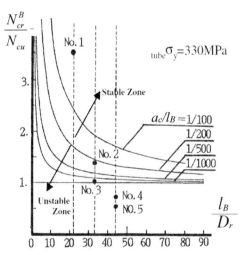

Figure 2.1.3 Stability Chart for BRBs [2.3]

This design criteria was validated by the first unbonded brace tests, which were carried out in 1987 [2.3]. Cross sections of the specimens are shown in Figure 2.1.4, with detailed descriptions summarized in Table 2.1.1 (N^B_{cr}/N_{cu} is described as P_E/P_y). Specimens No.1 to 3 satisfied Equation (2.1.13) with $_e\alpha = 0$, while No.4 and 5 did not. Observed hysteresis loops for Specimens No.1, 3, 4, 5 are shown in Figure 2.1.5. Specimens No.1-3 had safety factors of $_e\alpha > 1.03$ and achieved stable hysteresis through the full testing protocol of up to 1.5% core strain, while specimens with $N^B_{cr}/N_{cu} < 1.0$

16 Chapter 2. Restrainer Design and Clearances

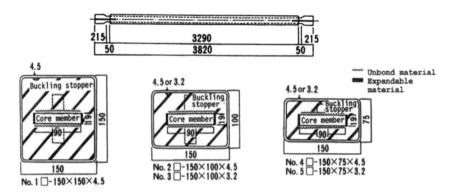

Figure 2.1.4 Specimens in the first BRB tests in 1987 [2.3]

Table 2.1.1 Criteria of buckling-restrain conditions and test results [2.3]

Specimen No.	Variable: Pipe Dimension B×D×t (mm)	Steel Pipe: Second Moment of Area I_k (cm⁴)	Steel Pipe: Buckling Load P_E (ton)	Core Member: Cross-sectional Area, A (cm²)	Core Member: Yield Load P_y (ton)	P_E/P_y	Tensile Yielding: Load P_t (ton)	P_t/P_y	Compressive Yielding: Load P_c (ton)	P_o/P_y	Buckling: Load P_{cr} (ton)	P_{cr}/P_y	P_{cr}/P_E
No. 1	150 × 150 × 4.5	896	171.0	16.84	48.50	3.53	48.6	1.00	51.5	1.06	-	-	-
No. 2	150 × 100 × 4.5	352	67.4	16.84	48.50	1.39	48.3	1.00	51.8	1.07	-	-	-
No. 3	150 × 100 × 3.2	262	50.2	16.88	48.61	1.03	47.6	0.98	49.3	1.01	-	-	-
No. 4	150 × 75 × 4.5	183	35.0	16.84	48.50	0.72	48.3	1.00	-	-	46.5	0.95	1.33
No. 5	150 × 75 × 3.2	137	26.2	16.62	47.87	0.55	47.9	1.00	-	-	43.1	0.90	1.65

Yield strength and rigidity of mortar were neglected because mortar theoretically cracks when subjected to repetitive loading.

Euler buckling load $P = \dfrac{\pi^2 E I_k}{l^2}$

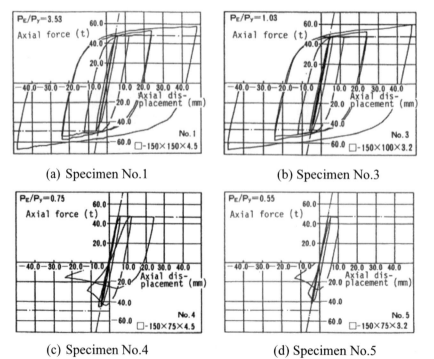

(a) Specimen No.1   (b) Specimen No.3

(c) Specimen No.4   (d) Specimen No.5

Figure 2.1.5 Axial Force-displacement relationship obtained in the tests

underwent global buckling prior to achieving a single stable hysteresis loop. The ratio of compressive overstrength (max compressive strength divided by tensile strength) was less than 1.1, achieved almost symmetric performance. As a result, the validity of Equations from (2.1.9) to (2.1.13) is confirmed.

2.2 DEBONDING GAP

The debonding material thickness or clearance between the core member and the restrainer greatly affects performance. The purpose of this layer is to prevent significant compressive loads from being passed to the restrainer, preventing it from buckling and ensuring a balance hysteresis. This is achieved by introducing a low friction interface, and by accommodating Poisson effect expansion of the core under compressive loads, either through provision of a suitable gap, compressible material or through elastic deformation of the restrainer material. However, the gap must be closely controlled as it is directly related to the higher mode buckling amplitude. Larger buckling amplitude results in increased normal force and friction (leading to compression load transfer), increased core curvature demands (concentrating strain demands and decreasing low cycle fatigue capacity), and increased transverse demands (potentially leading to restrainer bulging failure).

To determine an appropriate clearance (s_r) relative to the as-built core, the plastic Poisson ratio (for steel $v_p = 0.5$), maximum expected tensile strain (ε_{max}) and core width (B_c) for the respective axis may be used, with the expansion shared between each face. As the gap is typically $v_p \cdot \varepsilon_{max} = 0.5\sim2.0\%$ of the core width, resulting in a dimension of just a couple millimeters, strict fabrication control is required.

$$s_r \geq \frac{v_p \varepsilon_{max} B_c}{2} \text{ (per face)} \tag{2.2.4}$$

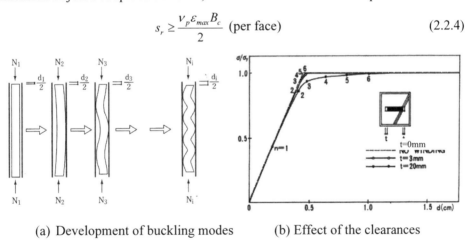

(a) Development of buckling modes   (b) Effect of the clearances

Figure 2.2.1 Effect of clearance on axial force – deformation relationship [2.3]

Higher mode buckling is observed in most BRB cores following plastic deformation in loading tests, depicted in Figure 2.2.1. As mentioned previously, this is an expected phenomenon and while the resultant curvature demands reduce the low cycle fatigue capacity to less than what a coupon test would suggest, as long as the amplitude is controlled this is still a highly effective energy dissipation mechanism. As a core is subjected to compressive force, it will begin to buckle in the first mode, but quickly strikes the restrainer wall. The restrainer will then act as a support and buckling will commence in the next lowest mode (Figure 2.2.1 (a)). Eventually a stable mode shape will form and determination of this final wavelength as a function of core strength and

18   Chapter 2. Restrainer Design and Clearances

dimensions is discussed further in Chapter 3, where it is a key parameter in determining restrainer bulging demands.

The effect of higher mode buckling on the axial stress-strain relationship was investigated [2.3]. For a theoretical 250×25 mm core with clearances of $s = 3$ or 20 mm, the additional axial displacement due to inelastic buckling was calculated assuming a sinusoidal waveform. The theoretical point at which the Nth buckling mode formed is indicated in Figure 2.2.1(b), as well as the ideal elasto-perfectly plastic curve. It is apparent that while the large 20 mm gap introduces significant nonlinearity, the more representative 3 mm gap closely matches ideal axial behavior and has a negligible influence on the stress-strain behavior.

2.3 CORE MATERIAL AND OVERSTRENGTH

Capacity design requires knowledge of the maximum overstrength demands of the yield mechanism for designing not only the restrainer, but connections and surrounding beams and columns. Given the axial yielding mechanism, it is relatively simple to reliably determine BRB overstrength, which consists of material overstrength due to variability in yield stress and strain hardening, and an experimentally determined compression overstrength factor β, accounting for force transfer to the restrainer through friction.

This book denotes the maximum compressive demand as N_{cu}, which includes the BRB-specific compression-tension overstrength factor β, as well as material overstrength due to strain hardening and variation in yield strength. In the US the material overstrength factors are denoted as ω and R_y, while in New Zealand ϕ_{OS} and ϕ_{OM} are used, respectively.

$$N_{cu} = {}_d\alpha N_y = \beta\omega R_y N_y \qquad (2.3.1)$$

If the debonding gap is properly designed to limit friction and bulging demands, values on the order of $\beta = 1.1$ are readily achieved, even at large strains of $\varepsilon \approx 3$ %. However, to ensure a competitive market and recognizing that good performance can still be achieved with larger compressive overstrength values, higher values are permitted by most major codes. In Japan, the BCJ specification permits $\beta \leq 1.2$, while the US standard AISC 341 recently relaxed the criteria from $\beta \leq 1.3$ (2010 edition) to $\beta \leq 1.5$ (2016 edition). However, such large compressive overstrengths are indicative of a poor debonding mechanism and the design procedures in this book are intended to achieve $\beta \leq 1.2$.

It is generally desirable to use core materials with a defined upper limit on the yield stress, but if this is not defined in the material code, the project specification should explicitly restrict the upper limit in some manners. Common steel grades and the permissible strength ranges are tabulated in Table 2.3.1 [2.4], [2.5].

Table 2.3.1 Steel materials for BRB core member [2.4], [2.5]

Steel grade	Standard	Min. yield stress (N/mm^2)	Max. yield stress (N/mm^2)	Tensile strength (N/mm^2)	Elongation (%)
LY 100	*LYS	80	120	200-300	50-
LY 225	*LYS	205	245	300-400	40-
SN400B	JIS	235	355	400-510	21-
SN490B	JIS	325	445	490-610	21-
A36**	ASTM	250	-	400–550	
A572Gr.50	ASTM	345	-	450-	21-

* Low yield strength steel qualification certified by the Minister of land, infrastructure, transportation and tourism, Japan

**Typically specified by engineer as 260-320MPa [2.7]

The shape of the stress-strain curve differs for various steel grades, with representative monotonic curves shown in Figure 2.3.1 for several common Japanese steels. Note the lack of a defined yield point for low (LY100) and high strength steels, as well as the substantial strain hardening for LY100. In Japan, low yield strength steels such as LY100 and LY225 are commonly used for hysteretic damping devices, although SN400 and SN490 are currently most popular for BRBs, followed by LY225. LY100 are less used because of their significant strength hardening.

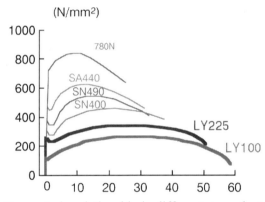

Figure 2.3.1 Stress-strain relationship in different strength steel materials

Core material is one several parameters that can be manipulated to achieve a desired yield drift. In particular, yielding can be achieved at smaller drifts by reducing the plastic length L_p or by increasing the area of the connection relative to the core. This can be desirable as the BRB starts dissipating energy earlier, but must be balanced against the increased strain demands. The relationship between drift angle Δ and core strain ε is shown in Figure 2.3.2.

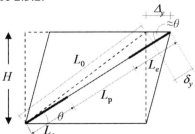

Figure 2.3.2 Core strain to story drift relationship

Assuming small drift angles and setting the panel and connection zone areas equal with $A_{pn} \approx A_e$, the BRB yield displacement δ_y and drift Δ_y are given by Equations (2.3.2) and (2.3.3), respectively.

$$\delta_y = \frac{N_y}{K_{eq}} \approx \left(\frac{L_p}{L_0} + \frac{A_c}{A_e} - \frac{A_c}{A_e}\frac{L_p}{L_0} \right) L_0 \varepsilon_y \tag{2.3.2}$$

$$\Delta_y = \frac{\delta_y}{H \cos\theta} \approx \left(\frac{L_p}{L_0} + \frac{A_c}{A_e} - \frac{A_c}{A_e}\frac{L_p}{L_0} \right) \frac{\varepsilon_y}{\cos\theta \sin\theta} = \left(\frac{L_p}{L_0} + 2\frac{A_c}{A_e}\frac{L_e}{L_0} \right) \frac{\varepsilon_y}{\cos\theta \sin\theta} \tag{2.3.3}$$

Note that when $\theta = 45°$, $L_p/L_0 = 0.5$ and $A_c/A_e = 0.5$, the story drift angle is 1.5 times the yield strain. This confirms that shorter plastic lengths and larger elastic areas decrease the yield drift, while a high yield strength core or shallower BRB angle θ will increase the yield drift. With $\varepsilon_y = 0.05\sim2\%$, $\theta = 20\sim45°$, $L_p/L_0 = 0.3\sim0.7$ and $A_c/A_e = 0.4\sim0.5$, yield drifts of $\Delta_y = 0.05\sim0.5\%$ are possible, although $\Delta_y = 0.1\sim0.25\%$ is more typical.

Once the core has yielded, the subsequent elastic deformations of the connection and panel zones may be assumed insignificant relative to the plastic deformation of the core. The relationship between drift Δ and plastic strain ε_p is given by Equation (2.3.4).

$$\Delta = \Delta_y + \frac{\delta}{H \cos\theta} \approx \Delta_y + \frac{L_p}{L_0} \cdot \frac{\varepsilon_p}{\cos\theta \sin\theta} \tag{2.3.4}$$

For large strains, Equation (2.3.4) can be further simplified as:

$$\Delta \approx \frac{L_p}{L_0} \cdot \frac{\varepsilon}{\cos\theta \sin\theta} \tag{2.3.5}$$

Alternatively, the core ductility demand can be related to drift ductility or design drift and yield strain.

$$\mu = \frac{\varepsilon}{\varepsilon_y} \approx \frac{\Delta}{\Delta_y}\left(1 + \frac{A_c}{A_e}\left(\frac{L_0}{L_p} - 1 \right) \right) = \frac{\Delta}{\varepsilon_y}\frac{L_0}{L_p}\cos\theta \sin\theta \tag{2.3.6}$$

2.4 HYSTERETIC MODELS FOR ANALYSIS

For analysis and design, BRBs are typically modelled using truss elements and elasto-plastic hysteresis rules. When using centerline models, the pure material behavior must be modified to account for the increased apparent core compressive yield and ultimate strength (β). If a single truss element is used for both the core and connections, the equivalent elastic axial stiffness as indicated by Figure 2.4.1 should be used. The transformed modelling parameters and conversions to determine the core demands are shown in Figure 2.4.2. The post-yield equivalent stiffness ratio is approximately $K_{eq,p} / K \approx L_p / L_0$, with the tangent modulus typically $E_t \approx 0.02\text{-}0.05\ E$.

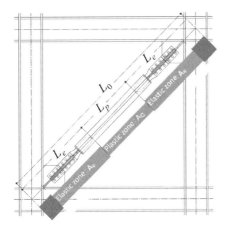

Equivalent axial stiffness:
$$K_{eq} = \frac{EA_c}{L_0} \cdot \frac{1}{\dfrac{L_p}{L_0} + 2\dfrac{L_e}{L_0}\dfrac{A_c}{A_e}}$$

Yield axial force: $N_y = A_c \cdot \sigma_y$
Yield axial deformation: $\delta_y = N_y / K_{eq}$
L_p: length of plastic zone
L_e: length of reinforced elastic zone
A_c: area of core in plastic zone
A_e: area of core in reinforced elastic zone

Figure 2.4.1 Equivalent axial elastic stiffness of BRB

Model	Direct	Core area Modification	Modulus Modification
	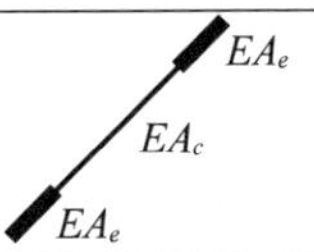 EA_e / EA_c / EA_e	 EA'_c	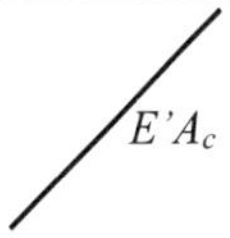 $E'A_c$
Core area A_c	A_c, A_e	$A_c \cdot K_{eq} / K$	A_c
Young's modulus E	E	E	$E \cdot K_{eq} / K$
Plastic modulus E_t	E_t	$E_t \cdot K / K_{eq} \cdot L_0 / L_p$	$E_t \cdot L_0 / L_p$
Yield stress σ_y	σ_y	$\sigma_y \cdot K / K_{eq}$	σ_y
Yield strain ε_y	ε_y	$\varepsilon_y \cdot K / K_{eq}$	$\varepsilon_y \cdot K / K_{eq}$
Analysis result			
Core stress σ	σ	$\sigma \cdot K_{eq} / K$	σ
Plastic strain[*] ε_p	ε_p	$\approx \varepsilon_p \cdot L_0 / L_p$	$\approx \varepsilon_p \cdot L_0 / L_p$

[*]actual local strain is amplified by a factor of 1~2.0 (Chapter 5)

Figure 2.4.2 BRB centerline models

As member degradation is generally precluded by the connection, debonding mechanism and restrainer design, relatively simple hysteresis rules can be used. One simple case is a bi-linear model composed of elastic stiffness, compressive and tensile yield strengths, and post-yielding stiffness. The simple bi-linear model captures kinematic hardening with a fixed yield line as shown in Figure 2.4.3, but this leads to significant error for some steel materials. This is especially apparent for LY100 (Figure 2.4.3a), where strain hardening leads to a stress almost twice of yield after cyclic loading [2.6].

To model cyclic hardening, isotropic hardening rules can be introduced. One such model is shown in Figure 2.4.4 where the yield point is controlled by an inclined yield line.

Greater precision can be achieved by modeling the skeleton (ie backbone curve) and yield lines by polynomial functions. The Menegotto-Pinto model uses this approach, as shown in Figure 2.4.5.

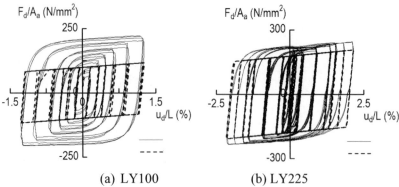

(a) LY100   (b) LY225
Figure 2.4.3 Bi-linear model with kinematic hardening

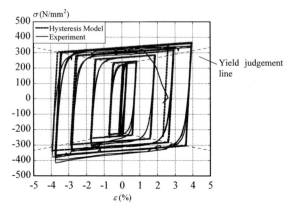

Figure 2.4.4 Bi-linear model with isotropic hardening

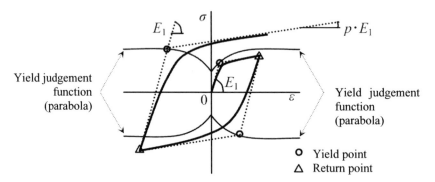

Figure 2.4.5 Menegotto-pinto model

The effects of compression overstrength (β) and slip are often difficult to include in the hysteresis model. In this case the expedient option may be to use symmetric yield points based on the tensile yield strength and to ignore slip. The detrimental effects of slip on damper efficiency are in part why slip critical bolted connection are ubiquitous in Japan, although pin connections are also common and these exhibit slip.

2.5 QUALITY REQUIREMENT FOR STABLE HYSTERESIS

Although steel ideally exhibits a smooth, symmetric and ductile hysteresis, whether BRBs achieve this performance depends on the buckling restraining system and fabrication quality. Two undesirable effects were previously mentioned, where a poorly designed debonding gap leads to excessive compression ($\beta > 1.2$), or where transverse demands due to higher mode buckling cause restrainer bulging (further discussed in Chapter 3). These are indicated in Figure 2.5.1. Further undesirable behavior includes global buckling with multiple hinges forming in the connections (further discussed in Chapter 4), or local buckling in the case of all-steel BRBs.

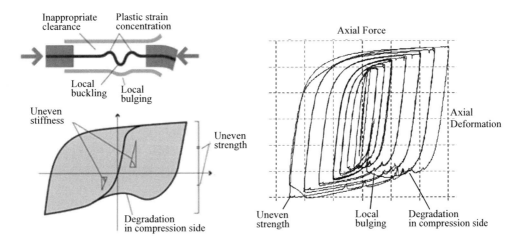

Figure 2.5.1 Bulging-induced failure

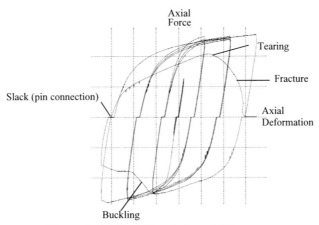

Figure 2.5.2 Buckling-induced failure

However, other effects commonly observed during experiments are generally not detrimental, such as slack (when changing from compression to tension), bolt slip, or sticking (friction at peak displacements). Finally, as performance is sensitive to fabrication quality, particularly with regard to the debonding mechanism, it is important to limit fabrication to shops whose quality has been confirmed through performance testing. Established BRB should keep the quality avoiding above failures, and the required conditions are discussed in the following Chapters.

References

[2.1]   Architectural Institute of Japan: *Recommendations for Stability Design of Steel Structures*, 1996.

[2.2]   Wada A, Nakashima M: From Infancy to Maturity of Buckling restrained Braces Research, *Proceedings of 13th World Conference on Earthquake Engineering*, 2004; (1732).

[2.3]   Fujimoto M, Wada A, Saeki E, Takeuchi T, Watanabe A: Development of Unbonded Brace, *Quarterly Column*, 1990; (115): 91-96.

[2.4]   Japanese Industrial Standard Committee: *JIS G 3136, Rolled steels for building structure*, 2012.

[2.5]   ASTM International: *ASTM A36 / A36M-14, Standard Specification for Carbon Structural Steel*, 2014.

[2.6]   Architectural Institute of Japan: *Recommended Provisions for Seismic Damping Systems applied to Steel Structures*, 2014.

[2.7]   AISC: *Seismic Design Manual, 2nd Edition, American Institute of Steel Construction*, 2012.

Chapter 3

LOCAL BULGING FAILURE

CHAPTER CONTENTS

3.1 FAILURE CAUSED BY LOCAL BUCKLING

3.2 ESTIMATION OF OUTWARD FORCE (DEMAND)

3.3 LOCAL BUCKLING WAVE LENGTH ESTIMATION

3.4 ESTIMATION OF STEEL TUBE CAPACITY

3.5 TEST RESULTS AND EVALUATIONS

3.6 REQUIRED MORTAR STRENGTH

3.7 LOCAL BULGING CRITERION FOR CIRCULAR RESTRAINER

3.8 SUMMARY

26   Chapter 3. Local Bulging Failure

3.1. FAILURE CAUSED BY LOCAL BUCKLING

Figure 3.1.1 below shows a BRB composed of a flat steel core plate and a rectangular steel tube infilled with mortar. The compressible debonding layer between the steel core and the restrainer provides a space for the flat steel core to form high mode buckling waves when the BRB is under compression. Figure 3.1.2(a) shows the typical BRB axial force and deformation relationships, Figures 3.1.2(b) and 3.1.2(c) show the transverse and longitudinal cross-sectional profile of the BRB, respectively. When the BRB is initially compressed (Figure 3.1.2(d)), the steel core flexural buckling waveforms within the space provided by the two debonding layers each has a thickness of s_{rw} or s_{rs}. After tension is applied and the BRB experienced the maximum tensile core strain (ε_t), because of the Poisson effect, the clearances between the core and restrainer increase to $s_{rs}+0.5 v_p B_c \varepsilon_t$ and $s_{rw}+0.5 v_p t_c \varepsilon_t$ in the core plate's in-plane and out-of-plane directions as shown in Figure 3.1.2(e), the tern v_p equals to 0.5 and is the Poisson's ratio when steel deforms inelastically. When the applied load is reversed, the number of buckling waves grows as the axial compression increases until it reaches the BRB's yield capacity (N_y). The in-plane ($l_{p,s}$) and out-of-plane ($l_{p,w}$) high mode buckling wavelengths form as the compression reaches N_y (Figure 3.1.2(f)) and the wavelengths would not significantly change as the compression continues increasing to the BRB's maximum axial force capacity (N_{cu}) (Figure 3.1.2(g)). The buckling wave crests squeeze the debonding layers and act outward forces on the restrainer. The maximum in-plane ($P_{d,s}$) and out-of-plane ($P_{d,w}$) outward forces are fully developed when BRB axial force reaches N_{cu} (Figure 3.1.2(g)).The in-plane or out-of-plane local bulging failure would occur if the steel tube strength is insufficient to sustain the in-plane or out-of-plane outward force (Figures 3.1.2(h)). Figures 3.1.3(a) and 3.1.3(b) show the in-plane and out-of-plane local bulging failure observed in component tests (Takeuchi et. al [3.1], Lin et. al [3.2]).

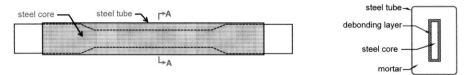

Figure 3.1.1 The BRB longitudinal and transverse cross-sectional configuration

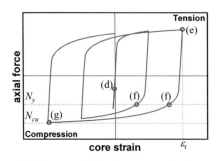
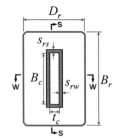

(a) Force and displacement relation   (b) Transverse cross-sectional section

Chapter 3. Local Bulging Failure   27

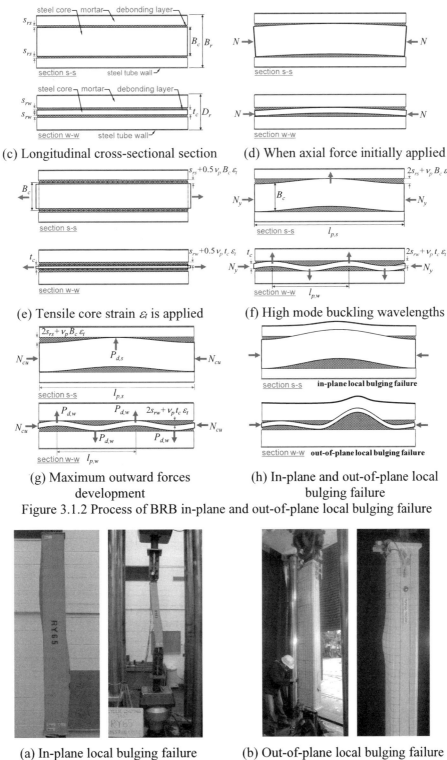

(c) Longitudinal cross-sectional section
(d) When axial force initially applied
(e) Tensile core strain ε_t is applied
(f) High mode buckling wavelengths
(g) Maximum outward forces development
(h) In-plane and out-of-plane local bulging failure

Figure 3.1.2 Process of BRB in-plane and out-of-plane local bulging failure

(a) In-plane local bulging failure
(b) Out-of-plane local bulging failure

Figure 3.1.3 Local bulging failure observed in component tests

3.2 ESTIMATION OF OUTWARD FORCE DEMAND

When the BRB is in tension, the steel core plate thickness (t_c) becomes thinner because of the Poisson effect as shown in Figure 3.1.2(e). When the applied load is reversed, compression could develop and the steel core deformation remains in tensile strain (Point (f) in Figure 3.1.2(a)). Thus, for a conservative estimation, the maximum in-plane ($P_{d,s}$) and out-of-plane outward force ($P_{d,w}$) are estimated based on the geometric relationships of the in-plane ($l_{p,s}$) and out-of-plane high buckling wavelengths ($l_{p,w}$), and the maximum clearances between steel core and restrainer. Figures 3.2.1(a) and 3.2.1(b) show the free body diagrams of the steel core in-plane and out-of-plane high mode buckling waves within the range of two adjacent wave crests. Neglecting the steel core bending moments at the wave crests, the maximum in-plane ($P_{d,s}$) and out-of-plane outward forces ($P_{d,w}$) can be computed by applying the moment equilibrium condition on the free body as follows:

$$P_{d,s} = \frac{4N_{cu}(2s_{rs} + v_p B_c \varepsilon_t)}{l_{p,s}} \quad (3.1a)$$

$$P_{d,w} = \frac{4N_{cu}(2s_{rw} + v_p t_c \varepsilon_t)}{l_{p,w}} \quad (3.1b)$$

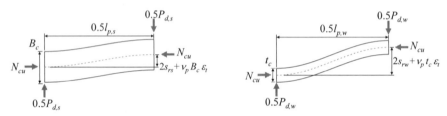

(a) In-plane high mode buckling (b) Out-of-plane high mode buckling
Figure 3.2.1 Steel core within a half wavelength range

3.3 LOCAL BUCKLING WAVELENGTH ESTIMATION

The high mode buckling wave length affects the accuracy on estimating the maximum outward force. Based on the experimental observations (Takeuchi et al. [3.1], Wu et al. [3.3]), the out-of-plane ($l_{p,w}$) and in-plane high mode buckling wavelengths ($l_{p,s}$) are about 10 to 12 times the steel core thickness ($l_{p,w} \approx 10t_c \sim 12t_c$) and 7 to 8 times the steel core width ($l_{p,s} \approx 7B_c \sim 8B_c$), respectively. This characteristic can be explained as follows. When the core plate buckles within the clearances between core member and restrainer, the number of wave increases while the compression increases (Point (e) to Point (f) in Figure 3.1.2(a)). However, it stops increasing at the point where the flexural buckling strength resulting from the tangent modulus of the core plate (σ_{cr}) reaches the core plate yield strength (σ_{cy}) [3.4], as described as follows,

$$\sigma_{cy} = \frac{N_y}{A_c} = \sigma_{cr} = \frac{\pi^2 E_t}{\bar{\lambda}_{c,s}^2} = \frac{\pi^2 E_t}{\bar{\lambda}_{c,w}^2} = \frac{\pi^2 E_t I_s}{A_c (l_{p,s}/2)^2} = \frac{\pi^2 E_t I_w}{A_c (l_{p,w}/2)^2} \quad (3.2)$$

where A_c and E_t are the sectional area and material tangent modulus of the core plate, respectively. I_s and I_w are the major and minor moment of inertia of the core plate. $\bar{\lambda}_{c,s}$ and $\bar{\lambda}_{c,w}$ are the equivalent slenderness ratios when in-plane and out-of-plane high mode buckling waves form, respectively. The in-plane ($l_{p,s}$) and out-of-plane ($l_{p,w}$) high mode buckling wavelengths are then determined as follows.

$$l_{p,s} = \sqrt{\frac{4\pi^2 E_{t,eq} I_s}{N_y}} = B_c \cdot \pi \sqrt{\frac{E_{t,eq}}{3\sigma_{cy}}} \tag{3.3a}$$

$$l_{p,w} = \sqrt{\frac{4\pi^2 E_{t,eq} I_w}{N_y}} = t_c \cdot \pi \sqrt{\frac{E_{t,eq}}{3\sigma_{cy}}} \tag{3.3b}$$

The in-plane or out-of-plane high mode buckling wavelengths can be expressed by the core plate width (B_c) or thickness (t_c) times a dimensionless factor of $\pi\sqrt{E_{t,eq}/3\sigma_{cy}}$. The tangent modulus E_t can be replaced by an averaged modulus ($E_{t,eq}$). Based on the past experimental results, Takeuchi et al. [3.1] used a tangent modulus of E_t equals to $0.02E$ for estimating the in-plane high mode buckling wavelengths, where E is the elastic Young's modulus of steel core material. Yoshida et al. [3.5] used tangent modulus of $E_t = 0.05E$ for out-of-plane high mode buckling wavelength estimations. Midorikawa et al. [3.6] proposed the reduced modulus in evaluating the out-of-plane high mode buckling wavelengths as follows,

$$E_{t,eq} = \frac{4E_t E}{\left(\sqrt{E_t}+\sqrt{E}\right)^2} \tag{3.4}$$

Lin et al [3.2] proposed an equivalent flexural stiffness (EI)$_{eff}$ for evaluating the in-plane high mode buckling wavelength. Figures 3.3.1(a) and 3.3.1(b) show the steel core cross section at the high mode buckling wave crests and the stress and strain relationships during loading and unloading procedures. It is anticipated that part of the cross-sectional area (A_{Et}) deforms in loading procedure and another part (A_E) deforms in unloading procedure. A_{Et} is assumed to be 76% of the entire cross-sectional area of the steel core and E_t equals to 0. Thus, the effective flexural stiffness (EI)$_{eff}$ is about $0.055EI$.

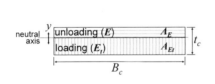
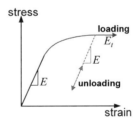

(a) Cross section of steel core   (b) Stress and strain relationships
Figure 3.3.1 Loading and unloading relationships

Afterwards, $E_{t,eq}=0.05E$ is adopted in Equation (3.3) for evaluating the out-of-plane and in-plane high mode buckling wavelengths. Table 3.3.1 summarizes the $l_{p,s}$ and $l_{p,w}$ obtained from Equation (3.3) when A36, A572, or SN490B steel material is adopted as the steel core.

Table 3.3.1 Numerical high mode buckling wavelengths

	$l_{p,s}$	$l_{p,w}$
A36 (σ_{cy} = 248MPa)	$11.5B_c$	$11.5t_p$
A572 Gr50 (σ_{cy} = 345 MPa)	$9.8B_c$	$9.8t_p$
SN490B (σ_{cy} = 325 MPa)	$10.1B_c$	$10.1t_p$

3.4 ESTIMATION OF STEEL TUBE CAPACITY

Based on the experimental observations [3.2], for the specimens with local bulging failure, the mortar near the local bulging region was always severely crushed. The mortar crush might be induced from the frictions generated at the high mode buckling wave crests. Thus, the mortar may not able in resisting the outward forces. Only the steel tube wall is considered in resisting the outward forces, and the mortar is only responsible in transferring the outward force to the steel tube wall inner surface. Figure 3.4.1 presents schematics of a segment of BRB within the range of an out-of-plane high mode buckling wavelength. The steel tube wall out-of-plane bulged is represented by a wedge shape as shown in the 3-D view in Figure 3.4.1. In order to form the bulged wedge shape, each of the nine boundary of the wedge should develop its flexural strength. The minimum out-of-plane outward force ($P_{c,w}$) required to form the bulged wedge shape is considered as the steel tube capacity in resisting the outward force induced form the out-of-plane high mode buckling waves.

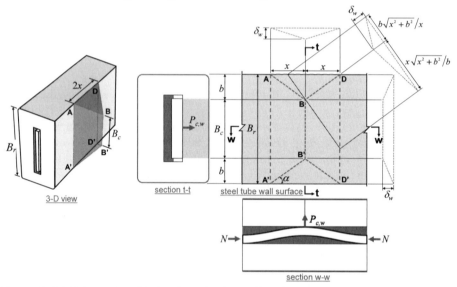

Figure 3.4.1 Schematic of bulged steel tube wall and the out-of-plane outward force from transverse and longitudinal cross section views

As shown in Figure 3.4.1, the length of boundary BB' is assumed to be equal to the core plate width (B_c). The lengths of boundaries AD and A'D' are $2x$. The boundaries AB, DB, A'B', and D'B' incline with respect to the longitudinal direction with incline angle of α. If δ_w is the maximum steel tube wall outward deformation. The rotation (θ) at each boundary can be computed as follows:

$$\theta_{BB'} = \frac{2\delta_w}{x}$$

$$\theta_{AA'} = \theta_{DD'} = \frac{\delta_w}{x}$$

$$\theta_{AD} = \theta_{A'D'} = \frac{\delta_w}{b}$$

$$\theta_{AB} = \theta_{A'B'} = \theta_{BD} = \theta_{B'D'} = \frac{\delta_w x}{b\sqrt{x^2+b^2}} + \frac{\delta_w b}{x\sqrt{x^2+b^2}} = \frac{\delta_w}{\sqrt{x^2+b^2}}\left[\frac{x}{b}+\frac{b}{x}\right]$$

The flexural capacity of the steel tube wall within a unit length of boundary line (m_p) can be computed as follows,

$$m_p = \frac{t_r^2}{4}\sigma_{ry} \tag{3.5}$$

where t_r and σ_{ry} are the steel tube wall thickness and material yield stress, respectively. The internal energy (E_9) that required to form all the nine yield lines along the wedge edges can be computed as follows,

$$E_9 = \left[B_c\theta_{BB'} + 2B_r\theta_{AA'} + 2(2x)\theta_{AD} + 4\sqrt{x^2+b^2}\,\theta_{AB} \right]m_p = 4m_p\delta_w\left(\frac{B_r}{x} + \frac{4x}{B_r - B_c} \right) \tag{3.6}$$

where b equals to $(B_r - B_c)/2$. However, the boundaries AD and A'D' are less capable in developing full flexural strength because of the presence of residual stress at the tube corners. In addition, the deformation curvatures along the longitudinal direction are relative small near the boundaries AA' and DD' based on the experimental observation [3.2]. Thus, the boundaries AA' and DD' may not be considered as yield lines. If the aforementioned boundaries (AD, A'D', A'A, and DD') are not considered to develop full flexural strength, the internal energy (E_5) can be computed as follows,

$$E_5 = \left[B_c\theta_{BB'} + 4\sqrt{x^2+b^2}\,\theta_{AB} \right]m_p = 2m_p\delta_w\left(\frac{B_r}{x} + \frac{4x}{B_r - B_c} \right) \tag{3.7}$$

Assuming that the mortar will not deform while transferring the outward force, the work (T) done by the out-of-plane outward force ($P_{c,w}$) is,

$$T = P_{c,w}\delta_w \tag{3.8}$$

By equating T to E_9 or E_5, the $P_{c,w}$ can be computed for four conditions by considering either E_9 [3.5] or E_5 [3.2], and the lengths of x and y are determined by either minimizing the internal energy [3.5] or assuming α equals to 45 degrees [3.2]. The geometries of the wedge boundaries and yield lines are shown in Figure 3.4.2.

Condition 1, Figure 3.4.2(a):
Consider all the nine yield lines on the wedge boundaries, the length of $2x$ is determined when E_9 is minimum, thus,

$$x = \frac{\sqrt{B_r(B_r - B_c)}}{2}, \quad P_{c,w} = 4m_p\left(\frac{B_r}{x} + \frac{4x}{B_r - B_c} \right) = \frac{4t_r^2\sigma_{ry}}{\sqrt{(1 - B_c/B_r)}} = Q_{w1}t_r^2\sigma_{ry} \tag{3.9a}$$

Condition 2, Figure 3.4.2 (b):
Consider all the nine yield lines on the wedge boundaries, and assume the incline angle α is 45 degrees, thus,

$$\alpha = 45°, \quad x = b, \quad P_{c,w} = 4m_p\left(\frac{B_r}{x} + \frac{4x}{B_r - B_c} \right) = \left(\frac{4 - 2B_c/B_r}{1 - B_c/B_r} \right)t_r^2\sigma_{ry} = Q_{w2}t_r^2\sigma_{ry} \tag{3.10a}$$

Condition 3, Figure 3.4.2 (c):
Consider only the five yield lines on the wedge boundaries, the length of $2x$ is determined when E_5 is minimum, thus,

$$x = \frac{\sqrt{B_r(B_r - B_c)}}{2}, \quad P_{c,w} = 2m_p\left(\frac{B_r}{x} + \frac{4x}{B_r - B_c} \right) = \frac{2t_r^2\sigma_{ry}}{\sqrt{(1 - B_c/B_r)}} = Q_{w3}t_r^2\sigma_{ry} \tag{3.11a}$$

Condition 4, Figure 3.4.2 (d):
Consider only the five yield lines on the wedge boundaries, and assume the incline angle α is 45 degrees, thus,

32   Chapter 3. Local Bulging Failure

$$\alpha = 45°, \; x = b, \; P_{c,w} = 2m_p\left(\frac{B_r}{x} + \frac{4x}{B_r - B_c}\right) = \left(\frac{2 - B_c/B_r}{1 - B_c/B_r}\right)t_r^2\sigma_{ry} = Q_{w4}t_r^2\sigma_{ry} \qquad (3.12a)$$

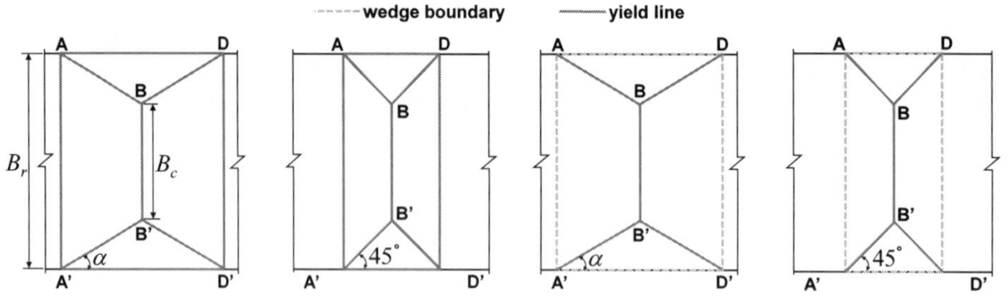

---- wedge boundary   —— yield line

(a) Condition 1   (b) Condition 2   (c) Condition 3   (d) Condition 4

Figure 3.4.2 Yield line distributions on out-of-plane bulged steel tube wall

Figure 3.4.3 shows schematics of a segment of BRB within the range of an in-plane high mode buckling wavelength ($l_{p,s}$). The length of boundary BB' equals to the core plate thickness (t_c). The same procedure can be done for evaluating the steel tube wall capacity ($P_{c,s}$) in resisting the in-plane outward force. The four conditions are shown in Figure 3.4.4 and the results are as follows,

Condition 1, Figure 3.4.4(a):
Consider all the nine yield lines on the wedge boundaries, the length of $2y$ is determined when the internal energy is minimum, thus,

$$y = \frac{\sqrt{D_r(D_r - t_c)}}{2}, \; P_{c,s} = 4m_p\left(\frac{D_r}{y} + \frac{4y}{D_r - t_c}\right) = \frac{4t_r^2\sigma_{ry}}{\sqrt{(1 - t_c/D_r)}} = Q_{s1}t_r^2\sigma_{ry} \qquad (3.9b)$$

Condition 2, Figure 3.4.4 (b):
Consider all the nine yield lines on the wedge boundaries, and assume the incline angle γ is 45 degrees, thus,

$$\gamma = 45°, \; y = c, \; P_{c,s} = 4m_p\left(\frac{D_r}{y} + \frac{4y}{D_r - t_c}\right) = \left(\frac{4 - 2t_c/D_r}{1 - t_c/D_r}\right)t_r^2\sigma_{ry} = Q_{s2}t_r^2\sigma_{ry} \qquad (3.10b)$$

Condition 3, Figure 3.4.4 (c):
Consider only the five yield lines on the wedge boundaries, the length of $2y$ is determined when the internal energy is minimum, thus,

$$y = \frac{\sqrt{D_r(D_r - t_c)}}{2}, \; P_{c,s} = 2m_p\left(\frac{D_r}{y} + \frac{4y}{D_r - t_c}\right) = \frac{2t_r^2\sigma_{ry}}{\sqrt{(1 - t_c/D_r)}} = Q_{s3}t_r^2\sigma_{ry} \qquad (3.11b)$$

Condition 4, Figure 3.4.4 (d):
Consider only the five yield lines on the wedge boundaries, and assume the incline angle γ is 45 degrees, thus,

$$\gamma = 45°, \; y = c, \; P_{c,s} = 2m_p\left(\frac{D_r}{y} + \frac{4y}{D_r - t_c}\right) = \left(\frac{2 - t_c/D_r}{1 - t_c/D_r}\right)t_r^2\sigma_{ry} = Q_{s4}t_r^2\sigma_{ry} \qquad (3.12b)$$

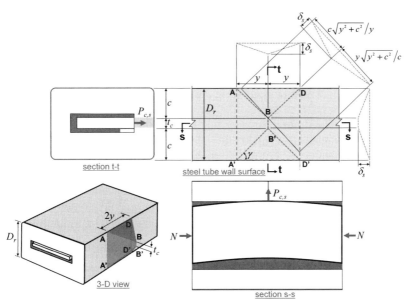

Figure 3.4.3 Schematic of bulged steel tube wall and the in-plane outward force from transverse and longitudinal cross sections

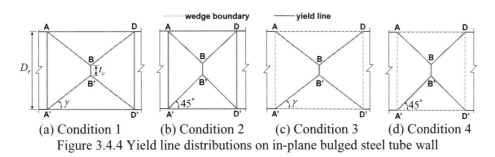

(a) Condition 1 (b) Condition 2 (c) Condition 3 (d) Condition 4
Figure 3.4.4 Yield line distributions on in-plane bulged steel tube wall

Takeuchi et al. [3.1] proposed $P_{c,s}=8m_p=2t_r^2\sigma_{ry}$, which agrees with the Equation (3.11b) and (3.12b) when $t_c/D_r=0$. As shown in Equation (3.9) to (3.12), the steel tube wall capacity can be expressed by a dimensionless resistance factor (Q_{wn} and Q_{sn}, $n = 1$ to 4) times $t_r^2\sigma_{ry}$. The effectiveness of the resistance factor Q_{wn} and Q_{sn} is evaluated by the test results in the following sections.

3.5 TEST RESULTS AND EVALUATIONS

In order to verify the effectiveness of the estimation methods in avoiding the local bulging failure, the test results of a total of 34 BRB specimens were examined. Among the 34 BRB specimens, 22 BRBs were tested in the Taiwan National Center for Research on Earthquake Engineering (NCREE) [3.2], 6 BRBs were tested at the Tokyo Institute of Technology (TokyoTech) [3.1], 6 BRBs were tested by the Kanagawa University (KU) [3.7]. 14 specimens exhibited out-of-plane local bulging failure and 5 specimens exhibited in-plane local bulging failure when the applied core strains were greater than 0.02. While the other 15 specimens exhibited steel core fracture at the end of each test. Figures 3.5.1(a) to 3.5.1 (c) show the cross sections of BRB specimens tested in NCREE, TokyoTech, and KU, respectively. Table 3.5.1 lists the dimensions and mechanical properties of the 34 BRB specimens. The purposes of the NCREE and TokyoTech BRB tests were to investigate the out-of-plane and in-plane local bulging failures, respectively. As shown in Figure 3.5.1(c), the KU BRB consists of a flat steel core plate and a restrainer assembled by a pair of steel channels each has different leg lengths. The s_{rw} can be controlled by adjusting the steel channel leg overlapped length. The two overlapped steel channel legs were connected by using fillet welds. A pair of spacers are arranged in order to prevent the formation of excessive in-plane high mode buckling waves. This configuration may not lead to the out-of-plane local bulging failure, thus, only the out-of-plane local bulging failures are examined for the KU BRBs.

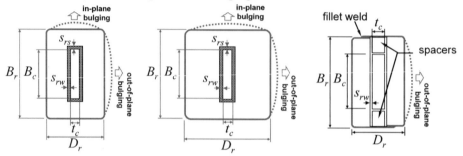

(a) NCREE specimens   (b) TokyoTech specimens   (c) KU specimens
Figure 3.5.1 Sections of BRB specimens

Each of the BRB specimen was tested by applying either increasing, decreasing, or constant axial cyclic strains. The effects of the maximum core strain applied (ε_t), the cumulative plastic deformation (CPD), and the loading sequences on the performances of the BRB specimens will be discussed. Figure 3.5.2 shows the loading protocols and the corresponding CPD gain. It should be noted that the CPD shown in Figure 3.5.2 is computed by assuming the core yield strain is 0.0017 (A572 Gr50). After the increasing or decreasing cyclic strains were applied, the fatigue cycles with constant strain amplitudes were applied until the BRB fails to sustain axial load.

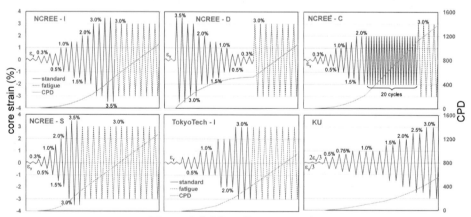

Figure 3.5.2 Loading protocols

The test result and loading protocol adopted by each of the test is listed in Table 3.5.2. The The $l_{p,s}$ and $l_{p,w}$ were computed based on Equation (3.3a) and (3.3b) by using $E_{t,eq}=0.05E$. $N_{cu,\exp}$ is the maximum compression measured during the tests. The experimental resistance factors for the steel tube capacities in resisting the in-plane

$(Q_{s,\exp})$ and out-of-plane $(Q_{w,\exp})$ outward forces are computed as follows,

$$Q_{s,\exp} = \frac{4N_{cu,\exp}\left(2s_{rs} + v_p B_c \varepsilon_t\right)}{l_{p,s} t_r^2 \sigma_{ry}} \tag{3.13a}$$

$$Q_{w,\exp} = \frac{4N_{cu,\exp}\left(2s_{rw} + v_p t_c \varepsilon_t\right)}{l_{p,w} t_r^2 \sigma_{ry}} \tag{3.13b}$$

Table 3.5.3 shows the resistance factors computed from the aforementioned four different conditions (Q_{wn} and Q_{sn}, Equation (3.9) to (3.12)) and obtained from the test results ($Q_{w,\exp}$ and $Q_{s,\exp}$, Equation (3.13a) and (3.13b). Figure 3.5.3 shows the relationships of the resistance factors between Q_{wn}, Q_{sn} and $Q_{w,\exp}$, $Q_{s,\exp}$. For the test results with core fracture, both the $Q_{s,\exp}$ and $Q_{w,\exp}$ are plotted. For the test results of in-plane local bulging failure, only the $Q_{s,\exp}$ are plotted. Similarly, for the test results of out-of-plane local bulging failure, only the $Q_{w,\exp}$ are plotted. Based on the test results, the effectiveness of resistance factors computed from four conditions are judged as follows,

(1) For the test results without local bulging failure until core fracture, if Q_{sn} is smaller than $Q_{s,\exp}$ (when ● is above Q_{sn} lines), the estimation is conservative. However, if Q_{sn} is greater than $Q_{s,\exp}$ (when ● is below Q_{sn} lines), the steel tube wall capacity is appropriately estimated by using Q_{sn}.

(2) For the test results without local bulging failure until core fracture, if Q_{wn} is smaller than $Q_{w,\exp}$ (when • is above Q_{wn} lines), the estimation is conservative. However, if Q_{wn} is greater than $Q_{w,\exp}$ (when ● is below Q_{wn} lines), the steel tube wall capacity is appropriately estimated by using Q_{sn}.

(3) For the test results of in-plane local bulging, if Q_{sn} is smaller than $Q_{s,\exp}$ (when ▲ is above the Q_{sn} lines), the steel tube wall capacity estimation by using Q_{sn} is smaller than that when bulging occurs, thus, the estimation is appropriate. However, if Q_{sn} is greater than $Q_{s,\exp}$ (when ▲ is below the Q_{sn} lines), the steel tube wall capacity estimation by using Q_{sn} is larger than that when bulging occurs, the estimation is dangerous.

(4) For the test results of out-of-plane local bulging, if Q_{wn} is smaller than $Q_{w,\exp}$ (when × is above the Q_{wn} lines), the steel tube wall capacity estimation by using Q_{wn} is smaller than that when bulging occurs, thus, the estimation is appropriate. However, if Q_{wn} is greater than $Q_{w,\exp}$ (when × is below the Q_{wn} lines), the steel tube wall capacity estimation by using Q_{wn} is larger than that when bulging occurs, the estimation is dangerous.

36   Chapter 3. Local Bulging Failure

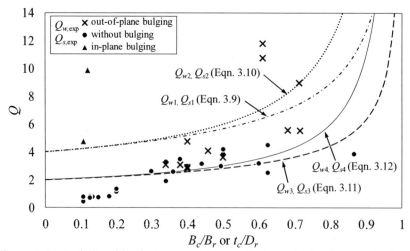

Figure 3.5.3 Relationships between resistance factors obtained numerically and experimentally and the ratios of B_c/B_r or t_c/D_r

Table 3.5.1 Dimensions and mechanical properties of the BRB specimens

Tester	Specimen	Steel tube ($B_r \times D_r \times t_r$, mm)	B_c (mm)	t_c (mm)	Core material	σ_{cy} (N/mm²)	σ_{ry} (N/mm²)	s_{rw} (mm)	s_{rs} (mm)	f_c' (N/mm²)	N_y (kN)	B_c/B_r	t_c/D_r	t_m/B_r
NCREE	W15G2-74-IN	150×100×9	74	15	A572Gr50	379	400	2	2	55	421	0.49	0.15	-
	W18G2-90-IN	150×100×9	90	18	A572Gr50	359	400	2	2	55	582	0.6	0.18	-
	W16G2-85-IN	250×150×9	85	16	A36	367	400	2	2	55	499	0.34	0.11	-
	W16G2-95-IN	250×150×9	95	16	A36	367	400	2	2	55	558	0.38	0.11	-
	W20G2-90-IN	250×150×9	90	20	A36	302	400	2	2	55	544	0.36	0.13	-
	W20G2-110-IN	250×150×9	110	20	A36	302	400	2	2	55	664	0.44	0.13	-
	R25G2-200-IN	400×200×12	200	25	A572Gr50	393	408	2	2	55	1965	0.5	0.13	-
	R40G2-200-IN	400×200×12	200	40	A572Gr50	398	408	2	2	55	3184	0.5	0.2	-
	F25G2-160-IN	400×200×12	160	25	A572Gr50	393	408	2	2	55	1572	0.4	0.13	-
	F25G4-160-IN	400×200×12	160	25	A572Gr50	393	408	4	4	55	1572	0.4	0.13	-
	R25G2-250-IN	400×200×12	250	25	A572Gr50	393	408	2	2	55	2456	0.63	0.13	-
	R25G1-250-IN	400×200×12	250	25	A572Gr50	393	408	1	1	55	2456	0.63	0.13	-
	C40G2-160-IN	350×150×12	160	40	A572Gr50	398	331	2	2	55	2547	0.46	0.27	-
	C25G2-250-IN	350×150×12	250	25	A572Gr50	393	331	2	2	55	2456	0.71	0.17	-
	F25G2-160-DN	400×200×12	160	25	A572Gr50	354	378	2	2	55	1416	0.4	0.13	-
	F25G2-160-IH	400×200×12	160	25	A572Gr50	354	378	2	2	97	1416	0.4	0.13	0.18
	R25G2-200-DN	400×200×12	200	25	A572Gr50	354	378	2	2	55	1770	0.5	0.13	-
	R40G2-120-IN	400×200×12	120	40	A572Gr50	381	378	2	2	55	1829	0.3	0.2	-
	R40G2-200-SN	400×200×12	200	40	A572Gr50	381	378	2	2	55	3048	0.5	0.2	-
	W16G2-85-IH	250×150×9	85	16	A36	392	430	2	2	97	533	0.34	0.11	0.22
	W16G2-95-IH	250×150×9	95	16	A572Gr50	388	430	2	2	97	590	0.38	0.11	0.22
	W16G2-85-CN	250×150×9	85	16	A36	270	430	2	2	55	367	0.34	0.11	-
TokyoTech	RY25	150×150×6	130	16	SS400	261	350	1	1	-	543	0.87	0.11	-
	RY65	150×150×2.3	130	16	SS400	261	351	1	1	-	543	0.87	0.11	-
	RY65G	150×150×2.3	130	16	SS400	261	351	1	6	-	543	0.87	0.11	-
	RrY125	100×100×0.8	90	12	SS400	276	288	1	1	-	298	0.9	0.12	-
	RrY125M	100×100×0.8	68	16	SS400	274	288	1	1	-	298	0.68	0.16	-
	RrY63	100×100×1.6	90	12	SS400	276	288	1	1	-	298	0.9	0.12	-
KU	N400-1	216.4×82×3.2	132	12	SN400B	279	325	1	-	37	442	0.61	0.15	-
	N490-1	216.4×82×3.2	132	12	SN490B	345	325	1	-	37	546	0.61	0.15	-
	N225-1	216.4×82×3.2	154	14	LY225	239	325	1	-	37	515	0.71	0.17	-
	N400-2	216.4×100×3.2	132	12	SN400B	279	325	1	-	37	442	0.61	0.12	-
	N490-2	216.4×100×3.2	132	12	SN490B	345	325	1	-	37	546	0.61	0.12	-
	N225-2	216.4×100×3.2	154	14	LY225	239	325	1	-	37	515	0.68	0.14	-

Chapter 3. Local Bulging Failure

Table 3.5.2 BRB test results

Specimen	Loading protocol	$l_{p,s}$ (mm)	$l_{p,w}$ (mm)	e_t	CPD	$N_{cu,\,exp}$ (kN)	Test result
W15G2-74-IN	NCREE-I	689	140	0.035	391	796	No bulging until core fracture
W18G2-90-IN	NCREE-I	862	172	0.035	491	1037	No bulging until core fracture
W16G2-85-IN	NCREE-I	805	151	0.035	397	886	Out-of-plane bulging
W16G2-95-IN	NCREE-I	899	151	0.035	317	885	Out-of-plane bulging
W20G2-90-IN	NCREE-I	939	209	0.035	669	1007	No bulging until core fracture
W20G2-110-IN	NCREE-I	1148	209	0.035	661	1239	No bulging until core fracture
R25G2-200-IN	NCREE-I	1830	229	0.035	439	2745	Out-of-plane bulging
R40G2-200-IN	NCREE-I	1818	364	0.035	583	4428	No bulging until core fracture
F25G2-160-IN	NCREE-I	1464	229	0.035	354	2134	Out-of-plane bulging
F25G4-160-IN	NCREE-I	1464	229	0.03	226	1920	Out-of-plane bulging
R25G2-250-IN	NCREE-I	2287	229	0.035	604	3432	No bulging until core fracture
R25G1-250-IN	NCREE-I	2287	229	0.035	767	3499	No bulging until core fracture
C40G2-160-IN	NCREE-I	1455	364	0.035	341	3767	Out-of-plane bulging
C25G2-250-IN	NCREE-I	2287	229	0.035	522	3402	Out-of-plane bulging
F25G2-160-DN	NCREE-D	1542	241	0.035	690	2155	Out-of-plane bulging
F25G2-160-IH	NCREE-I	1542	241	0.035	420	2216	No bulging until core fracture
R25G2-200-DN	NCREE-D	1928	241	0.035	547	2863	No bulging until core fracture
R40G2-120-IN	NCREE-I	1115	372	0.035	394	2838	No bulging until core fracture
R40G2-200-SN	NCREE-S	1858	372	0.035	413	4545	No bulging until core fracture
W16G2-85-IH	NCREE-I	779	147	0.035	486	987	No bulging until core fracture
W16G2-95-IH	NCREE-I	875	147	0.035	491	1056	No bulging until core fracture
W16G2-85-CN	NCREE-C	938	177	0.03	1922	701	No bulging until core fracture
RY25	TokyoTech-I	1460	180	0.03	550	977	No bulging until core fracture
RY65	TokyoTech-I	1460	180	0.02	286	977	In-plane bulging
RY65G	TokyoTech-I	1460	180	0.02	286	977	In-plane bulging
RrY125	TokyoTech-I	983	131	0.03	518	536	In-plane bulging
RrY125M	TokyoTech-I	746	175	0.03	522	536	In-plane bulging
RrY63	TokyoTech-I	983	131	0.03	518	536	In-plane bulging
N400-1	KU	1433	130	0.02	410	550	Out-of-plane bulging
N490-1	KU	1289	117	0.015	226	891	Out-of-plane bulging
N225-1	KU	1807	164	0.025	813	565	Out-of-plane bulging
N400-2	KU	1433	130	0.025	558	595	Out-of-plane bulging
N490-2	KU	1289	117	0.02	280	727	Out-of-plane bulging
N225-2	KU	1807	164	0.03	978	345	Out-of-plane bulging

Table 3.5.3 Comparison of resistance factors between numerical and test results

Specimen	Test result	Q_{w-exp}	Q_{s-exp}	Out-of-plane Q_{wn}				In-plane Q_{sn}				DCR_s	DCR_w	DCR_{wh}
				Q_{w1}	Q_{w2}	Q_{w3}	Q_{w4}	Q_{s1}	Q_{s2}	Q_{s3}	Q_{s4}			
W15G2-74-IN	Core fracture	3	0.75	5.62	5.95	2.81	2.97	4.34	4.35	2.17	2.18	0.35	1.01	-
W18G2-90-IN	Core fracture	3.21	0.83	6.32	7	3.16	3.5	4.42	4.44	2.21	2.22	0.37	0.92	-
W16G2-85-IN	Out-of-plane bulging	3.09	-	4.92	5.03	2.46	2.52	-	-	-	-	0.35	1.23	-
W16G2-95-IN	Out-of-plane bulging	3.09	-	5.08	5.23	2.54	2.61	-	-	-	-	0.32	1.18	-
W20G2-90-IN	Core fracture	2.59	0.74	5	5.13	2.5	2.56	4.3	4.31	2.15	2.15	0.34	1.01	-
W20G2-110-IN	Core fracture	3.19	0.79	5.35	5.57	2.67	2.79	4.3	4.31	2.15	2.15	0.37	1.14	-
R25G2-200-IN	Out-of-plane bulging	3.63	-	5.66	6	2.83	3	-	-	-	-	0.36	1.21	-
R40G2-200-IN	Cre fracture	3.9	1.24	5.66	6	2.83	3	4.47	4.5	2.24	2.25	0.55	1.3	-
F25G2-160-IN	Out-of-plane bulging	2.82	-	5.16	5.33	2.58	2.67	-	-	-	-	0.31	1.06	-
F25G4-160-IN	Out-of-plane bulging	4.79	-	5.16	5.33	2.58	2.67	-	-	-	-	0.43	1.79	-
R25G2-250-IN	Core fracture	4.53	0.86	6.53	7.33	3.27	3.67	4.28	4.29	2.14	2.14	0.4	1.24	-
R25G1-250-IN	Core fracture	2.54	0.66	6.53	7.33	3.27	3.67	4.28	4.29	2.14	2.14	0.31	0.69	-
C40G2-160-IN	Out-of-plane bulging	4.09	-	5.43	5.68	2.71	2.84	-	-	-	-	0.63	1.44	-
C25G2-250-IN	Out-of-plane bulging	5.54	-	7.48	9	3.74	4.5	-	-	-	-	0.48	1.23	-
F25G2-160-DN	Out-of-plane bulging	2.92	-	5.16	5.33	2.58	2.67	-	-	-	-	0.33	1.09	-
F25G2-160-IH	Core fracture	3	0.72	5.16	5.33	2.58	2.67	4.28	4.29	2.14	2.14	0.34	1.12	0.49
R25G2-200-DN	Core fracture	3.87	0.82	5.66	6	2.83	3	4.28	4.29	2.14	2.14	0.38	1.29	-
R40G2-120-IN	Core fracture	2.64	1.14	4.78	4.86	2.39	2.43	4.47	4.5	2.24	2.25	0.51	1.09	-
R40G2-200-SN	Core fracture	4.22	1.35	5.66	6	2.83	3	4.47	4.5	2.24	2.25	0.6	1.41	-
W16G2-85-IH	Core fracture	3.31	0.8	4.92	5.03	2.46	2.52	4.23	4.24	2.12	2.12	0.38	1.32	0.49
W16G2-95-IH	Core fracture	3.52	0.79	5.08	5.23	2.54	2.61	4.23	4.24	2.12	2.12	0.37	1.35	0.43
W 16G2-85-CN	Core fracture	1.93	0.45	4.92	5.03	2.46	2.52	4.23	4.24	2.12	2.12	0.21	0.77	-
RY25	Core fracture	3.87	0.84	10.95	17	5.48	8.5	4.23	4.24	2.12	2.12	0.4	0.46	-
RY65	In-plane bulging	-	4.76	-	-	-	-	4.23	4.24	2.12	2.12	2.25	2.98	-
RY65G	In-plane bulging	-	19.18	-	-	-	-	4.23	4.24	2.12	2.12	9.05	2.98	-
RrY125	In-plane bulging	-	39.6	-	-	-	-	4.26	4.27	2.13	2.14	18.54	17.57	-
RrY125M	In-plane bulging	-	47.08	-	-	-	-	4.36	4.38	2.18	2.19	21.49	35.98	-
RrY63	In-plane bulging	-	9.9	-	-	-	-	4.26	4.27	2.13	2.14	4.63	4.39	-
N400-1	Out-of-plane bulging	10.75	-	6.4	7.13	3.2	3.56	-	-	-	-	0.71	3.02	-
N490-1	Out-of-plane bulging	19.09	-	6.4	7.13	3.2	3.56	-	-	-	-	1.14	5.36	-
N225-1	Out-of-plane bulging	8.99	-	7.45	8.94	3.72	4.47	-	-	-	-	0.67	2.01	-
N400-2	Out-of-plane bulging	11.79	-	6.4	7.13	3.2	3.56	-	-	-	-	0.85	3.31	-
N490-2	Out-of-plane bulging	15.8	-	6.4	7.13	3.2	3.56	-	-	-	-	1.05	4.43	-
N225-2	Out-of-plane bulging	5.58	-	7.07	8.25	3.54	4.13	-	-	-	-	0.46	1.35	-

As shown in Table 3.5.3 and Figure 3.5.3, the Q_{w1} and Q_{w2} overestimate the steel tube capacities for nine specimens exhibited out-of-plane local bulging failure (W16G2-85-IN, W16G2-95-IN, R25G2-200-IN, F25G2-160-IN, F25G4-160-IN, C40G2-160-IN, C25G2-250-IN, F25G2-160-DN, and N225-2). This suggests that Q_{w1} and Q_{w2} provide dangerous estimation for design purpose. In addition, if compare Q_{w3} with Q_{w4} or Q_{s3} with Q_{s4}, the Q_{w3} and Q_{s3} provide smaller steel tube capacity estimations so that the design results may be over-conservative when the B_c/B_r or t_c/D_r is large. Therefore, the resistance factors computed by Condition 4 (Q_{w4} and Q_{s4}) are recommended for the BRB design in avoiding the local bulging failure. The demand-to-capacity ratio (DCR) for evaluating the in-plane (DCR_s) and out-of-plane (DCR_w) local bulging failures can be computed from the following equations. Both DCR_s and DCR_w should be no greater than 1.0 in order to avoid the local bulging failure,

$$DCR_s = \frac{P_{d,s}}{P_{c,s}} = \frac{(D_r - t_c)}{(2D_r - t_c)t_r^2 \sigma_{ry}} \cdot \frac{4N_{cu}(2s_{rs} + v_p B_c \varepsilon_t)}{l_{p,s}} < 1.0 \qquad (3.14)$$

$$DCR_w = \frac{P_{d,w}}{P_{c,w}} = \frac{(B_r - B_c)}{(2B_r - B_c)t_r^2 \sigma_{ry}} \cdot \frac{4N_{cu}(2s_{rw} + v_p t_c \varepsilon_t)}{l_{p,w}} < 1.0 \qquad (3.15)$$

As indicated in Equation (3.12a) and (3.12b), the steel tube capacity increases dramatically when the B_c/B_r or t_c/D_r is close to 1.0. However, the lengths of inclined yield lines (AB, BD, A'B', and B'D') become shorter as B_c/B_r or t_c/D_r increases. As the inclined yield lines near the steel tube corners are less capable in developing full flexural strength because of the residual stress effect, the maximum steel tube capacity when B_c/B_r or t_c/D_r is close to 1.0 should be set. Among the 15 test results of steel core fracture, the maximum ratio of B_c/B_r is 0.87. Thus, when using the Equation (3.14) and (3.15) in evaluating the BRB local bulging failure, it is suggested that the B_c/B_r and t_c/D_r should be no greater than 0.85 for conservative design purpose. This indicates that when the BRB configuration with B_c/B_r or t_c/D_r greater than 0.85, the maximum steel tube wall capacity $P_{c,w}$ or $P_{c,s}$ is limited to $7.7 t_r^2 \sigma_{ry}$. The comparisons between test results and the proposed equations are shown in Figure 3.5.4. The DCR_s and DCR_w for each specimen are shown in Table 3.5.3. The effects of steel tube thickness (t_r), debonding layer thickness (s_{rs} and s_{rw}), loading sequences, and infill mortar compressive strength on the test results are discussed in the following sections.

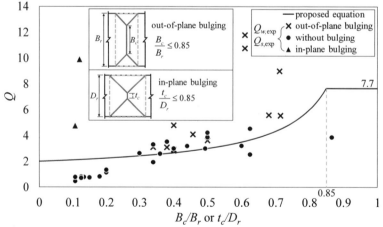

Figure 3.5.4 Comparisons between test results and proposed equations

Effects of steel tube wall thickness and debonding layer thickness

As indicated in Equation (3.14) and (3.15), the thicker steel tube wall thickness (t_r) can efficiently increase the capacity of the steel tube wall in resisting the outward forces. This can be verified by comparing the specimens RY25 to RY65, the in-plane local bulging failure was observed on the specimen RY25 with the steel tube wall thickness of 2.3mm. However, the local bulging failure was successfully avoided on the specimen RY65 by using a steel tube with thicker wall thickness (6mm). The proposed estimation also correctly predicts the test results (the DCR_s equal to 0.40 and 2.25 for RY25 and RY65, respectively).

As indicated in Equation (3.1), the outward forces are proportional to the clearances between the surfaces of steel core plate and mortar (s_{rs} and s_{rw}). Comparing the specimens F25G4-160-IN (DCR_w=1.79) to F25G2-160-IN (DCR_w=1.06), they have the same cross section dimensions and the loading protocol except the s_{rs} and s_{rw}. The out-of-plane local bulging failures were found on the specimens F25G4-160-IN and F25G2-160-IN when the 0.03 and 0.035 core strain cycles were applied, respectively. As shown in Figure 3.5.5, the specimen F25G4-160-IN(s_{rs}=s_{rw}=4mm) exhibited out-of-plane local bulging failure earlier than the specimen F25G2-160-IN(s_{rs}=s_{rw}=2mm). Thus, the specimen F25G4-160-IN gained less CPD (226) than the specimen F25G2-160-IN (354). In addition, before the local bulging failure occurred, the maximum axial force developed by specimen F25G4-160-IN (1920kN) is only 90% of specimen F25G2-160-IN (2134kN). Moreover, if compare the specimen R25G2-250-IN with specimen R25G1-250-IN, both of the two specimen exhibited steel core fracture and developed similar maximum axial force capacity ($N_{cu,\exp}$). The specimen with thinner debonding layer thickness (R25G1-250-IN) gained more CPD (767) than specimen R25G2-250-IN (CPD = 604). In conclusion, the thicker debonding layer thickness (s_{rs} or s_{rw}) would increase the risk of local bulging failure. In addition, when s_{rs} or s_{rw} is too large (4mm for example), it may lead to early development of local bulging failure and insufficient development of maximum axial force capacity ($N_{cu,\exp}$).

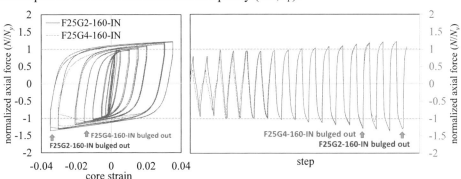

Figure 3.5.5 Test results of specimens F25G2-160-IN and F25G4-160-IN

Effects of loading sequence

Comparing the specimens R25G2-200-IN with R25G2-200-DN, they have the identical steel core and steel tube dimensions, each of the specimen was subjected to NCREE-I or NCREE-D loading protocol, respectively. The DCR_w are 1.21 and 1.29 for the specimens R25G2-200-IN and R25G2-200-DN, respectively. However, only the specimen R25G2-200-IN exhibited out-of-plane local bulging failure. Comparing the loading protocols NCREE-I and NCREE-D as shown in Figure 3.5.2, when the 0.035

42   Chapter 3. Local Bulging Failure

core strain was applied, the maximum outward force could be fully developed. However, the mortar in the specimen adopting NCREE-I loading protocol (R25G2-200-IN) has experienced more cycles of acting outward forces than the one adopting NCREE-D loading protocol (R25G2-200-DN). Thus, the mortar in the specimen R25G2-200-IN may be damaged more severely than the specimen R25G2-200-DN. This could explain why the specimen R25G2-200-IN exhibited out-of-plane local bulging failure but the specimen R25G2-200-DN did not. Similar results can be found by comparing the specimens F25G2-160-IN (DCR_w=1.06) with F25G2-160-DN (DCR_w=1.09). Before the steel tubes bulged out, the specimen adopting the NCREE-I loading protocol (F25G2-160-IN, CPD=354) gained less CPD than the one adopting NCREE-D loading protocol (F25G2-160-DN, CPD=690).

Effects of mortar compressive strength

According to the study [3.2], the steel tube of each specimen was removed after the tests in order to inspect the damaged mortar. For the specimens' restrainers infilled mortar with compressive strength (f'_c) of 97MPa (14000psi), the mortar remains in large chunks with only a few cracks. Thus, it is anticipated that the mortar with higher compressive strength would be less damaged by the high mode buckling waves before the steel core fractures. Based on the experimental observations [3.2] [3.7], when the out-of-plane outward forces are acting, the mortar cracks tended to extend form the contact line at the wave crests to the steel tube wall inner surface in both longitudinal and transverse directions with an incline angle of 45 degrees. The crack surfaces form a wedge shape mortar chunk. The mortar chunk assists in transferring the outward force to the steel tube wall. The outward force then acts as a surface load on the steel tube wall inner surface within a rectangular area of $2t_m$ long in the longitudinal direction and b' wide in the transverse direction as shown in Figure 3.5.6, where t_m is the mortar thickness and b' equals to B_c+2t_m. It should be reasonable to assume the yield lines to distribute along the outward force loading region edges as shown in Figure 3.5.6. Similar to the aforementioned steel tube wall bulged shape, the boundaries AD, A'D', AA', and DD' are not considered as yield lines. In addition, the ratio of b'/B_r should be no greater than 0.85 in order to avoid overestimating steel tube capacity when the inclined yield lines are too short. The internal energy (E_{wh}) resulted from the eight yield lines can be computed as follows,

$$E_{wh} = \left(\frac{8B_r - 4b' + 8t_m}{B_r - b'} \right) \delta_{wh} m_p, \quad b' = B_c + 2t_m \leq 0.85B_r \tag{3.16}$$

where δ_{wh} is the maximum outward deformation of the steel tube wall. The steel tube wall capacity $P_{c,wh}$ is as follows,

$$P_{c,wh} = \left(\frac{2B_r - b' + 2t_m}{B_r - b'} \right) t_r^2 \sigma_{ry} = Q_{wh} t_r^2 \sigma_{ry}, \quad b' = B_c + 2t_m \leq 0.85B_r \tag{3.17}$$

where Q_{wh} is the resistance factor considering the mortar spreading the outward forces to the steel tube wall surface in 45 degrees. The corresponding demand-to-capacity ratio (DCR_{wh}) can be computed as follows,

$$DCR_{wh} = \frac{P_{d,w}}{P_{c,wh}} = \frac{B_r - b'}{\left(2B_r - b' + 2t_m\right)t_r^2 \sigma_{ry}} \cdot \frac{4N_{cu}\left(2s_{rw} + v_p t_c \varepsilon_t\right)}{l_{p,w}}, \quad b' \leq 0.85B_r \tag{3.18}$$

Table 3.5.3 and Figure 3.5.7 show the DCR_{wh} and the relationships between Q_{wh} and $Q_{w,exp}$ for the specimens with f'_c greater than 97MPa. The numbers in Figure 3.5.7 indicate the t_m/B_r ratio of each specimen.

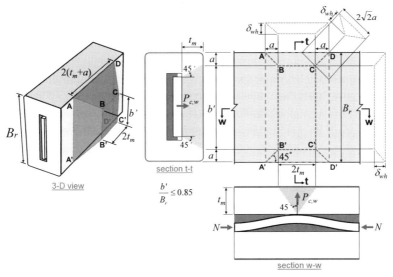

Figure 3.5.6 Schematic of bulged steel tube wall and the in-plane spreading outward force from transverse and longitudinal cross section views

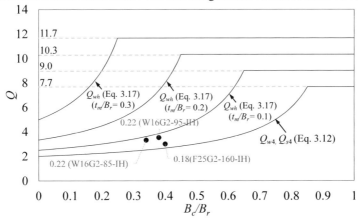

Figure 3.5.7 Relationships between $Q_{w,\exp}$ and Q_{wh} when t_m/B_r=0.1, 0.2, and 0.3

For the three BRB specimens with f'_c greater than 97MPa, all the DCR_w are greater than 1.0, but none of them exhibited out-of-plane local bulging failure. This suggests that the DCR_w may be over-conservative when the f'_c is greater than 97MPa. The revised DCR_{wh} could help in explaining the three BRBs did not exhibit out-of-plane local bulging failure. However, the design criterion of using DCR_{wh} needs to be verified by further investigations. Based on the test results, the DCR_w would be conservative when the f'_c is higher. In addition, it is suggested that the DCR_{wh} can be adopted only when the mortar compressive strength is greater than 97MPa.

3.6 REQUIRED MORTAR STRENGTH

As mentioned in the previous sections, the outward force is assumed to act as a line load at the contact region between the steel core wave crests and mortar. However, the contact region becomes from a line to a surface as the applied compression continues increasing. When the in-filled mortar in the restrainer does not have enough strength, it could be crushed by the acting outward forces. As shown in Figure 3.6.1, if the contact surface is B_c long and l_c wide, the criterion could be expressed as Equation (3.19).

$$\frac{P_{d,w}}{l_c B_c} < f'_c \tag{3.19}$$

where, f'_c is the allowable compressive strength of the in-filled mortar. Although the value of l_c requires more researches, it can be estimated generally as $l_c \approx t_c$. Using concrete or lower stiffness/strength materials for infill is not recommended for local crush are reported in the experiments using concrete infill instead of mortar.

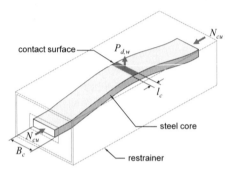

Figure 3.6.1 Schematic of local crush of in-filled material

3.7 LOCAL BULGING CRITERION FOR CIRCULAR RESTRAINER

Although no local bulging failure is reported for circular hollow section restrainers in the past, the criterion is proposed by Takeuchi et al. [3.8]. An estimated collapse mechanism with a circular restrainer is shown Figure 3.7.1. From this estimation, the ultimate perpendicular force component along in-plane direction, $P_{c,s}$ is calculated as Equation (3.20).

$$P_{c,s} = 2P_{ry}\cos\theta = \pi\sigma_{ry} t_r B_r \cos\theta, \qquad \cos\theta = \frac{c_m t_m + t_c}{B_r - 2t_r} \tag{3.20}$$

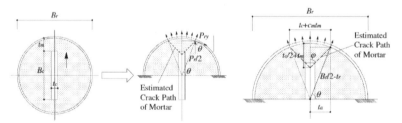

Figure 3.7.1 Plane yielding of circular restraint tube

where t_m represents the mortar thickness in the in-plane direction and the c_m is estimated as 2.5 in ref. [3.8] for mortar strength greater than 43MPa. Therefore, the demand-to-capacity ratio for circular hollow restrainer in resisting the steel core in-plane outward force (DCR_{sc}) can be computed as follows,

$$DCR_{sc} = \frac{P_{d,s}}{P_{c,s}} = \frac{(B_r - 2t_r)}{(c_m t_m + t_c)\pi t_r B_r \sigma_{ry}} \cdot \frac{4N_{cu}(2s_{rs} + v_p B_c \varepsilon_t)}{l_{p,s}} < 1.0 \tag{3.21}$$

Usually the criterion for out-of-plane local bulging becomes less critical than in-plane. Also local bulging failure with core plates with cruciform sections is not reported. Therefore, BRBs with cruciform, CHS, or H sectioned core plates are usually not required local bulging check, instead of local buckling concentration caused by friction between core and restrainer directly pushing the restrainer skin.

3.8 SUMMARY

The BRB local bulging failure should be avoided because it may lead to the BRB lose its compressive force carrying capacity. Based on the BRB test results, a simple procedure to evaluate the risk of local bulging is discussed in this chapter. The summaries are drawn as follows.

(1) When the steel core is in compression, the core plate forms both in-plane and out-of-plane high mode buckling waves. The steel core act outward forces on the restrainer at each wave crest. If the restrainer's strength is insufficient in resisting the outward forces, the steel tube wall may locally bulge out and lose its buckling-restrained ability.

(2) The outward force demand can be computed based on the BRB axial force and the geometric relationships between debonding layer thickness and high mode buckling wavelengths. Both the in-plane and out-of-plane high mode buckling wavelengths can be approached from the Euler buckling equations by using the BRB's yield axial force as buckling load and an averaged modulus of 5% of the elastic Young's modulus. The thicker debonding layer thickness and the larger BRB axial force applied, the larger outward forces would develop.

(3) Based on the experimental observations, the mortar in the restrainer was always severely crushed by the steel core high mode buckling waves near the local bulging region. Thus, only the steel tube wall strength is considered when estimating the restrainer capacity in resisting the outward forces. The mortar is only responsible in transferring the outward force from the steel core high mode buckling wave crests to the steel tube wall.

(4) The bulged steel tube wall can be represented as a wedge shape. The minimum outward force required to form the wedge shape with its five boundaries developing full flexural strength is considered as the capacity.

(5) When the infill mortar compressive strength is high, the out-of-plane local bulging failure estimation tends to be conservative. A modified wedge shape of the bulged steel tube wall can be adopted in computing the capacity when the infill mortar compressive strength is greater than 97MPa.

(6) Among the 34 BRB test specimens, 14 and 5 specimens exhibited out-of-plane and in-plane local bulging failures, respectively. The recommended estimation method correctly predicts all the local bulging results, and additional 11 over-conservative out-of-plane local bulging failure estimations. The estimation method is conservative and could be adopted for the BRB design in severe seismic services.

References:

[3.1]   Takeuchi T., Hajjar JF, Matsui R., Nishimoto K, and Aiken ID: Local buckling resistant condition for core plates in buckling restrained braces, *Journal of Constructional Steel Research*, 2010; **66**(2):139-149.

[3.2]   Lin PC, Tsai KC, Chang CA, Hsiao YY, Wu AC: Seismic design and testing of buckling-restrained braces with a thin profile, *Earthquake Engineering and Structural Dynamics*, 2016; **45**(3):339-358.

[3.3]   Wu AC, Lin PC, and Tsai KC: High-mode buckling responses of buckling-restrained brace core plates, *Earthquake Engineering and Structural Dynamics*, 2013; **43**(3):375-393.

[3.4]   Koetaka Y, Byakuno Y, Inoue K: Experimental verification of design criteria of knee brace damper, *The 4th International Symposium on Steel Structures*, 2006.

[3.5]   Yoshida F, Okamoto Y, Murai M, Iwata M: A study on local failure of buckling restrained braces using steel mortar planks (Part-1: local failure), *Summaries of technical papers of Annual Meeting Architectural Institute of Japan*, 2010; C-1, Structure III:961-962. *(in Japanese)*

[3.6]   Midorikawa M, Sasaki D, Asari T, Murai M, Iwata M: Experimental study on buckling-restrained braces using steel mortar planks - Effects of the clearance between core plate and restraining member on compressive strength and estimation of the number of buckling mode related to compressive strength, *AIJ J. Struct. Constr. Eng.*, 2010; **75**(653): 1361-1368. *(in Japanese)*

[3.7]   Okamoto Y, Yoshida F, Murai M, Iwata M: A study on local failure of buckling restrained braces using steel mortar planks (Part-2: cyclic loading test), *Summaries of technical papers of Annual Meeting Architectural Institute of Japan*, 2010; C-1, Structure III:963-964. *(in Japanese)*

[3.8]   Takeuchi T, Hajjar JF, Matsui R, Nishimoto K, Aiken ID: Effect of local buckling core plate restraint in buckling restrained braces, *Engineering Structures*, 2012; **44**:304-311.

Chapter 4

CONNECTION DESIGN AND GLOBAL STABILITY

CHAPTER CONTENTS

4.1 TYPICAL CONNECTION DETAILS AND DESIGN FORCES

4.2 GLOBAL INSTABILITY INCLUDING CONNECTIONS

4.3 STABILITY CONDITION FOR BRBS WITH ONE-WAY CONFIGURATION

4.4 STABILITY CONDITION FOR BRBS WITH CHEVRON CONFIGURATION

4.5 EVALUATIONS FOR KEY PARAMETERS

4.6 CONNECTION DESIGN AGAINST IN-PLANE DEFORMATION

4.1 TYPICAL CONNECTION DETAILS AND DESIGN FORCES

Typical connections used for BRBs are shown in Figure 4.1.1. Bolted connections are commonly used for ease of installation and to enable the braces to be replaced following a severe earthquake. These may use either slip critical or bearing type bolts. Welded connections produce a compact connection, but require site welding. Pinned connections are used to avoid in-plane bending moment transfer and enhanced aesthetics, but require tight tolerances and precise alignment to avoid excessive slack and the resultant pinched hysteresis shape. Although bolted connections are easily replaceable, global stability tends to become the governing design criteria.

(a) Bolted connection

(b) Welded connection   (c) Pinned connection

Figure 4.1.1 Typical connections used for BRBs

BRBs are unique in that the axial overstrength is larger in compression than tension. While core buckling is restrained, Pδ 'buckling' moments are still present due to small initial imperfections and slack between the neck and restrainer. Therefore, a critical design action should consider combined compression and bending (NM) with stability that is governing limit state.

The designer must therefore consider both strength and stiffness, with the requirements in some cases more onerous than for conventional braced frame connections. Strength checks include the section, weld and bolt capacities of the gusset, splice, neck, and restrainer end, as indicated in Figure 4.1.2(a). Minimum stiffness criteria (Figure 4.1.2(b)) are primarily related to out-of-plane stability, a unique aspect of BRB connection design that is the primary focus of this chapter.

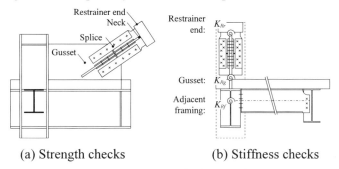

(a) Strength checks   (b) Stiffness checks

Figure 4.1.2 Key design checks

4.2 GLOBAL INSTABILITY INCLUDING CONNECTIONS

While BRB stability calculations have traditionally been limited to the restrainer design, numerous studies have highlighted the risk of global out-of-plane buckling initiated by inelasticity in the gussets, necks and/or restrainer ends (Figure 4.2.1). This mode of instability is distinct from global restrainer buckling (Chapter 2), local gusset plate buckling, and restrainer bulging (Chapter 3), as depicted in Figure 4.2.1.

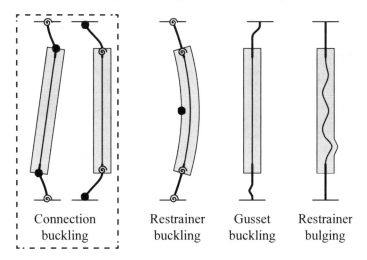

Fig. 4.2.1 Out-of-plane buckling mode

Buckling-restrained braces (BRBs) are expected to exhibit stable hysteresis when subjected to in-plane cyclic axial loading; however, numerous studies have highlighted the risk of global BRB buckling initiated by inelasticity in the gussets, necks and/or restrainer ends, sometimes prior to core yielding (Figure 4.2.1). For instance, Saeki et al. (1997) [4.1] reported that the specimen would become unstable when cores were not tapered to restrict yielding within the restrainer. Out-of-plane buckling was observed during large scale frame tests, highlighting the importance of gusset out-of-plane stiffness and restrainer end continuity (Tsai et al. (2002, 2008) [4.2], [4.3]). Several studies have investigated the effect of low adjacent framing out-of-plane rotational or translational stiffness, a critical aspect for chevron and multi-tier configurations (Koetaka et al. (2008) [4.4], Chou et al. (2012) [4.5], Hikino et al. (2013) [4.6]). A related focus of research has been the potential for out-of-plane instability following softening of adjacent beams under large in-plane demands, both in steel (Uriz et al. (2008) [4.7], Palmer et al. (2014) [4.8]) and reinforced concrete frames (Mahrenholtz et al. (2015) [4.9]). Various beam-pin or gusset isolation details have been proposed to eliminate the in-plane compatibility demands (Walters et al. (2004) [4.10], Berman et al. (2009) [4.11], Wigle et al. (2010) [4.12], Prinz et al. (2014) [4.13]), with similar details for RC applications discussed in Chapter 7. Recent results have demonstrated that initial out-of-plane drift is important both due to the imposed flexural demands, and in enforcing the critical anti-symmetric imperfection pattern (Takeuchi et al. (2014, 2016) [4.14], [4.15]).

Fig. 4.2.2 Global BRB buckling including connections and vulnerable connection detail examples

Code Requirements

Few design codes provide analytical methods to assess BRB connection stability, with prototype testing adopted as the primary means of validation. The commentary to AISC 341-16 (2016) [4.21] states:

Recent testing in stability and fracture has demonstrated that gusset-plate connections may be a critical aspect of the design of BRBF (Tsai et al., 2003; Lopez et al., 2004). The tendency to instability may vary depending on the flexural stiffness of the connection portions of the buckling-restrained brace and the degree of their flexural continuity with the casing. This aspect of BRBF design is the subject of continuing investigation and designers are encouraged to consult research publications as they become available. The stability of gussets may be demonstrated by testing, if the test specimen adequately resembles the conditions in the building. AISC 341-16 C-F4.6c (2016) [4.21]

However, several *Architectural Institute of Japan* publications (2009, 2013, 2014, 2017) [4.16-4.19] offer perhaps the most detailed treatment of this topic, including quantitative evaluation methods to supplement the *Building Centre of Japan* (BCJ) prequalification specification (2017) [4.20]. This chapter is primarily based on these provisions and the research behind their development. For engineers practicing outside of Japan, the method described in Section 4.4 is similar to the design provisions in AIJ *Recommendations for stability design of steel structures: Chapter 3.5 buckling-restrained braces* (2017).

Design Concept

Two stability design concepts were proposed in the 2009 AIJ *Recommendations for Stability Design of Steel Structures* [4.16], and are shown in Figure 4.2.3. The primary stability design concept should be clearly identified at the outset of design based on discussions with the supplier.

(1) *Cantilever Connection Concept*: Effectively rigid adjacent framing and gussets are provided, such that restrainer end continuity can be neglected. Stability is ensured by designing the connection zone as a simple cantilever [Figure 4.2.3 (a)].

(2) *Restrainer Continuity Concept*: Full restrainer end moment transfer capacity is provided, permitting more flexible gusset or adjacent framing details. Buckling analysis is more complex, with the critical hinge located either at the neck or gusset. [Figure 4.2.3 (b)].

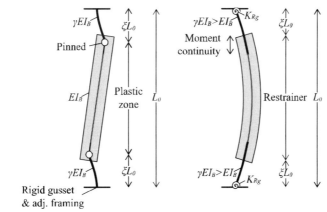

(a) Cantilever Connection   (b) Restrainer Continuity

Figure 4.2.3 BRB stability condition concepts

(*AIJ Recommendations for Stability Design of Steel Structures,* 2009) [4.16]

The out-of-plane stiffness of several key components distinguish the AIJ stability concepts: the gusset rotational stiffness K_{Rg}, adjacent framing rotational stiffness K_{Rf}, and the restrainer end rotational stiffness K_{Rr}.

Gusset rotational stiffness K_{Rg}

The *Cantilever Connection Concept* (a) primarily relies on the gusset and adjacent framing rotational stiffness. The gusset rotational stiffness K_{Rg} is largely governed by the stiffener topology, which is classified in Figure 4.2.4. First, consider the case where the connection is a cruciform section with flexural stiffness γEI_B. If the cruciform is extended full-depth (Gusset Type D), the gusset introduces no additional flexibility and results in a rigid boundary conditions. Gussets with full-depth edge stiffeners (Gusset

Type C) are only slightly more flexible, and so either Gusset Type C or D can be employed if *Cantilever Connection Concept* is selected.

However, if full-depth stiffeners are omitted (Gusset Type A or B), the connection stiffness rapidly decreases, with out-of-plane rotation concentrating at the gusset. This has a dramatic effect on the elastic buckling load, which can easily be less than 30% of the pure cantilever buckling load.

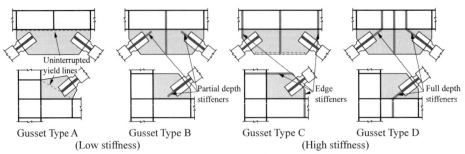

Figure 4.2.4 – Gusset plate types and out-of-plane stiffness

Adjacent framing rotational stiffness K_{Rf}

In some cases the adjacent framing rotational stiffness (K_{Rf}) may be of a similar magnitude or more flexible than the gusset. This reduces the gusset rotational stiffness This usually occurs at the beam connection of BRB arranged in a chevron configuration, as shown in Figure 4.2.5(b). In this case, standard buckling length L_0 should be taken from the adjacent beam centroid.

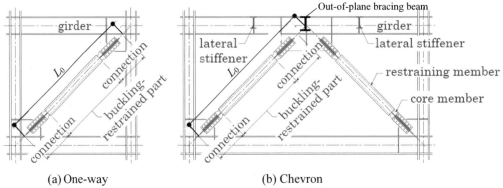

(a) One-way (b) Chevron
Figure 4.2.5 – BRB configurations in frame

Restrainer end rotational stiffness K_{Rr}

The *Restrainer Continuity Concept* requires calculation of the restrainer end rotational stiffness (K_{Rr}), including the effects of local deformations of the restrainer or collar tube. Special details are required to prevent transmission of axial loads into the restrainer, resulting in a bearing type connection (Figure 4.2.6). Flexural continuity is established by a rigid elastic inner member bearing against the restrainer. If the insert or overlap length L_{in} is short, this imposes relatively large out-of-plane bearing forces, which can easily deform the thin tube.

Chapter 4. Connection Design and Global Stability   53

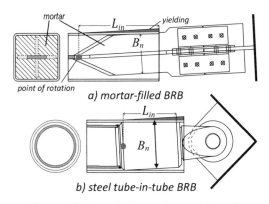

Figure 4.2.6 Typical restrainer end details

For cruciform inserts (Figure 4.2.6a), Matsui et al. (2014) [4.24] found that the degree of continuity is closely related to the cruciform out-of-plane width (B_n) and insert length (L_{in}). For short insert lengths ($L_{in}/B_n<1.0$) the detail essentially acts as a pin once the core yields, while longer inserts ($L_{in}/B_n>1.5$~2.0) transfer a significant portion of the neck flexural capacity. Intermediate ratios tend to be governed by local yielding of the restrainer end casing, as indicated by Figure 4.2.7.

While most BRBs have mortar infill, this should be assumed to be fully cracked and effective only in transmitted the bearing forces. This is consistent with cyclic test data. Another important aspect of the restrainer end detail is the potentially large clearance between the neck and restrainer, which is required to limit friction. This introduces an apparent geometric imperfection, as the connection must undergo large out-of-plane displacements prior to engaging the restrainer in flexure.

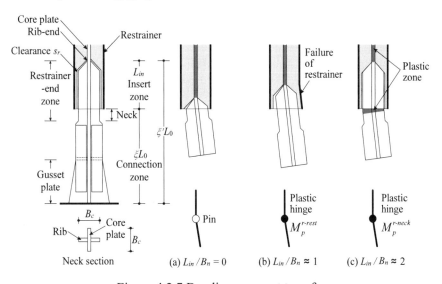

Figure 4.2.7 Bending moment transfer

4.2.1 CANTILEVER CONNECTION CONCEPT

Several researchers have proposed evaluation methods based on the *Cantilever Connection* Concept. These are simple to apply, but most only consider elastic stability. Because continuity at the restrainer end is ignored, a stiff gusset (Gusset Type C or D) with rigid adjacent framing (fixed end transverse beam) is usually required. These methods are a good starting point to check the general feasibility of a connection arrangement.

Tsai and Nakamura's proposal (2002)

One of the earliest evaluation methods for out-of-plane stability was proposed by Tsai et al. (2002) [4.2] and is listed in the textbook by Bruneau et al. (2011) [4.25]. This is an elastic buckling check based on the neck section with an effective length taken as twice the beam/column centroid to restrainer end distance, as shown in Figure 4.2.8. However, neither a rigorous theoretical basis, nor detailed explanation is provided.

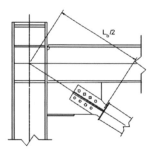

Figure 4.2.8 – Tsai and Nakamura's proposal [4.2]

Koetaka and Inoue's proposal (2008)

Koetaka et al. (2008) [4.4] discussed the elastic buckling limit for a BRB in the chevron configuration, including a rotational and horizontal sway spring at the upper (beam) connection as shown in Figure 4.2.9. In this model, bending-moment transfer capacity at the restrainer ends is neglected and assumed to be pinned, while the beam/column end is assumed fixed. Note that the brace is assumed to deflect in an anti-symmetric mode shape, accounting for the destabilizing shear resulting from the inclined restrainer. $r_J EI_B$ is the bending stiffness at connections expressed as a percentage of the restrainer out-of-plane flexural stiffness [4.4].

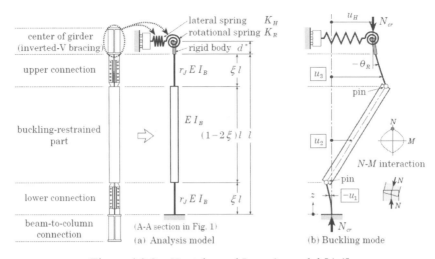

Figure 4.2.9 – Koetaka and Inoue's model [4.4]

The stability limit is defined as a combination of translation and rotation at the upper (beam) connection. When the upper connection is braced by a fixed-end secondary beam or by fly bracing and slab, both the rotational and horizontal springs, K_R and K_H, respectively, are large and the elastic buckling strength is defined by:

$$N_{cr} = \frac{\pi^2 (1-2\xi) r_J E I_B}{(2\xi L_0)^2} \qquad (4.2.1)$$

When a diaphragm restrains the translational component, but offers insufficient rotational stiffness K_R to provide full restraint, the stability limit is evaluated by:

$$N_{cr} = \frac{(1-2\alpha_N \xi)l}{(1+d^* - \alpha_N \xi l)(d^* + \alpha_N \xi l)} \cdot K_R \qquad (4.2.2)$$

Where $\alpha_N = 1/\left(1 - N_{Max}/N_J^E\right)$, $N_J^E = \dfrac{\pi^2 r_J E I_J}{(2\xi l)^2}$

where a_N, the displacement amplitude factor, is defined as $a_N=1/(1-N_{max}/N_J^E)$. When this effect is negligible, a_N approaches 1, and Equation (4.2.2) reduces to Equation (4.2.3), referring to Figure 4.2.9 for the definition of connection length proportions ξ_1 (lower) and ξ_2 (upper), and brace length L_0.

$$N_{cr} = \frac{1-\xi_1-\xi_2}{(1-\xi_1)\cdot \xi_2 L_0} \cdot K_R \qquad (4.2.3)$$

Hikino and Okazaki's proposal (2013)

Hikino et al. (2013) [4.6] discussed stability conditions of a BRB with similar boundary conditions as Koetaka et al. (2008) [4.4], but modelled the restrainer and connection segments shown in Figure 4.2.9 (b) as rigid bodies. When a diaphragm restrains the translational component, the proposed equation becomes equivalent to Equation (4.2.3).

$$N_{cr} = \frac{K_R}{L_1}\frac{L_1}{L_1+L_2} = \frac{K_R}{\xi l + d^*} \cdot \frac{1-2\xi-d^*}{1-\xi} = \frac{1-\xi_1-\xi_2}{(1-\xi_1)\cdot \xi_2 L_0}\cdot K_R \qquad (4.2.4)$$

Takeuchi's proposal (2014)

Recognizing that the *Cantilever Connection Concept* will often require non-slender sections, Takeuchi et al. (2014) [4.14] proposed using code column buckling curves to account for inelasticity. Idealizing the gusset as a concentrated rotational spring, the elastic buckling load is given by Equation (4.2.5). Note that the connection length is taken to the end of the insert and the connection stiffness γEI_B can conservatively be taken to exclude splice plates.

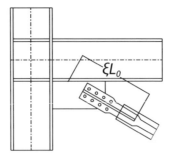

Figure 4.2.10 Effective length

$$N_{cr}^R = (1-2\xi) \cdot \frac{\pi^2 \gamma_J EI_B}{(2\xi L_0)^2} \cdot \frac{{}_\xi \kappa_{Rg}}{{}_\xi \kappa_{Rg} + 24/\pi^2} \quad (4.2.5)$$

${}_\xi \kappa_{Rg}$ is the normalized rotational stiffness at the gusset defined in Equation (4.3.1) later. A generalized equivalent slenderness covering all gusset types is given by Equations (4.2.6 a-c), where I' and A' correspond to the effective gusset section. The inelastic buckling load is then determined from an appropriate code column buckling curve, and is denoted N_{cr}^r.

$$\lambda = \frac{L_e}{i_c}, \; L_e = 2\xi L_0 \cdot \frac{\gamma_J I_r}{I'} \cdot \sqrt{\frac{{}_\xi \kappa_{Rg} + 24/\pi^2}{(1-2\xi) {}_\xi \kappa_{Rg}}}, \; i_c = \sqrt{\frac{I'}{A'}} \quad (4.2.6 \text{ a-c})$$

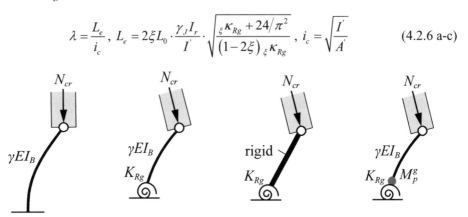

Tsai and Nakamura   Koetaka and Inoue   Hikino and Okazaki   Takeuchi

Figure 4.2.11 *Cantilever Connection Concepts*

A schematic of these methods is depicted in Figure 4.2.11, indicating the key parameters and simplifying assumptions. While analysis is simplified by assuming the restrainer end is pinned, greater economy can be achieved by directly considering restrainer end continuity, the *Restrainer Continuity Concept*.

4.3 STABILITY CONDITION WITH ONE-WAY CONFIGURATION [4.14]

The *Restrainer Continuity Concept* described in Figure 4.2.3 (b) is based on the analysis of the full BRB with continuity provided at the restrainer ends. As it is more common for only partial continuity to be provided, this analysis can be generalized to consider a semi-rigid connection with restrainer end rotational stiffness K_{Rr}. The modeling idealization is shown in Figure 4.3.1.

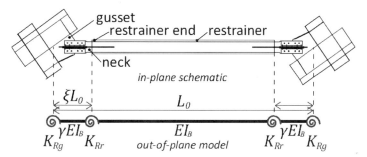

Figure 4.3.1 Spring model idealization

The stability limit of this model is more complex to analyze than for typical columns, as the restrainer does not resist significant axial loads. This shifts the critical hinge to the connection region where the Pδ moment distribution and cross section capacity varies. The critical plastic hinge can be assumed to be located at the gusset or neck, which are represented by discrete elasto-plastic springs in Figure 4.3.1. It is useful to normalize the initial rotational stiffness of these springs as follows:

$$_\xi\kappa_{Rg} = \frac{K_{Rg}\xi L_0}{\gamma_J EI_B}, \quad _\xi\kappa_{Rr} = \frac{K_{Rr}\xi L_0}{\gamma_J EI_B} \quad (4.3.1)$$

Initial Imperfections

Another important consideration when restrainer end continuity is assumed is the presence of rotational slack between the neck and restrainer. While the debonding gap or compressible material thickness along the neck may be small, the connection must undergo some out-of-plane rotation before the restrainer flexural stiffness is engaged. Because geometric imperfections introduced during fabrication and construction are typically only on the order of L/1000, the out-of-plane displacement required to achieve continuity can greatly reduce the critical inelastic buckling load.

A conservative approximation of the total geometric imperfection (a_r) was proposed by Takeuchi et al. [4.14], including eccentricity of the applied load (e), fabrication tolerance anlge (θ_0), and slack due to the debonding gap (s_r).

$$a_r = e + s_r + \xi L_0 \left(\theta_0 + \frac{2s_r}{L_{in}} \right) \quad (4.3.2)$$

Equation (4.3.2) assumes the linear rotation shown in Figure 4.3.2. The lateral displacements from a recent test readily illustrate this large apparent geometric imperfection (Figure 4.3.3). Construction tolerances were confirmed to be negligible ($\theta_0 \le$ L/1000) and yet a large initial imperfection a_r=13mm (L/35) is clearly visible.

58   Chapter 4. Connection Design and Global Stability

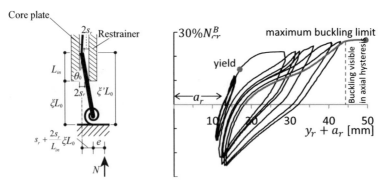

Figure 4.3.2 Initial imperfections   Figure 4.3.3 Axial force by lateral displacement
(specimen MCL2.0S2 [4.14])

While the proportions of this specimen exaggerate the effect, imperfections of full-size BRBs can easily be on the order of L/100. Consult with suppliers on the appropriate debonding thickness.

Elastic Buckling Properties

Given that imperfection is generated at the restrainer end, which is also one of the potential plastic hinge location, this will be taken as the reference lateral displacement y_r. The elastic buckling properties and Pδ moment distribution of this system can then be determined analytically, as described by Matsui et al. (2010) [4.24].

Representing the elastic buckling load by an effective length factor, these values are tabulated in Table 4.3.1 for the first two modes over the typical range of normalized stiffness encountered in practice. It is clear that at least either the gusset or restrainer end must have substantial stiffness to control the effective length, but that there are diminishing returns to making both stiff.

For comparison, values in Table 4.3.1 are highlighted where the effective length is longer than that proposed by Tsai and Nakamura, and Table 4.3.2 shows the effective length with respect to the full brace.

Furthermore, the Pδ moment distribution as a function of the restrainer end lateral displacement is illustrated in Figure 4.3.4 and Appendix A.4. Note that the moment at the sensitive restrainer end is larger for the anti-symmetric mode case, providing some indication as to why this mode might govern for inelastic buckling.

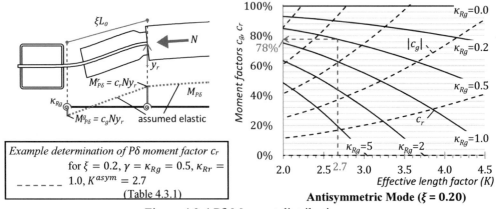

Figure 4.3.4 Pδ Moment distribution

Chapter 4. Connection Design and Global Stability

Table 4.3.1 Effective length factor (K)

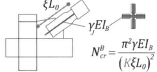

$$N_{cr}^B = \frac{\pi^2 \gamma EI_B}{(K\xi L_0)^2}$$

$K > (1.5 \cdot)K_{Nakamura}$ $\gamma_J = 0.5$

K			Symmetric Mode					Asymmetric Mode			
ξ	K_{Rg} \ K_{Rr}	0.25	0.5	1.0	2.0	5.0	0.25	0.5	1.0	2.0	5.0
0.15	0.0	7.5	6.2	5.5	5.1	4.9	5.7	4.4	3.5	3.1	2.8
	0.2	5.2	4.8	4.5	4.4	4.3	4.7	3.8	3.2	2.8	2.6
	0.5	4.1	4.0	3.9	3.8	3.8	4.0	3.4	2.9	2.6	2.4
	1.0	3.5	3.4	3.4	3.4	3.4	3.4	3.0	2.6	2.4	2.3
	2.0	3.2	3.2	3.2	3.1	3.1	2.9	2.6	2.3	2.2	2.1
	5.0	3.1	3.0	3.0	3.0	2.9	2.4	2.2	2.1	2.0	1.9
0.20	0.0	7.1	5.6	4.7	4.2	3.9	5.2	3.9	3.1	2.6	2.3
	0.2	5.0	4.4	3.9	3.6	3.5	4.5	3.6	2.9	2.5	2.2
	0.5	3.9	3.6	3.3	3.2	3.1	3.9	3.2	2.7	2.3	2.1
	1.0	3.2	3.0	2.9	2.8	2.7	3.4	2.9	2.4	2.1	1.9
	2.0	2.7	2.6	2.5	2.5	2.5	2.9	2.6	2.2	2.0	1.8
	5.0	2.3	2.3	2.2	2.2	2.2	2.5	2.2	2.0	1.8	1.6
0.25	0.0	6.9	5.3	4.3	3.7	3.4	4.7	3.5	2.8	2.3	2.0
	0.2	4.9	4.2	3.6	3.3	3.0	4.2	3.3	2.6	2.2	1.9
	0.5	3.9	3.5	3.1	2.9	2.7	3.8	3.0	2.5	2.1	1.8
	1.0	3.1	2.9	2.7	2.5	2.4	3.4	2.8	2.3	2.0	1.7
	2.0	2.6	2.4	2.3	2.2	2.1	3.0	2.5	2.1	1.8	1.6
	5.0	2.2	2.1	2.0	1.9	1.9	2.6	2.2	1.9	1.7	1.4

Gusset Type A ↑
Gusset Type D ↓

Thin RHS rest. $L_{in}/D < 1$ → Thick CHS rest. $L_{in}/D > 2$

Table 4.3.2 Global effective length factor (K_{global}) with respect to full length

$K_{Global} = K \cdot \xi / \sqrt{\gamma_J}$

$\gamma_J = 0.5$

$K_{global} > 1.0$

$$N_{cr}^B = \frac{\pi^2 EI_B}{(K_{global} L_0)^2}$$

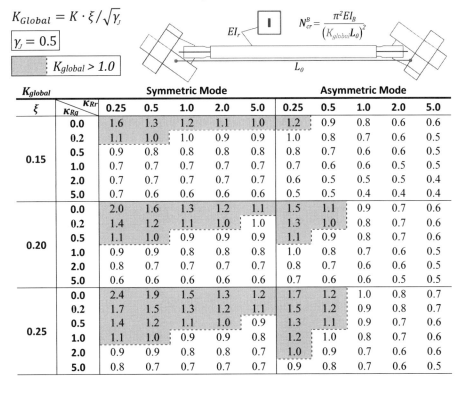

K_{global}			Symmetric Mode					Asymmetric Mode			
ξ	K_{Rg} \ K_{Rr}	0.25	0.5	1.0	2.0	5.0	0.25	0.5	1.0	2.0	5.0
0.15	0.0	1.6	1.3	1.2	1.1	1.0	1.2	0.9	0.8	0.6	0.6
	0.2	1.1	1.0	1.0	0.9	0.9	1.0	0.8	0.7	0.6	0.5
	0.5	0.9	0.8	0.8	0.8	0.8	0.8	0.7	0.6	0.6	0.5
	1.0	0.7	0.7	0.7	0.7	0.7	0.7	0.6	0.6	0.5	0.5
	2.0	0.7	0.7	0.7	0.7	0.7	0.6	0.5	0.5	0.5	0.4
	5.0	0.7	0.6	0.6	0.6	0.6	0.5	0.5	0.4	0.4	0.4
0.20	0.0	2.0	1.6	1.3	1.2	1.1	1.5	1.1	0.9	0.7	0.6
	0.2	1.4	1.2	1.1	1.0	1.0	1.3	1.0	0.8	0.7	0.6
	0.5	1.1	1.0	0.9	0.9	0.9	1.1	0.9	0.8	0.7	0.6
	1.0	0.9	0.9	0.8	0.8	0.8	1.0	0.8	0.7	0.6	0.5
	2.0	0.8	0.7	0.7	0.7	0.7	0.8	0.7	0.6	0.6	0.5
	5.0	0.6	0.6	0.6	0.6	0.6	0.7	0.6	0.6	0.5	0.5
0.25	0.0	2.4	1.9	1.5	1.3	1.2	1.7	1.2	1.0	0.8	0.7
	0.2	1.7	1.5	1.3	1.2	1.1	1.5	1.2	0.9	0.8	0.7
	0.5	1.4	1.2	1.1	1.0	0.9	1.3	1.1	0.9	0.7	0.6
	1.0	1.1	1.0	0.9	0.9	0.8	1.2	1.0	0.8	0.7	0.6
	2.0	0.9	0.9	0.8	0.8	0.7	1.0	0.9	0.7	0.6	0.6
	5.0	0.8	0.7	0.7	0.7	0.7	0.9	0.8	0.7	0.6	0.5

Elasto-plastic Buckling

Despite the unique characteristics of BRBs, the fundamental equations governing buckling of beam-columns with initial geometric imperfection are still applicable. For simplicity, we first consider an elasto-perfectly plastic system.

The first important equation defines the relationship between the lateral displacement (y_r) and compressive load (N). It is assumed that the pattern of initial imperfections and displacements due to simultaneous transverse demands matches the mode shape associated with an elastic buckling load $N^B{}_{cr}$. Importantly, both forms of initial lateral displacement are increasingly amplified as the elastic buckling load is approached ($N \to N^B_{cr}$).

$$\underbrace{y_r + a_r}_{\text{total disp.}} = \underbrace{(a_r + y_{N=0})}_{\text{initial imperf.}} \cdot \underbrace{1/(1 - N/N^B_{cr})}_{\text{amplification}} \qquad (4.3.5)$$

The lateral displacement generates Pδ moments, which act in combination with the applied first order moments from the transverse actions. However, the effect of end fixity reduces the Pδ moment at the restrainer end to $c_r \cdot N \cdot y_r$ with c_r a moment distribution factor. The total moment at the restrainer end is then given by Equation 4.3.6:

$$M^r = M_0^r + c_r N(y_r + a_r) \qquad (4.3.6)$$

$M_0{}^r$ is additionally imposed bending moment at restrainer end due to out-of-plane drift, described later in 4.5.3. After the total moment exceeds yield, the stiffness degrades and lateral displacements are amplified at an increased rate (refer Figure 4.3.5). For inelastic buckling this is a gradual process as the plastic hinge softens, but generally the *collapse path* converges to the residual system's elastic buckling limit, $N^R_{cr}(\kappa_{Rr} \to 0)$. Whether the slope is positive or negative depends on the magnitude of N^R_{cr}. Substituting N^R_{cr} for N^B_{cr} and rearranging Equation (4.3.5):

$$N = N^R_{cr} \frac{y_r - y_{N=0}}{y_r + a_r} \qquad (4.3.7a)$$

Including the hinge's net locked-in plastic buckling moment $(M_p^r - M_0^r)$, with corresponding axial load related by $\beta_{(g,r)}$, the post-yield collapse path becomes:

$$N = N^R_{cr} \frac{y_r - y_{N=0}}{y_r + a_r} + \beta_{(g,r)} \frac{M_p^r - M_0^r}{y_r + a_r} \qquad (4.3.7b)$$

Equations (4.3.5)-(4.3.7) are depicted in Figure 4.3.5. The critical buckling load N_{cr} can then be solved from Equations (4.3.5) and (4.3.6) (critical moment), or from Equations (4.3.5) and (4.3.7b) (intersection of elastic and collapse paths).

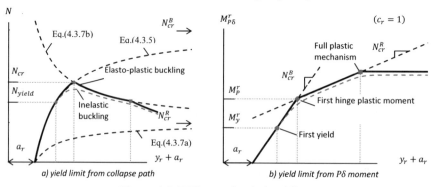

Figure 4.3.5 Elasto-plastic buckling

Note that this elasto-plastic system gives only an approximate indication of the true inelastic buckling capacity. As described in Galambos and Surovek (2008) [4.26], for trivially simple cases the moment-load-curvature (M-N-φ) can be analytically determined and directly solved. However, for practical systems this relationship is highly nonlinear and best assessed numerically using a finite element model with fibre elements.

4.3.2 TAKEUCHI's PROPOSAL (2014)

Takeuchi et al. (2014) [4.14] proposed to evaluate the buckling capacity from the plastic collapse mechanism. This is graphically depicted by Figure 4.3.6.

First, recognizing that displacements due to out-of-plane drift are much less than initial imperfections, Equation 4.3.5 is approximated as:

$$N = \frac{y_r}{y_r + a_r} N_{cr}^B \qquad (4.3.8)$$

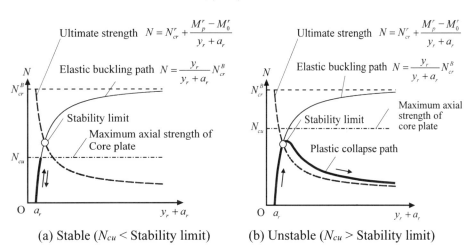

(a) Stable (N_{cu} < Stability limit)   (b) Unstable (N_{cu} > Stability limit)

Figure 4.3.6 BRB stability concepts and limits

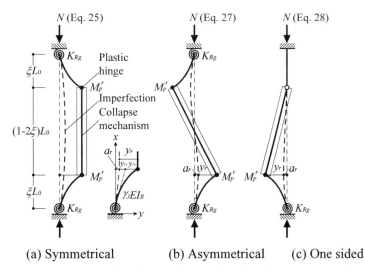

(a) Symmetrical   (b) Asymmetrical   (c) One sided

Figure 4.3.7 Collapse mechanisms with rotational springs at gusset plates

Interestingly, the general form of Equation (4.3.7b) can be directly derived by analyzing the plastic mechanism using the Energy Method. Three potential collapse modes were considered.

This method adopts a sinusoidal imperfection pattern as a function of the restrainer end displacement y_r:

$$y = \frac{a_r x}{\xi L_0} + y_r \left[1 - \cos\left(\frac{\pi x}{2\xi L_0} \right) \right]$$ (4.3.9)

The energy balance equation is then assembled, with the strain energy from spring rotation (U_s) and connection flexural action (U_ε), plastic strain energy from the restrainer end hinge (U_p), and axial work done (T) for each end given by:

$$U_\varepsilon = 0.5\gamma EI_r \int \ddot{y}^2 , \ U_S = 0.5K_g\Delta\theta_r , \ U_p = M_p^r\Delta\theta_r , \ T = N\Delta u_g$$ (4.3.10)

The stability limit is determined from the energy differential and repeated for each mode.

$$\frac{\partial(U_\varepsilon + U_p + U_s - T)}{\partial y_r} = 0$$ (4.3.11)

Solving for N, the symmetric mode reduces to:

$$N = \frac{\pi^2 \gamma_J EI_B}{(2\xi L_0)^2} \frac{\xi \kappa_{Rg}}{\xi \kappa_{Rg} + 24/\pi^2} \cdot \frac{y_r}{y_r + 8a_r/\pi^2} + \frac{4}{\pi} \frac{\xi \kappa_{Rg} + 6/\pi}{\xi \kappa_{Rg} + 24/\pi^2} \cdot \frac{M_p^r}{y_r + 8a_r/\pi^2}$$ (4.3.12)

Not coincidentally, the first term in this equation is the elastic buckling load of the post-yield system N^R_{cr}, with a pin substituted for the plastic hinge. Further approximating $8/\pi^2 \approx 1$, and setting the residual terms equal to β, the same form as Equation (4.3.7) is obtained.

$$N \approx N^R_{cr} \frac{y_r}{y_r + a_r} + \beta_{(g,r)} \frac{M_p^r}{y_r + a_r}$$ (4.3.13)

A similar analysis can be conducted for the anti-symmetric and one-sided modes, leading to the same general form. Furthermore, the factor relating flexure-to-axial load $\beta \approx 1$, and M^r_p can be directly reduced by the first-order flexural demands due to out-of-plane drift. For further details refer to Takeuchi et al. (2014) [4.14]. As the cross point of elastic buckling strength path and ultimate strength in Figure 4.3.6, the stability limit is defined as:

$$N_{lim1} = \frac{\left(M_p^r - M_0^r \right)/a_r + N_{cr}^r}{\left(M_p^r - M_0^r \right)/a_r N_{cr}^B + 1} > N_{cu}$$ (4.3.14)

Where, N^r_{cr} is elasto-plastic buckling load of N^R_{cr}, and $M_p^r - M_0^r$ should be taken as zero if the difference is negative. Equation (4.3.14) is lead from the approximation of Equation (4.3.13) to yield to $N_{lim1}=N^r_{cr}$ when $M_p^r - M_0^r = 0$.

To satisfy Equation (4.3.14), two approaches can be followed.

(1) When the gusset stiffness $_\xi \kappa_{Rg}$ is sufficiently large, the left part of Equation (4.3.14) tends towards zero. This corresponds to the *Cantilever Connection* concept discussed earlier (Figure 4.2.2a)

Chapter 4. Connection Design and Global Stability   63

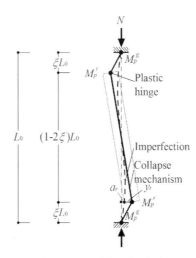

Figure 4.3.8 Collapse mechanisms with plastic hinges at gusset plates

(2) Decrease M_0^r and N_{cr}^r by decreasing $_\xi \kappa_{Rg}$, and provide sufficient bending strength M_p^r to satisfy Equation (4.3.14). This approach corresponds to transferring the bending moment at the restrainer-end zone (Figure 4.2.2b).

The proposed stability condition in Equation (4.2.14) is based on the condition that the gusset plates remain elastic. When plastic hinges are produced at the gusset plates, a different global buckling mode as shown in Figure 4.3.8 comes into play. The stability condition for this collapse mode can be expressed as follows.

$$N_{lim2} = \frac{\left[(1-2\xi)M_p^g + M_p^r - 2M_0^r\right]/a_r}{\left[(1-2\xi)M_p^g + M_p^r - 2M_0^r\right]/(a_r N_{cr}^B)+1} > N_{cu} \qquad (4.3.15)$$

where M_p^g is the plastic bending strength of the gusset plate including the axial force effect, and $(1-2\xi)M_p^g - M_0^r$ or $M_p^r - M_0^r$ should be taken as zero if the difference is negative.

In this evaluation method, the full plastic capacity is adopted, reduced for the effects of expected axial load. At the restrainer end, either the neck NM capacity, or restrainer moment transfer mechanism may govern.

$$M_p^r = \min\left\{M_p^{r-neck}, M_p^{r-rest}\right\} \qquad (4.3.16)$$

For cruciform sections, the NM interaction is highly parabolic. The analytical solution is well approximated by Equation 4.3.17, which is adopted for minor axis bending of I/H sections in AIJ [4.16]. Note that this becomes unconservative for large web areas ($N_{wy}^c/N_u^c > 0.5$).

$$M_p^{r-neck} = \left\{1 - \left(\frac{N_{cu} - N_{wy}^c}{N_u^c - N_{wy}^c}\right)^2\right\} Z_{cp} \sigma_{cy} \qquad (4.3.17)$$

where N_{wy}^c denotes the yield axial force cruciform web (width × thickness), N_u^c denotes the gross section squash load, Z_{cp} denotes the plastic section modulus, and σ_{cy} denotes the yield stress.

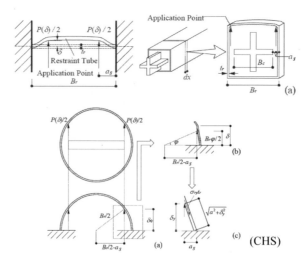

Figure 4.3.9 Collapse mechanism at Restrainer Ends

The moment transfer capacity M_p^{r-rest} for cruciform inserts in mortar-filled steel tube restrainers was investigated by Matsui et al. (2010) [4.24]. A simplified expression is given by Equation 4.3.18:

$$M_p^{r-rest} = \begin{cases} \min\{Z_{rp}\sigma_{ry}, \alpha_p^r[K_{Rr1}\theta_{y1}' + K_{Rr2}(\theta_{y2} - \theta_{y1}')]\} & \text{(Rectangular Tube)} \\ \min\{Z_{rp}\sigma_{ry}, \alpha_p^r K_{Rr1}\theta_y\} & \text{(Circular Tube)} \end{cases} \quad (4.3.18)$$

$$\alpha_p^r = 4.5 - 1.5(L_{in}/B_c) \quad (0.5 \le L_{in}/B_c < 2)$$

where Z_{rp} denotes the plastic section modulus of the restrainer tube, σ_{ry} denotes restrainer yield stress, K_{Rr1} denotes the restrainer elastic rotational stiffness about the rib-end, which can be evaluated with the following equations (Figure 4.3.9).

$$K_{Rr1} = \frac{EB_r t_r^3 L_{in}^3}{3(2B_r a_s^3 - 3a_s^4)} \text{ (RHS)}, \quad K_{Rr1} = \frac{2\sigma_{ry} t_r L_{in}^3}{3\sqrt{a_s^2 + \delta_y^2}} \cdot \frac{\delta_y}{\delta_y - \delta_0} \text{ (CHS)} \quad (4.3.19)$$

K_{Rr2} denotes the post-yielding rotational stiffness of the restrainer about the rib-end

$$K_{Rr2} = 0.11 \sigma_{ry} B_r^3 (L_{in}/W_1)^3 \text{ (RHS)} \quad (4.3.20)$$

θ_{y1}' denotes the pseudo initial yield angle of the rectangular restraint tube, θ_{y2} denotes the angle at which the plastic hinge occurs, θ_y denotes the yield angle of the circular restraint tube, and B_c denotes the core plate width.

$$\theta'_{y1} = 1.64 \times 10^{-3} \left(\frac{\sigma_{ry}}{E}\right)\left(\frac{B_r}{t_r}\right)\left(\frac{W_1}{L_{in}}\right), \quad \theta_{y2} = \frac{B_r}{L_{in}}\sqrt{\left(\frac{\sigma_{ry}}{2E}\right)^2 + \left(\frac{a_s \sigma_{ry}}{B_r E}\right)} \text{ (RHS)} \quad (4.3.21)$$

$$\theta_y = (\delta_y - \delta_0)/L_{in}, \quad \delta_y = \sqrt{\left(\frac{\pi B_r \sigma_{ry}}{4E} + \frac{B_r}{2}\cos^{-1}\left(\frac{B_r - 2a_s}{B_r - 2t_r}\right)\right)^2 - a_s^2},$$

$$\delta_0 = \frac{B_r}{2}\sin\left[\cos^{-1}\left(\frac{B_r - 2a_s}{B_r - 2t_r}\right)\right] \approx \sqrt{\left(\frac{B_r}{2} - t_r\right)^2 - \left(\frac{B_r}{2} - a_s\right)^2} \text{ (CHS)} \quad (4.3.22)$$

Experimental Validation

To confirm the proposed stability evaluation method, gradually increasing cyclic loading tests of up to 3% core strain were conducted following application of an initial 1% out-of-plane drift [4.14]. The test configuration and loading protocol are shown in Figures 4.3.10-12, and the restrainer shape, debonding gap, gusset type, and neck insert length were varied as follows:

- Core: 90x12mm plate, JIS-SN400B (σ_y = 270 MPa)
- Neck: 90x90x12mm cruciform
- Restrainer: square 125x2.3mm or circular 139.8x3.2mm mortar-filled tube.
- Debonding gap: 1.0 or 2.0mm (per face)
- Gusset: low stiffness ($_\xi\kappa_{Rg}$ = 0.04, Type A), or edge-stiffened ($_\xi\kappa_{Rg}$ = 0.3, Type C)
- Insert length of L_{in} = 90mm (L_{in}/D_{neck}=1.0) or L_{in} = 180mm (L_{in}/D_{neck}=2.0).

Further details are provided in Table 4.3.1, with the specimens labeled M-(R: Rectangular, C: Circular) -L (Insert length ratio) -S (Clearance) -H (Stiffened type gusset plate).

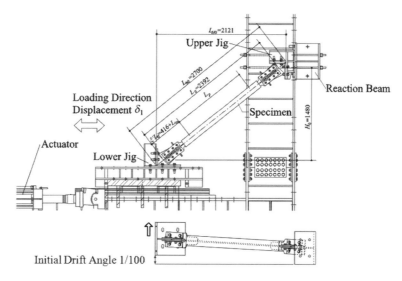

Figure 4.3.10 Cyclic loading test setup

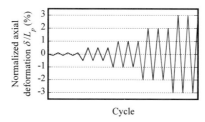

Figure 4.3.11 Loading protocol

Chapter 4. Connection Design and Global Stability

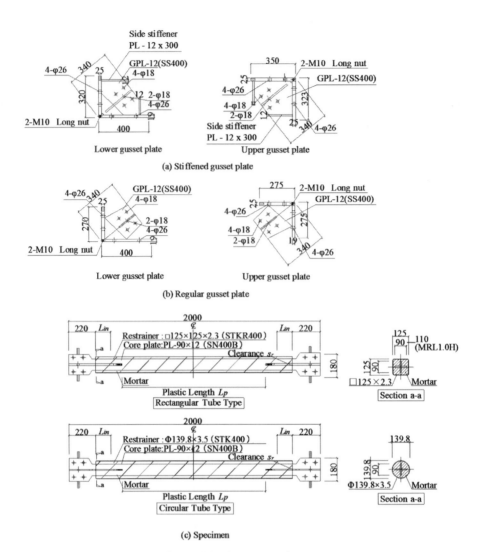

Figure 4.3.12 Test specimen

Table 4.3.1 Specimen details

Specimen	A_c (mm^2)	σ_{cy} (N/mm^2)	EI_B (Nmm)	σ_{ry} (N/mm^2)	K_{Rg} (Nmm)	$\gamma_J EI_B$ (Nmm)	L_0 (mm)	L_{in} (mm)	L_p (mm)	s_r (mm)	ξL_0 (mm)	$\xi' L_0$ (mm)
MRL1.0S1H	1080	266.0	5.81×10^{11}	305.0	6.90×10^8	1.20×10^{12}	2392	90	1380	1	416	506
MRL2.0S1	1080	266.8	5.81×10^{11}	385.8	9.73×10^7	1.20×10^{12}	2392	180	1200	1	416	596
MRL2.0S2	1080	266.8	5.81×10^{11}	391.5	9.73×10^7	1.20×10^{12}	2392	180	1200	2	416	596
MCL2.0S2	1080	269.7	7.14×10^{11}	365.7	9.73×10^7	1.20×10^{12}	2392	180	1200	2	416	596
MRL1.0S1	1080	266.8	5.81×10^{11}	391.5	9.73×10^7	1.20×10^{12}	2392	90	1380	1	416	506
MRL1.0S2	1080	266.8	5.81×10^{11}	391.5	9.73×10^7	1.20×10^{12}	2392	90	1380	2	416	506

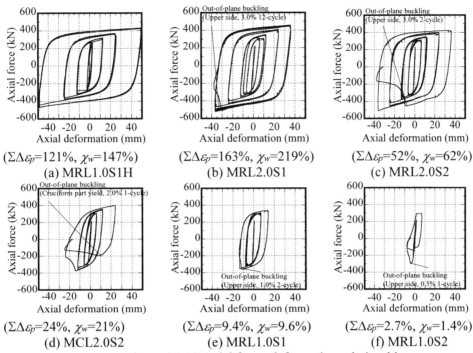

Figure 4.3.13 Axial force–deformation relationship

Despite imminent buckling, the axial hysteresis loops shown in Figure 4.3.13 are full and stable prior to the cycle where global buckling is observed. While this confirms that inelasticity is not detrimental to the axial energy dissipation capacity as long as stability is ensured, lateral displacements should be directly monitored (shown later in Figure 4.3.14). In this experiment the lateral buckling displacements were visible once yielding commenced, though this is in part due to the large debonding gap relative to the BRB size, giving large initial imperfection as summarized in Table 4.3.2.

Cumulative plastic strain $\Sigma\Delta\varepsilon_p=\Sigma\Delta\delta_p/L_p$, and normalized cumulative absorbed energy $\chi_w=E_d/\sigma_y A_c$ are also listed in Figure 4.3.13. Generally these are proportional to the safety factor against buckling, with most cases requiring significant strain hardening to reach the critical buckling load, while one specimen (MRL1.0S2) buckled at yield. However, real earthquakes do not feature gradually increasing loading protocols, and only MRL1.0S1H and MRL2.0S1 would have achieved the first stage of the Japanese BCJ loading protocol (though MRL2.0S1 would still be unacceptable due to the instability), which is discussed latter in Chapter 6.

Gusset stiffness

Only a single specimen (MRL1.0S1H) was provided with full depth stiffeners, and was the only one to not buckle. This specimen effectively had a pinned restrainer end ($L_{in}/D_{neck}=1.0$), and so stability relied on the *Cantilever Connection* design concept.

Of the five specimens which buckled, all featured the unstiffened Gusset Type A, with varying degrees of restrainer end continuity and debonding gap sizes.

Restrainer end continuity

The three specimens with longer insert ratios (MRL2.0S1, MRL2.0S2, MCL2.0S2, with L_{in}/D_{neck}=2.0) all substantially outperformed those with shorter insert ratios (MRL1.0S1, MRL1.0S2, with L_{in}/D_{neck}=1.0). This is unsurprising, as the latter two are basically mechanisms if one considers that L_{in}/D_{neck}<1.0 is a near-pin condition. Additional specimens tested with L_{in}/D_{neck}=0.5 exhibited nearly identical hysteresis loops as the specimens with L_{in}/D_{neck}=1.0 [4.14].

Longer insert lengths have the dual benefit of reducing the apparent initial imperfection, as the initial rotation to establish flexural continuity ($2s_r/L_{in}$) has a dominant contribution. However, this factor can be controlled by comparing specimens with the same imperfection, but different insert lengths (MRL2.0S2 vs MRL1.0S1). In this case the longer insert length resulted in a 450% increase in cumulative plastic strain and 40% increase in buckling load.

Debonding gap size & out-of-plane drift

Not only were the measured lateral displacements following application of out-of-plane drift directly proportional to the debonding gap-to-insert length ratio, the cumulative plastic strain and buckling loads also varied accordingly. For each insert length, specimens with the 1.0mm debonding gap buckled earlier than those with 2.0mm debonding gaps (MRL2.0S2 vs MRL2.0S1, MRL1.0S2 vs MRL1.0S1).

Restrainer Shape

Somewhat counterintuitively, the circular specimen (MCL2.0S2) performed worse than the otherwise identical square specimen (MRL2.0S2), buckling at 70% of the load and 45% of the cumulative plastic strain. Despite this unexpected low capacity, the circular restrainer yielded in the neck, unlike the square specimen (MRL2.0S2), which experienced a restrainer end failure. It is also notable that the restrainer section stiffness was substantially larger for the circular specimen, confirming that this is not a key variable.

This is the only specimen where the proposed stability criteria overestimated the capacity and the lateral displacement plot indicates that the elastic stiffness was far lower than expected. it is likely that thought that there was a fabrication mishap.

These test results indicate that BRB stability is significantly affected by the gusset stiffness, restrainer end continuity and debonding gap in the neck, as is expected from the proposed Equations (4.3.14) and (4.3.15). The predicted buckling capacities and comparison to observed values are shown in Table 4.3.4 and Figures 4.3.14-15. The proposed evaluation method conservatively predicts the buckling capacity in all cases except for MCL2.0S2.

Chapter 4. Connection Design and Global Stability 69

Table 4.3.2 Initial imperfection angle

Specimen	L_{in} (mm)	s_r (mm)	$\theta_0 = 2s_r / L_{in}$ (rad)
MRL1.0S1H	90	1	0.02
MRL2.0S1	180	1	0.01
MRL2.0S2	180	2	0.02
MCL2.0S2	180	2	0.02
MRL1.0S1	90	1	0.02
MRL1.0S2	90	2	0.04

Table 4.3.3 Bending capacities at restrainer ends

Specimen	Yield bending strength of cruciform zone (kNm)	Yield bending strength of restrainer (kNm)	M_p^r (kNm)
MRL1.0S1H	1.42	2.97	1.42
MRL2.0S1	5.50	8.38	5.50
MRL2.0S2	6.56	8.56	6.56
MCL2.0S2	6.50	35.68	6.50
MRL1.0S1	6.78	4.28	4.28
MRL1.0S2	6.78	4.28	4.28

Table 4.3.4 Stability evaluations using proposed equation

Specimen	N_{cr}^B (kN)	a_r (mm)	N_{cr}^r (kN)	N_{cu} (kN)	M_0^r (kNm)	Failure cycle at experiment	Stability limit (kN) N_{lim1} (Eq.4.3.14)	Stability limit (kN) N_{lim2} (Eq.4.3.15)	Failure axial force in experiment (kN)
MRL1.0S1H	1880	11.4	695	431	0.00	None	818	1390	(452)
MRL2.0S1	1158	6.80	82	432	0.09	3.0%-12cycle	520	520	535
MRL2.0S2	1158	12.4	82	432	0.00	3.0%-2cycle	419	410	507
MCL2.0S2	1389	12.4	82	437	0.00	1.0%-2cycle	440	432	375
MRL1.0S1	1158	11.4	111	432	0.00	0.5%-1cycle	367	345	362
MRL1.0S2	1158	21.7	111	432	0.00	0.5%-1cycle	264	217	300

*N_{cu} is estimated as $1.5A_c\sigma_{cy}$ (approximately equivalent to axial forces of the first 3% normalized axial deformation).
( ): Exceptionally, MRL1.0S1H did not fail, so only the maximum applied axial force is shown above.

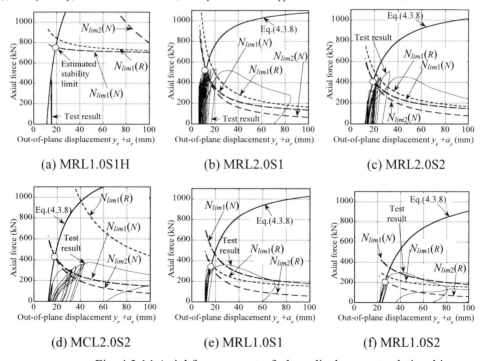

(a) MRL1.0S1H (b) MRL2.0S1 (c) MRL2.0S2

(d) MCL2.0S2 (e) MRL1.0S1 (f) MRL1.0S2

Fig. 4.3.14 Axial force vs. out-of-plane displacement relationship

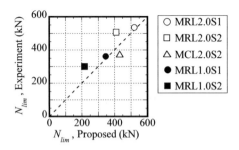

Figure 4.3.15 Distribution of proposed/ experimental accuracy by specimen type

4.4 STABILITY CONDITION WITH CHEVRON CONFIGURATIONS [4.15]

Chevron configurations can lead to significantly different end connections, primarily due to the rotational flexibility of the transverse framing at the beam connection. One method of analysis is to simply assume the more onerous conditions at each end and apply the equations from the previous section. Alternatively, a less conservative design can be obtained by directly analyzing the full generalized system. While the lack of symmetry introduces additional nonlinearity, complicating analysis, an approximate evaluation method is presented in this section.

Similar to Section 4.3, several inelastic buckling modes are analyzed, as shown in Figure 4.4.2.

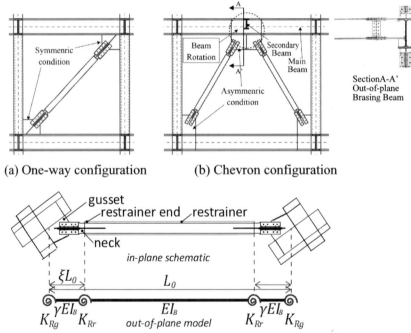

(a) One-way configuration (b) Chevron configuration

(c) Idealized Chevron Model

Figure 4.4.1 One-way vs Chevron Configuration

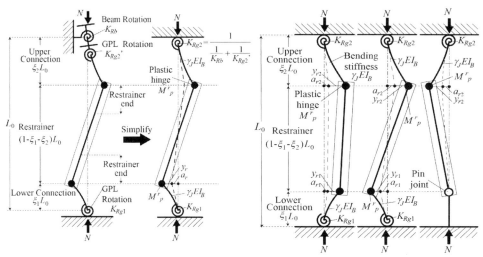

Figure 4.4.2 Collapse model for chevron configuration

(a) symmetric, (b) asymmetric, (c) one-sided
Figure 4.4.3 Collapse mechanism modes

Connection Stiffness

The model in Figure 4.4.1 requires the gusset and adjacent framing to be represented by a single spring. However, the rotation of the connected beam(s) has the effect of increasing the equivalent connection length and decreasing the gusset rotational stiffness. A modified rotational stiffness K_{Rg2} can be obtained by summing the adjacent beam and gusset rotational stiffness in series, given by Equation (4.4.1).

$$K_{Rg2} = \frac{1}{(1/K_{Rb}) + (1/K'_{Rg2})} \quad (4.4.1) \quad {_\xi}K_{Rg1} = \frac{K_{Rg1}\xi_1 L_0}{\gamma_J EI_B}, \quad {_\xi}K_{Rg2} = \frac{K_{Rg2}\xi_2 L_0}{\gamma_J EI_B} \quad (4.4.2)$$

where, K_{Rb} is the total out-of-plane rotational stiffness of the attached beam(s), and K'_{Rg2} is the rotational stiffness of the upper gusset plate.

Conservatively, the length beam connection $\xi_2 L_0$ can be taken from the beam centroid to restrainer end. However, if a fixed-end transverse beam is provided with a large adjacent framing rotational stiffness K_{Rb} relative to the gusset stiffness K'_{Rg2}, the connection effective length can be reduced. From the experiment described later in this section, rotation generally occurs about the bottom of the transverse beams, if present.

Three simple models are proposed, valid for a range of beam-to-gusset stiffness ratios, as shown in Figure 4.4.4:

Model 1: combined stiffness K_{Rg2}, length taken to bottom of transverse beam
  ($K_{Rb}/K'_{Rg2} < a$)
Model 2: combined stiffness K_{Rg2}, length taken to gusset base ($a < K_{Rb}/K'_{Rg2} < b$)
Model 3: gusset stiffness K'_{Rg2}, length taken to gusset base ($K_{Rb}/K'_{Rg2} > b$)
Where $a = \xi_2/\xi_g - 1$, $b = 10$

Elasto-plastic buckling capacity

Similar to Section 4.3, the ultimate strength is calculated for three critical mode shapes shown in Figure 4.4.3. However, the displaced shape and associated strain energies at each end are no longer equal in magnitude, with the restrainer end

Chapter 4. Connection Design and Global Stability

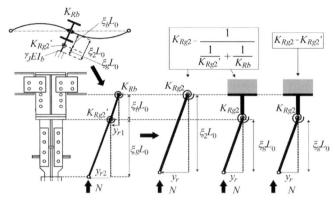

(a) Double-spring, (b) Model-1, (c) Model-2, (d) Model-3
Figure 4.4.4 Mechanical model at upper connection

displacements $|y_{r1}| \neq |y_{r2}|$ and ratio $r_a = y_{r1}/y_{r2}$. As inelastic buckling progresses r_a will vary, with inelasticity typically concentrating at one end. While the same general form as Equation 4.3.13 can be obtained, N^r_{cr} and β become highly nonlinear functions.

$$N = N^r_{cr} + \beta \frac{M^r_p - M^r_0}{y_r + a_r}$$

$$\beta = \frac{4}{\pi} \cdot \frac{\dfrac{r_a}{\xi_1} \dfrac{{}_\xi\kappa_{Rg1} + 6/\pi}{{}_\xi\kappa_{Rg1} + 3} + \dfrac{1}{\xi_2}\dfrac{{}_\xi\kappa_{Rg2} + 6/\pi}{{}_\xi\kappa_{Rg2} + 3}}{\dfrac{r_a^2}{\xi_1}\dfrac{{}_\xi\kappa_{Rg1} + 24/\pi^2}{{}_\xi\kappa_{Rg1} + 3} + \dfrac{1}{\xi_2}\dfrac{{}_\xi\kappa_{Rg2} + 24/\pi^2}{{}_\xi\kappa_{Rg2} + 3}} \approx 1 \qquad (4.4.3)$$

$$N^r_{cr} = \frac{\pi^2 \gamma_J EI_B}{(2L_0)^2} \frac{\dfrac{r_a^2\,{}_\xi\kappa_{Rg1}}{\xi_1^3({}_\xi\kappa_{Rg1}+3)} + \dfrac{{}_\xi\kappa_{Rg2}}{\xi_2^3({}_\xi\kappa_{Rg2}+3)}}{\dfrac{r_a^2}{\xi_1}\dfrac{{}_\xi\kappa_{Rg1}+24/\pi^2}{{}_\xi\kappa_{Rg1}+3} + \dfrac{1}{\xi_2}\dfrac{{}_\xi\kappa_{Rg2}+24/\pi^2}{{}_\xi\kappa_{Rg2}+3}} \qquad (4.4.4)$$

By a similar process, the anti-symmetric collapse mode of Figure 4.4.3 (b), Equation (4.4.4) becomes

$$N^r_{cr} = \frac{\pi^2 \gamma_J EI_B}{(2L_0)^2} \frac{C_2}{C_1}, \qquad C_2 = \frac{r_a^2\,{}_\xi\kappa_{Rg1}}{\xi_1^3({}_\xi\kappa_{Rg1}+3)} + \frac{{}_\xi\kappa_{Rg2}}{\xi_2^3({}_\xi\kappa_{Rg2}+3)},$$

$$C_1 = \frac{({}_\xi\kappa_{Rg1}+24/\pi^2)(r_a^2 + r_a\xi_1 - r_a^2\xi_2)}{\xi_1(1-\xi_1-\xi_2)({}_\xi\kappa_{Rg1}+3)} + \frac{({}_\xi\kappa_{Rg2}+24/\pi^2)(1+r_a\xi_2 - \xi_1)}{\xi_2(1-\xi_1-\xi_2)({}_\xi\kappa_{Rg2}+3)}$$

$$= \frac{(1+\xi_1/r_a - \xi_2)}{(1-\xi_1-\xi_2)} \frac{r_a^2}{\xi_1}\frac{{}_\xi\kappa_{Rg1}+24/\pi^2}{{}_\xi\kappa_{Rg1}+3} + \frac{(1+r_a\xi_2 - \xi_1)}{(1-\xi_1-\xi_2)} \frac{1}{\xi_2}\frac{{}_\xi\kappa_{Rg2}+24/\pi^2}{{}_\xi\kappa_{Rg2}+3} \qquad (4.4.5)$$

For the one-sided collapse mode shown in Figure 4.4.3 (c), Equation (4.4.4) becomes

$$N^r_{cr} = \frac{\pi^2(1-\xi_1-\xi_2)\gamma_J EI_B}{(2\xi_2 L_0)^2} \frac{{}_\xi\kappa_{Rg2}}{(1-\xi_1)({}_\xi\kappa_{Rg2}+24/\pi^2)} \qquad (4.4.6)$$

Comparing Equations (4.4.4), (4.4.5), and (4.4.6), the minimum $N_{cr}{}^r$ is determined by the asymmetrical or one-sided mode. As a result, the stability limit—determined by the cross point of Equation (4.3.3) and Equation (4.4.6)—can be expressed as Equation (4.4.7).

$$N_{lim1} = \frac{(M_p^r - M_0^r)/a_r + N_{cr}^r}{(M_p^r - M_0^r)/(a_r N_{cr}^B) + 1} > N_{cu} \tag{4.4.7}$$

$N_{cr}{}^r$ can be obtained using the equivalent slenderness ratio, given as follows:

$$\lambda_r = \frac{2L_0}{i_c} \cdot \sqrt{\frac{C_1}{C_2}} \quad (Asymmetrical\ mode) \tag{4.4.8}$$

$$\lambda_r = \frac{2\xi_2 L_0}{i_c} \sqrt{\frac{(1-\xi_1)(\xi \kappa_{Rg2} + 24/\pi^2)}{(1-\xi_1-\xi_2)\xi \kappa_{Rg2}}} \quad (One-sided\ mode) \tag{4.4.9}$$

C_1 and C_2 in Equation (4.4.8) are defined in Equation (4.4.5).

Furthermore, the stability limit with plastic hinges at the gusset plates, N_{lim2}, can be expressed as follows:

$$N_{lim2} = \frac{(M_p^r - M_0^r + C_3)/a_r}{(M_p^r - M_0^r + C_3)/(a_r N_{cr}^B) + 1}, \quad C_3 = \left(\frac{M_p^{g1} - M_0^r}{\xi_1} + \frac{M_p^{g2} - M_0^r}{\xi_2}\right)\frac{1}{1/\xi_1 + 1/\xi_2 + 4/(1-\xi_1-\xi_2)}$$

$$(Asymmetrical\ mode) \tag{4.4.10}$$

$$N_{lim2} = \frac{\left[(1-\xi_1-\xi_2)(M_p^{g2} - M_0^r)/(1-\xi_1) + M_p^r - M_0^r\right]/a_r}{\left[(1-\xi_1-\xi_2)(M_p^{g2} - M_0^r)/(1-\xi_1) + M_p^r - M_0^r\right]/(a_r N_{cr}^B) + 1} \quad (One-sided\ mode) \tag{4.4.11}$$

It can easily be confirmed that Equations (4.4.10) and (4.4.11) become Equations (4.3.14) and (4.3.15), respectively, when $\xi_1 = \xi_2$, $\xi \kappa_{Rg1} = \xi \kappa_{Rg2}$ and $r_a = 1$.

Experimental verification

To validate the proposed stability equations, gradually increasing cyclic loading tests of up to 3% strain were conducted with various beam connection details, as shown in Figure 4.4.5-4.4.8. An initial 1% out-of-plane drift was applied, with various transverse beams attached at the beam connection.

- Core: 90x12mm plate, JIS-SN400B (average $\sigma_y = 293$ MPa)
- Neck: 90x90x12mm cruciform
- Restrainer: square 125x4.5mm or circular 165.2x4.5mm mortar-filled tube.
- Debonding gap: 1.0mm (per face)
- Transverse beam: diaphragm restraint ($\xi \kappa_{Rg2} = 0.19$), half depth beam ($\xi \kappa_{Rg2} = 1.46$) or full depth beam ($\xi \kappa_{Rg2} = 2.73$)
- Restrainer end: Insert length of $L_{in} = 180$mm ($L_{in}/B_n = 2.0$), or with rib or collar reinforcement.

The specimens were labelled as (H, M, or L: stiffness at the beam connection)-(R: rectangular restrainer, C: circular restrainer)-(N: standard cruciform insert, F: ribs, C: collars)-2 (ratio of the insert zone length to the core plate width).

Chapter 4. Connection Design and Global Stability

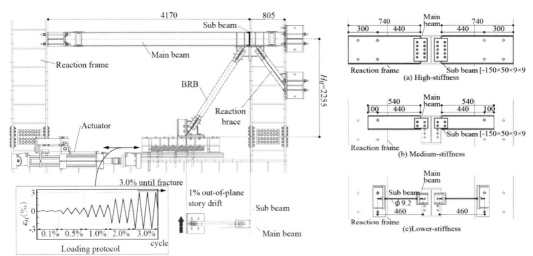

Figure 4.4.5 Test setup and loading protocol Figure 4.4.6 Types of secondary beams

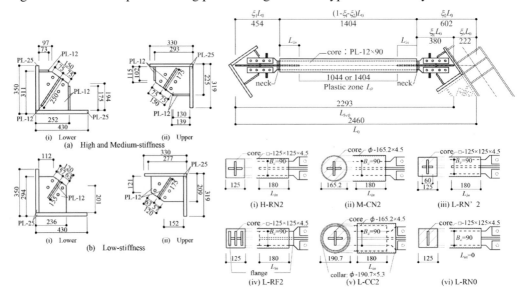

Figure 4.4.7 Types of gusset plates (mm)   Figure 4.4.8 BRB specimens with various restrainer ends (mm)

Table 4.4.1. Test matrix

Specimen	Core area A_c (mm^2)	Core yield strength σ_{cy} (N/mm^2)	Restrainer stiffness EI_B (kNm^2)	Lower spring K_{Rg1} (kNm)	Upper spring K_{Rg2} (kNm)	Upper GL spring K_{Rg2}' (kNm)	Beam Spring K_{Rb} (kNm)	Connection stiffness* $\gamma_J EI_B$ (kNm^2)	Total length L_0 (mm)	Insert length L_{in} (mm)	Plastic zone length L_p (mm)	Lower connection length $\xi_1 L_0$ (mm)	Upper connection length $\xi_2 L_0$ (mm)	Clearance s_r (mm)	upper normalized spring ξK_{Rg2}
H-RN2	1080	293	1080	11426	3153	3585	26174	696	2460	180	1044	454	602	1.0	2.73
M-CN2	1080	293	1500	11426	1691	3585	3202	696	2460	180	1044	454	602	1.0	1.46
L-RN'2	1080	293	1080	306	221	351	598	696	2460	180	1044	454	602	1.0	0.19
L-RF2	1080	293	1080	306	221	351	598	696	2460	180	1044	454	602	1.0	0.19
L-CC2	1080	293	1500	306	221	351	598	696	2460	180	1044	454	602	1.0	0.19
L-RN0	1080	293	1080	306	221	351	598	696	2460	0	1404	454	602	1.0	0.19

*Contribution of the splice plate section to the connection stiffness is neglected

Table 4.4.2 Stability evaluations using proposed equation

Specimen	Bending moment				Elasttic buckling strength	Initial imperfec-tion	Connection buckling strength	Slender-ness ratio	Connec-tion radius	Core yield strength	Stability limit				Experimental results
	Restrai-ner ends	Initial	Lower GPL	Upper GPL							Calculated				
											Elastic	Plastic	Min.	Judge	
	$M_p^{\,r}$	$M_0^{\,r}$	$M_p^{\,g1}$	$M_p^{\,g2}$	$N_{cr}^{\,B}$	a_r	$N_{cr}^{\,r}$	λ_r	i_r	N_{cu}	$N_{lim\,1}$	$N_{lim\,2}$	N_{lim}	N_{lim}	$N_{lim}^{\,exp}$
	(kNm)	(kNm)	(kNm)	(kNm)	(kN)	(mm)	(kN)		(mm)	(kN)	(kN)	(kN)	(kN)	$>N_{cu}$	(kN)
H-RN2	4.27	0.0	355	274	5241	4.0	428	63	31.3	475	1237	4717	1237	OK	No collapse
M-CN2	4.27	0.0	355	274	4369	4.8	389	75	31.3	475	1060	3932	1060	OK	No collapse
L-RN'2	1.75	0.0	2.48	2.49	2151	5.6	112	170	31.3	475	370	450	370	NG	527
L-RF2	23.0	0.0	2.48	2.49	2151	4.0	112	170	31.3	475	1595	1591	1591	OK	No collapse
L-CC2	45.1	0.0	2.48	2.49	2054	5.0	112	170	31.3	475	1693	1683	1683	OK	No collapse
L-RN0	0.51	0.0	2.48	2.49	2151	3.1	112	170	31.3	475	257	485	257	NG	339

The resultant hysteresis loops and example trace of the out-of-plane displacement at each end are shown in Figures 4.4.9 and 4.4.10, including the achieved cumulative plastic deformation, $\Sigma\Delta\varepsilon_p = \Sigma\Delta\delta_p/L_p$, and the normalized cumulative absorbed energy, $\chi_w = E_d/\sigma_y A_c$. The buckling capacities were also predicted using the proposed equations, as shown in Table 4.4.2.

Mode shape

Out-of-plane buckling was observed in only two of the six specimens (LRN'2 and LRN0), both with low transverse framing stiffness (translational fixity only) and lower restrained end stiffness. While buckling was initiated at the upper beam connection in both cases, the final mode shape was anti-symmetric, with the final displacements larger at the lower connection.

Transverse beam stiffness

Three specimens had similar restrainer end stiffness consisting of cruciform inserts with $L_{in}/D_{neck}=2.0$, but different degrees of rotational fixity at the beam connection. H-RN2 and M-CN2 had short transverse beams and were stable until core fracture. L-RN'2 was designed with only translational stiffness and buckled at a cumulative plastic strain of $\Sigma\Delta\varepsilon_p=28\%$, with buckling rotations occurring about the centroid of the translational restraint.

A further comparison can be made between L-RN'2 ($s_r=1.0$mm) in this study and MRL2.0S1 ($s_r=1.0$mm) and MRL2.0S2 ($s_r=2.0$mm) from Section 4.3. All three specimens had similar brace designs, but the latter two had rigid adjacent framing and achieved significantly greater cumulative plastic strains of $\Sigma\Delta\varepsilon_p=163\%$ and 52% before buckling.

Thus, the rotational restraint provided by transverse beam affects both the buckling effective length and rotational spring stiffness.

76 Chapter 4. Connection Design and Global Stability

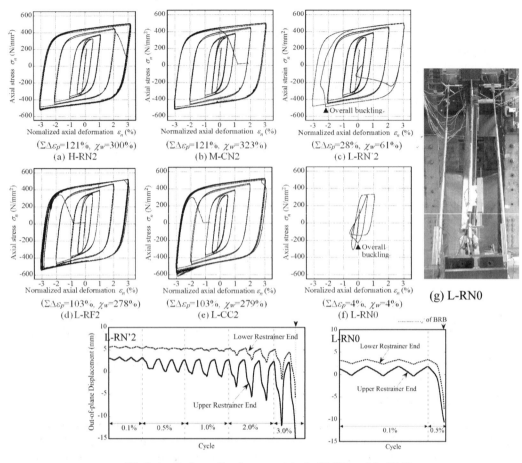

(h) Out-of-plane displacement in L-RN'2 and L-RN0
Figure 4.4.9 Normalized axial force–deformation relationship

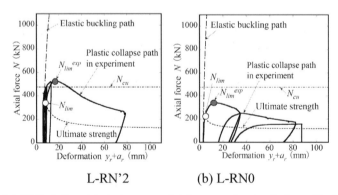

L-RN'2   (b) L-RN0
Figure 4.4.10 Relationship between axial force and out-of-plane displacement

Restrainer End reinforcement

Similarly, three specimens with flexible adjacent framing details were provisioned with various restrainer end details. While specimen L-RN'2 had an insert length nominally sufficient (L_{in}/D_{neck}=2.0) to transfer to neck moment capacity, this performed worse than specimens L-RF2 and L-CC2, which had additional out-of-plane stiffeners and a thick collar (190.7x5.3mm encasing a 165.2x4.3 circular restrainer), respectively. Neither of the reinforced specimens buckled, while L-RN'2 buckled with a hinge forming in the neck. Furthermore, a forth specimen (L-RN0) with a flexible restrainer end detail (L_{in}/D_{neck}=0) buckled almost immediately at $\Sigma\Delta\varepsilon_p$=4%, with rotation occurring about the core.

Between the two types of restrainer end reinforcement: additional out-of-plane stiffeners or thick collar, both performed well with regards to buckling. The additional stiffeners were effective in eliminating the weak neck and the hysteresis (Figure 4.4.8(iv)) appeared stable and symmetric. However, the collar specimen (L-CC2) exhibited increased compressive overstrength at large drifts (3%) due to friction between the collar and the restrainer, visible in Figure 4.4.8(v). The collar thickness (5.3mm) was also relatively large, precluding a tearing type failure, and was welded directly to a cruciform neck. The fabricator noted that both of these details were expensive and more difficult to assemble.

These specimens demonstrate that restrainer end reinforcements can be effective in achieving a stable design, even if the adjacent framing is flexible.

Figure 4.4.11 Neck hinges of specimens L-RN'2 and L-RN0

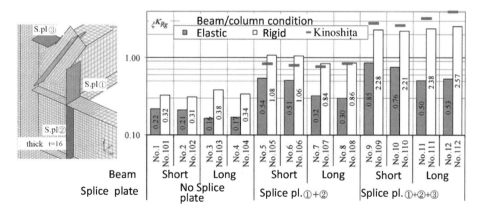

Figure 4.5.1 $_\xi\kappa_{Rg}$ values for beam-column connections [4.27]

4.5 EVALUATIONS FOR KEY PARAMETERS

4.5.1 GUSSET ROTATIONAL STIFFNESS ($_\xi K_{Rg}$)

As the gusset out-of-plane flexibility is modelled as a concentrated spring, the flexural stiffness must be estimated. The normalized rotational spring $_\xi K_{Rg}$ values for a typical beam/column connections were evaluated using FEM analysis [4.27] and the results shown in Figure 4.5.1. This figure indicates that an analytical method based on yield line analysis proposed by Kinoshita et al. (2008) (Appendix A.2) [4.28] provides a reasonable approximation for edge stiffened gusset topologies. In the later case, additional beam/column deformation must also be included by apply a series summation, similar to the procedure conducted for chevron beam connections. In general, gusset plates with low stiffness (Gusset Type A and B: no full depth stiffeners) give $_\xi K_{Rg}$ values of around 0.2, and those with high stiffness (Gusset Type C: edge stiffeners) give $_\xi K_{Rg}$ values of around 1.0. If the neck cruciform extends full depth (Gusset Type D), the normalized stiffness is theoretically infinite, although the adjacent framing introduces some nominal flexibility. If the gusset stiffness is extremely large, further increases in provides no further gain in buckling capacity.

A similar finite element study was of normalized rotational spring stiffness $_\xi K_{Rg2}$ was conducted for chevron beam connection [4.29], as shown in Figure 4.5.2. The resultant rotational stiffness is far lower if no or nominally pined transverse beams are provided, falling between $_\xi K_{Rg2}$=0.06~0.2. If fixed-end secondary beams with 0.5~0.7 times the depth of the primary beam and a stiffened gusset (Gusset Type C or D) is provided, the rotational stiffness increases to $_\xi K_{Rg2}$=0.4~0.6. More precise evaluation method for K_{Rb} is also explained in Appendix A.2.

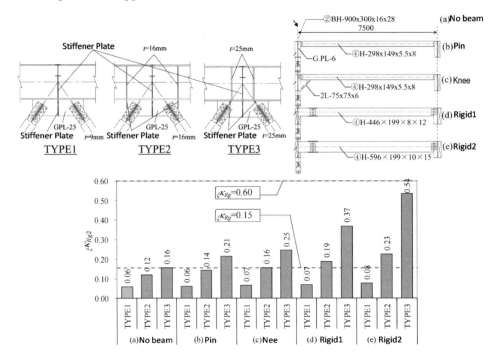

Figure 4.5.2 $_\xi K_{Rg2}$ values for beam-side connections in chevron configurations

4.5.2 ELASTIC BUCKLING CAPACITY N^B_{cr}

The global elastic buckling strength of a BRB, $N_{cr}{}^B$, including the effects of the connection zone's bending stiffness and the gusset plate's rotational stiffness, can be estimated from numerical analysis as described in Appendix A.3 by using the model shown in Figure 4.5.3, or by using the following equations. For chevron configuration, $K_{Rg} = \min[K_{Rg1}, K_{Rg2}]$, and $\xi = \max[\xi_1, \xi_2]$ can be used.

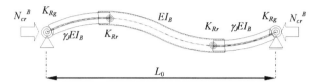

Figure 4.5.3 Buckling mode including springs

$$N^B_{cr} = \alpha^2 EI \quad (4.5.1)$$

where, α is the value satisfying the following equations.

$$\alpha^2(EI_B)^2 S_1 C_4 + \alpha EI_B\left(K_{Rr}S_1S_4 - \frac{K_{Rg}+K_{Rr}}{\sqrt{\gamma_J}}C_1C_4\right) - K_{Rg}K_{Rr}\left(\frac{1}{\gamma_J}S_1C_4 + \frac{1}{\sqrt{\gamma_J}}C_1S_4\right) = 0 \quad (\textit{Symmetric Mode})$$

$$\alpha^3(EI_B)^2 L_0 S_1 S_4 - \alpha^2 EI_B L_0\left(K_{Rr}S_1C_4 + \frac{K_{Rg}+K_{Rr}}{\sqrt{\gamma_J}}C_1S_4\right) + 2\alpha EI_B K_{Rg}S_1S_4 + \alpha K_{Rg}K_{Rr}L_0\left(\frac{1}{\sqrt{\gamma_J}}C_1C_4 - \frac{1}{\gamma_J}S_1S_4\right)$$

$$-2K_{Rg}K_{Rr}\left(S_1C_4 + \frac{1}{\sqrt{\gamma_J}}C_1S_4\right) = 0 \quad (\textit{Asymmetric Mode}) \quad (4.5.2)$$

$$S_1 = \sin\frac{\alpha}{\sqrt{\gamma_J}}\xi L_0, \ C_1 = \cos\frac{\alpha}{\sqrt{\gamma_J}}\xi L_0, \ S_4 = \sin\alpha L_0\left(\frac{1}{2}-\xi\right), \ C_4 = \cos\alpha L_0\left(\frac{1}{2}-\xi\right)$$

When K_{Rr} is infinity and $\gamma_J = 1$, the solution approaches the simpler approximate formula in Ref. [4.14].

$$N^B_{cr} = \frac{4\pi^2 EI_B}{L_0{}^2}\frac{{}_L\kappa_{Rg}^2 + 10{}_L\kappa_{Rg} + 16}{{}_L\kappa_{Rg}^2 + 14{}_L\kappa_{Rg} + 64} \quad (4.5.3)$$

where, ${}_L\kappa_{Rg} = \frac{K_{Rg}L_0}{EI_B}$. Note that N^B_{cr} becomes $\pi^2 EI_B/L_0{}^2$ when ${}_L\kappa_{Rg}=0$, and $N^B_{cr} = 4\pi^2 EI_B/L_0{}^2$ when ${}_L\kappa_{Rg}=\infty$.

4.5.3 BENDING MOMENT DUE TO OUT-OF-PLANE DRIFT M'_0

Given the asymmetric stiffness conditions, the moment due to out-of-plane drift can be determined from numerical analysis. Alternatively, it can be approximated using Equation (4.5.4), with ${}_\xi\kappa_{Rg} = \max[{}_\xi\kappa_{Rg1}, {}_\xi\kappa_{Rg2}]$, and $\xi' = \min[\xi'_1, \xi'_2]$.

Chapter 4. Connection Design and Global Stability

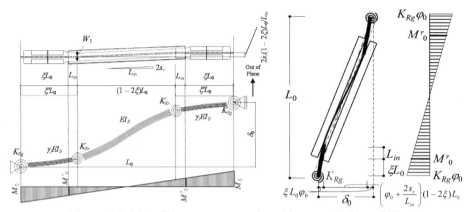

Figure 4.5.4 Bending moment produced by out-of-plane drift

$$M_0^r = (1-2\xi)\left\{\frac{\delta_0}{L_0} - \frac{2s_r}{L_{in}}(1-2\xi)\right\} \cdot \frac{EI_B}{L_0} \cdot \frac{6\gamma_J}{2\xi'(3-6\xi'+4\xi'^2)+\gamma(1-2\xi')^3 + \dfrac{6\xi}{\xi K_{Rg}} + \dfrac{6\gamma_J(1-2\xi')^2}{L K_{Rr}}} \geq 0 \quad (4.5.4)$$

When $K_{Rr} \to \infty$, $EI_B/L_0 \to \infty$, $\gamma = 1$ and $\xi' = \xi$, this equation reduces to the simpler equation as shown in the right of Figure 4.5.4 and presented in [4.14].

$$M_0^r = (1-2\xi)\left\{\frac{\delta_0}{L_0} - \frac{2s_r}{L_{in}}(1-2\xi)\right\} K_{Rg} \geq 0 \quad (4.5.6)$$

4.5.4 FAST CHECK

Prior to the detailed check from 4.2 to 4.4, we recommend to check the following.

1) Avoid obvious unstable details without out-of-plane brace at chevron layout or slender connections as shown in Figure 4.2.2
2) If satisfying $\xi<0.2$, $\gamma EI_B>0.5EI_B$, $L_{in}/B_c>2.0$, gusset plate being stiffened (Type C or D in Figure 4.2.4), and fixed end transverse beam (height $>2/3$ of the main beam) being provided at chevron connections, the out-of-plane stability problem is not likely to occur.

4.6 CONNECTION DESIGN AGAINST IN-PLANE DEFORMATION

Various beam-pin or gusset isolation details have been proposed to eliminate the responsible in-plane compatibility demands (Walters et al. (2004) [4.10], Berman et al. (2009) [4.11], Wigle et al. (2010) [4.12], Prinz et al. (2014) [4.13]), with similar details for RC applications discussed in Chapter 7.

The stability conditions of BRB in in-plane directions are more moderate than out-of plane direction because of the rotational stiffness in in-plane directions are usually much higher than out-of-plane directions, and considered as rotationally rigid. However, due to the asymmetrical in-plane rotation at the fixing point of connections along the story drift as shown in Figure 4.6.1 causes in-plane bending moment at the connections.

Therefore, AIJ: Recommended Provisions for Seismic Damping Systems applied to Steel Structures (2014) [4.18] requires splice plate design against the following in-plane bending moment.

$$M_{Ji} = \frac{N_{cu} \cdot l_J \cdot \theta_{Ji}}{1 - N_{cu} / N_{cr}^J} \quad (4.6.1)$$

Where, Rotation angle: $\theta_{Ji} = \frac{\cos^2 \varphi}{1 - 2\xi} R$, Elastic buckling: $N_{cr}^J = \frac{\pi^2 E I_J}{4 l_J^2}$ (4.6.2)

and R: story drift angle.

Gussets tend to act as a rigid haunch, stiffening the beam-column connection in the in-plane direction with the effect of shifting the plastic hinge zone away from the beam end and amplifying connection demands. Frame pinching and opening effects have been noted to cause concentrated buckling, yielding and fracture in adjacent beams and columns, and gusset weld fractures, respectively [4.16~20].

Typical damage patterns during brace tension and compression cycles are shown in Figure 4.6.2

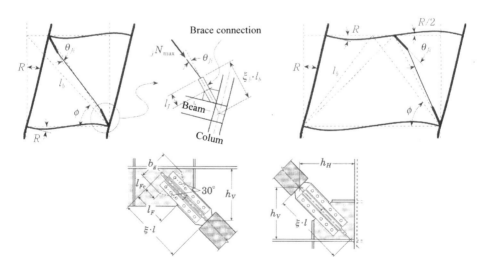

Figure 4.6.1 In-plane rotation at connections [4.18]

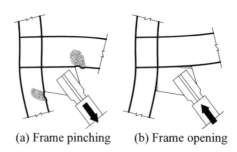

(a) Frame pinching   (b) Frame opening

Figure 4.6.2 Frame effects due to in-plane drift

Uriz et al. (2008) [4.7] reviewed testing of 3 bolted specimens in chevron and single diagonal frame configurations, with 25mm rectangular gussets attached with full-penetration butt welds to a welded moment frame with stiffeners and 15mm (beam) / 21mm (column) webs. The purpose of this testing was to determine the performance of the gussets and overall frame under in-plane drift. Significant yielding was observed in the adjacent framing elements and gusset during all tests. In the two single diagonal brace tests, cracks formed at the gusset/framing weld and beam fracture occurred at the gusset tip. This precipitated out-of-plane connection instability at 2.25% drift.

Palmer et al. (2014) [4.8] tested 6 bolted BRBs in a single diagonal frame configuration with 19mm gussets. These gussets were attached with a bolted end plate or with 12mm fillet welds on both sides to a welded moment frame. The beam and columns had 9mm and 11mm webs, respectively, with no stiffeners. An additional 4 pinned specimens were tested in a 2 storey 3D frame in a single diagonal configuration. The purpose of the test was to investigate gusset demands under in-plane drift, varying the taper (0°, 15°, 35°) and connection type. Significant yielding was observed in the adjacent framing elements and gussets in all tests. Gusset weld fracture and local buckling of the beam flange was observed in the single frame tests with the local buckling creating a softened condition that led to out-of-plane connection instability at ~2% drift.

Lin et al. (2016) [4.22] reviewed testing of a 3 story frame in a chevron configuration with 15mm non-tapered gussets attached with fillet welds to a welded moment frame with 11 to 13mm beam and 16mm column webs. The purpose was to confirm the performance of various BRB types and connection performance. Though gussets were designed according to normal AISC design provisions, the fracture of the gusset-to-flange welds occurred prior to exhausting the BRB ductility capacity.

Kasai et al. (2015) [4.23] tested 10 specimens in a subassembly with 9 or 12mm webs, 16 or 22mm flanges and 9 or 19mm non-tapered gussets both with (Type B) and without (Type D) stiffeners. At 0.7%~2% drift, extensive web yielding, local buckling and fracture was observed for cases where the web was thinner than the gusset, and a gusset cracked when it was sized thinner than the web.

Final damage states and corresponding interstory drift ratios of selected recent tests are shown in Figure 4.6.3

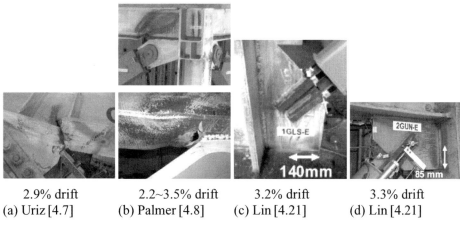

| 2.9% drift | 2.2~3.5% drift | 3.2% drift | 3.3% drift |
| (a) Uriz [4.7] | (b) Palmer [4.8] | (c) Lin [4.21] | (d) Lin [4.21] |

Figure 4.6.3 Damage to adjacent framing and gussets due to in-plane drift

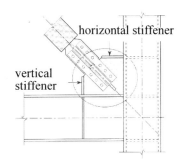

Figure 4.6.4 Recommended Connection [4.18]

In-plane frame action imposes compatibility demands on the gusset, which if not accounted for in design, results in yielding, local buckling, and fracture of the adjacent elements and gussets. Extensive yielding of the beams and columns may initiate out-of-plane BRB instability and global failure. Damage to the beams and columns also hinders post-earthquake repair.

This can be addressed by strengthening the members and designing for the compatibility demands, or by using special details that release the compatibility demands. To directly accommodate the frame rotation compatibility demands, Palmer et al. (2008) [4.8] and Kasai et al. (2015) [4.23] suggested to design the gusset-to-flange welds for gusset strength and to balance the gusset and framing web thickness. Lin et al. (2014) [4.22], Chou et al. (2012) [4.5] and Mhur et al. (2014) [4.31] proposed modifications to the Uniform Force Method that account for both axial and framing rotation-induced forces. Kasai et al. [4.22] reporting the recommended connection (Figure 4.6.4) with the same web thickness as GPL withstand 100cycles of 1.0% story drift angle and 40cycles of 3.0% story drift angle.

Modified details include reducing gusset fixity or introducing a hinge. Palmer et al. (2014) [4.8] studied the effect of tapering the gusset to reduce the length of the weld to the beam/column flanges and observed that this reduced or delayed, but did not eliminate, damage to the adjacent framing elements. Berman et al. (2009) [4.11] proposed to attach the gusset only to the beam (Figure 4.6.5 (a)) and then to design for the additional eccentricities. Wigle et al. [4.12] proposed to incorporate a beam hinge at the end of the gusset (Figure 4.6.5 (b)), releasing frame rotations. Note that all of these approaches reduce frame action by eliminating the gusset haunch effect, with the effect of reducing the structure's post-yield stiffness.

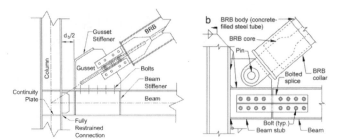

(a) Eccentric Gusset Concept [4.11] (b) Beam Pin Splice Concept [4.12]

Figure 4.6.5 Connection details releasing frame demands on gusset

References

[4.1]   Saeki E, Maeda Y, Nakamura H, Midorikawa M, Wada A: Experimental study on practical-scale unbonded braces. *AIJ J. of Struct. and Constr. Eng.*, 1995; **60**(476): 149-158. (*in Japanese*)

[4.2]   Tsai KC, Huang YC, Weng CS, Shirai T, Nakamura H: Experimental tests of large scale buckling restrained braces and frames. *Proceedings, 2nd Passive Control Symposium,* Tokyo Institute of Technology, 2002.

[4.3]   Tsai KC, Hsiao PC: Psuedo-dynamic test of a full-scale CFT/BRB frame – Part II Seismic performance of buckling-restrained braces and connections. *Earthquake Engineering and Structural Dynamics*, 2008; **37**:1099-1115.

[4.4]   Koetaka Y, Kinoshita T, Inoue K, Iitani K: Criteria of buckling-restrained braces to prevent out-of-plane buckling. *Proceedings of 14th World Conference on Earthquake Engineering,* 2008.

[4.5]   Chou CC, Liu JH: Frame and brace action forces on steel corner gusset plate connections in buckling-restrained braced frames. *Earthquake Spectra*, 2012; **28**:531-551.

[4.6]   Hikino T, Okazaki T, Kajiwara K, Nakashima M: Out-of-Plane stability of buckling-restrained braces placed in chevron arrangement. *Journal of Structural Engineering, ASCE,* 2013; **139**(11):DOI:10.1061/(ASCE)ST.1943-641X.0000767.

[4.7]   Uriz P, Mahin SA: Toward earthquake-resistant design of concentrically braced steel-frame structures. *Technical Report PEER 2008/08*, Pacific Earthquake Engineering Research Center, Berkeley, USA, 2008.

[4.8]   Palmer K, Christopulos A, Lehman D, Roeder C: Experimental evaluation of cyclically loaded, large-scale, planar and 3D buckling-restrained braced frames, *Journal of Constructional Steel Research*, 2014; **191**: 415-425.

[4.9]   Mahrenholtz C, Pao-Chun L, Wu AC, Tsai KC, Hwang SJ, Lin RY, Bhayusukma M: Retrofit of reinforced concrete frames with buckling-restrained braces, *Earthquake Engineering and Structural Dynamics*, 2015; **44**:59-75.

[4.10] Walters M, Maxwell B, Berkowitz R: Design for improved performance of buckling-restrained braced frames. *Proceedings 2004 SEAOC Convention*, Structural Engineers Association of California, Sacramento. 507-513, 2004.

[4.11] Berman J, Bruneau M: Cyclic testing of a buckling restrained braced frame with unconstrained gusset connections, *Journal of Structural Engineering, ASCE,* 2009; **135**(12):1499-1510.

[4.12] Wigle VR, Fahnestock LA: Buckling-restrained braced frame connection performance. *Journal of Constructional Steel Research*, 2010; **66**:65-74.

[4.13] Prinz G, Coy B, Richards P: Experimental and numerical investigation of ductile top-flange beam splices for improved buckling-restrained brace frame behaviour. *Journal of Structural Engineering*, 2014; **140**(9).

[4.14] Takeuchi T, Ozaki H, Matsui R, Sutcu F: Out-of-plane Stability of Buckling - Restrained Braces including Moment Transfer Capacity. *Earthquake Engineering & Structural Dynamics*, 2014; **43**(6):851–869, DOI:10.1002/eqe.2376.

[4.15] Takeuchi T, Matsui R, Mihara S: Out-of-plane stability assessment of buckling-restrained braces including connections with chevron configuration. *Earthquake Engineering & Structural Dynamics*, 2016; **45**(12):1895–1917, DOI: 10.1002/eqe.2724.

[4.16] Architectural Institute of Japan: *Recommendations for stability design of steel structures*, Sec. 3.5 Buckling-restrained braces, 2009;74–79. (*in Japanese*)

[4.17] Architectural Institute of Japan: *Stability problems of steel structures 2013*, Sec. 2 Stability of buckling-restrained braces including connections, 2013;19-38. (*in Japanese*)

[4.18] Architectural Institute of Japan: *Recommended provisions for seismic damping systems applied to steel structures*, Sec. 3 buckling restrained braces, Architectural Institute of Japan, 2014;24-59. (*in Japanese*)

[4.19] Architectural Institute of Japan: *Recommendations for stability design of steel structures*, Sec. 3.5 Buckling-restrained braces, Architectural Institute of Japan. 2017. *(in Japanese)*

[4.20] Building Center of Japan: *Specifications for BRB certification*, 2017. (*in Japanese*)

[4.21] AISC: *Seismic Provisions for Structural Steel Buildings*, AISC 341-16, 2016.

[4.22] Lin PC, Tsai KC, Wu AC, Chuang MC: Seismic design and test of gusset connections for buckling-restrained braced frames. *Earthquake Engineering & Structural Dynamics*, 2014; **43**:565-587.

[4.23] Kasai K, Matsuda Y, Motoyui S, Kishiki S: Fundamental study using new test loading scheme for steel frame subassembly with damper connection details. *AIJ J. Struct. Constr. Eng.*, 2015; **80**(708):309-319. (*in Japanese*)

[4.24] Matsui R, Takeuchi T, Nishimoto K, Takahashi S, Ohyama T: Effective Buckling Length of Buckling Restrained Braces Considering Rotational Stiffness at Restrained Ends, *Proc. of Seventh Int. Conf. on Urban Earthquake Eng.*, 2011;1245-1254.

[4.25] Bruneau M, Uang CM, Sabelli RSE: *Ductile design of Steel Structures, Chap.11, Ductile design of Buckling-restrained frames.* McGraw-Hill, 2nd edition, 2011.

[4.26] Galambos t, Surovek A: *Structural stability of steel: concepts and applications for structural engineers.* John Wiley and Sons, 2008.

[4.27] Ida M, Takeuchi T, Matsui R, Konishi Y, et al: Stability Assessment of Buckling Restrained Braces Taking Connections into Account (Part.2 Evaluation of Rotational Stiffness of Brace Connections). *Summaries of technical papers of Annual Meeting Architectural Institute of Japan*, 2013; **C-1, Structure III**:1247-1248. (*in Japanese*)

[4.28] Kinoshita T, Koetaka Y, Inoue I, Iitani K: Out-of-plane stiffness and yield strength of cruciform connections for buckling-restrained braces. *AIJ J. of Struct. Constr. Eng.*, 2008; **73**(632):1865-1873. DOI.org/10.3130/aijs.73.1865. (*in Japanese*)

[4.29] Ohyama S, Takeuchi T, Matsui R, Konishi Y, et al.: Stability Assessment of Buckling Restrained Braces Taking Connections into Account, (Part.15 Calculation Methods of Rotational Stiffness of Brace Connections in Chevron Configuration). *Summaries of technical papers of Annual Meeting Architectural Institute of Japan*, 2015; C-1, Structure III:1095-1096. (*in Japanese*)

[4.30] Sitler B, MacRae G, Takeuchi T, Matsui R, Westeneng B, Jones A: BRB performance issues. *16th World Conference on Earthquake Engineering,* 2016.

[4.31] Muir L, Thornton W: Vertical bracing connections – analysis and design. *Steel Design Guide 29 American Institute of Steel Construction,* 2014.

Chapter 5

CUMULATIVE DEFORMATION CAPACITY

CHAPTER CONTENTS

5.1 LOW-CYCLE FATIGUE FRACTURE

5.2 EFFECT OF THE DEBONDING CLEARANCE

5.3 EFFECT OF THE PLASTIC CORE LENGTH

5.1 LOW-CYCLE FATIGUE FRACTURE

In the Tohoku Great Earthquake in 2011 and Kumamoto Earthquake in 2016 Japan, multiple main shock and hundreds of aftershock continuously took place afterwards. Also there was large excitation of high-rise buildings in far distance cities for long duration up to several ten minutes. Therefore, engineers will be asked to determine if the yielded BRBs can survive such cumulative plastic amplitudes and whether BRB must be replaced afterwards. While prequalification tests regularly exceed minimum code requirements, in some cases the residual low cycle fatigue capacity must be calculated directly. This chapter discusses the fatigue properties of typical BRBs and methods to assess the cumulative damage index. In particular, as the effect of higher mode buckling amplifies the local strain demand, fatigue curves appropriate for BRBs are presented in Section 5.2, although generally these will be supplier specific.

Fatigue capacity under constant amplitude

Under constant amplitude loading, Manson (1954) [5.7] and Tavernelli and Coffin (1962) [5.8] indicated that the number of cycles to fracture N_f can be expressed as a function of the strain range, with separate coefficients used for the elastic and plastic ranges:

$$\Delta\varepsilon_e = C_1 \cdot N_f^{m_1} \tag{5.1.1}$$

$$\Delta\varepsilon_p = C_2 \cdot N_f^{m_2} \tag{5.1.2}$$

$$\Delta\varepsilon_t = C_1 \cdot N_f^{m_1} + C_2 \cdot N_f^{m_2} \tag{5.1.3}$$

where $\Delta\varepsilon_e$ = the elastic strain range; $\Delta\varepsilon_p$ = the plastic strain range; $\Delta\varepsilon_t$ = the total strain range; and C_i and m_i are constants that depend on the material.

The strain notations and correspondence between a typical BRB hysteresis and equivalent elasto-perfectly plastic idealization are shown in Figure 5.1.1.

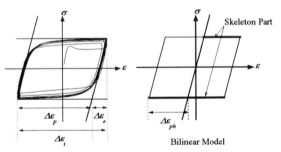

Fig. 5.1.1 Hysteretic loop and model

For seismic members the number of elastic cycles is generally far less than the limit, and so the plastic strain contribution dominates. Previous studies (e.g., Maeda et al. (1998) [5.9]; Nakagomi et al. (2000) [5.10]) have shown that these equations can be applied to BRB cores. This is premised on plastic strains being well-distributed along the full core length, sufficient restraint is provided against first-mode buckling and the core maintains positive tangent stiffness once yielded.

Also, plastic fatigue capacity differs little between materials. This is demonstrated by constant amplitude fatigue testing of BRBs with various steel grades (LY100, LY225, SN400) and shown in Figure 5.1.2.

Chapter 5. Cumulative Deformation Capacity   89

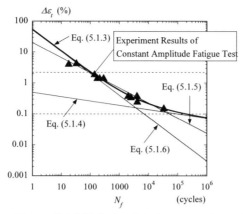

Figure 5.1.2 Relationship between $\Delta\varepsilon_t$ and N_f [5.1],[5.9]

As higher mode buckling introduces additional flexural strains, the Coffin-Manson coefficients for BRBs will be significantly less than for the base material. While these coefficients will vary from supplier-to-supplier and by BRB type and size, an approximate set proposed during the original development of BRBs is given by Equations 5.1.4~5.1.6 [5.1].

$$\Delta\varepsilon_t(\%) = 0.5 \cdot N_f^{-0.14} \, (\Delta\varepsilon_t < 0.1\%) \qquad (5.1.4)$$

$$\Delta\varepsilon_t(\%) = 20.48 \cdot N_f^{-0.49} \, (0.1\% \leq \Delta\varepsilon_t < 2.2\%) \qquad (5.1.5)$$

$$\Delta\varepsilon_t(\%) = 54.0 \cdot N_f^{-0.71} \, (2.2\% \leq \Delta\varepsilon_t) \qquad (5.1.6)$$

Fatigue capacity under variable amplitude loading

Testing protocols are generally conducted with gradually increasing amplitudes and real earthquakes impose variable amplitudes in a random sequence. One popular method of analyzing a variable amplitude sequence is to order and simply the sequence using the rainflow method and then to apply the damage index proposed by Miner (1945) [5.12].

The rainflow method is used rearrange a random sequence of stress or strain peaks into a reduced set, repeatedly searching for the largest total range. This is commonly described using the metaphor of rain dripping down a pagoda. The principle of this method is shown in Figure 5.1.3, with time a strain given on the two axes.

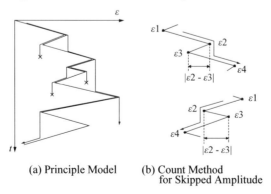

(a) Principle Model   (b) Count Method for Skipped Amplitude

Figure 5.1.3 Principle of rain-flow method

Miner's rule then a simple linear summation, with cycle counts at each strain range $\Delta\varepsilon_i$ compared against the corresponding limit predicted by the Coffin-Manson equation. Fatigue-induced fracture is predicted when the cumulative damage reaches 1.0.

$$D = \sum_{i=1}^{n} \frac{n_i}{N_{fi}} = 1.0 \tag{5.1.7}$$

where n_i = the number of cycles for the strain range $\Delta\varepsilon_i$; N_{fi} = the number of failure cycles for $\Delta\varepsilon_i$; and D = the damage index. While the original concept was developed for elastic stresses, in this case it is being applied to plastic strains, as shown previously in Figure 5.1.2.

However, in many cases the accuracy of Miner's rule can be poor. This is readily illustrated by a series of fatigue tests conducted on BRBs with different types of loading protocols:

- Constant amplitude
- Gradually increasing amplitude
- Variable/random amplitude

A typical distribution of strain range from the shaking table test (variable/random amplitude) is shown in Figure 5.1.4. The testing configuration, core materials and loading protocol are shown in Figure 5.1.5 and summarized in Table 5.1.1 [5.1]. All tests were conducted to the point of fracture, defined as a strength degradation of 25% from the peak.

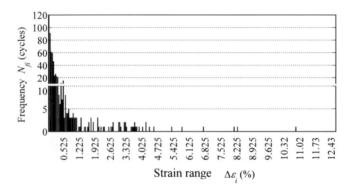

Figure 5.1.4 Strain range and frequency of shaking table test

Chapter 5. Cumulative Deformation Capacity 91

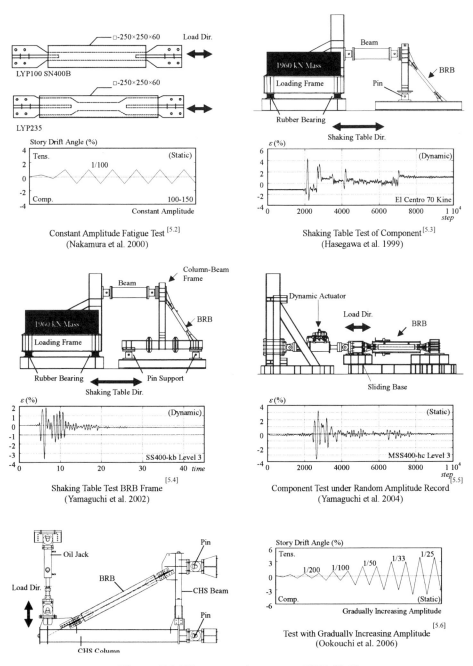

Figure 5.1.5 Past experiments on BRB [5.1]

Table 5.1.1 Specimen Summary of Past Tests on BRB [5.1]

Test	Specimen	Steel	Core Plate	Thickness (mm)	Width (mm)	Length (mm)	Input ε (%)	ε_{max} (%) Tens.	ε_{max} (%) Comp.	$\overline{\Delta\varepsilon_{ph}}$ (%)
Constant Amplitude Fatigue Test	100-150	LY100	—	25	100	960	1.5	0.76	-0.79	0.68
	100-016	LY100	—	25	100	960	0.16	0.10	-0.08	0.02
	100-040	LY100	—	25	100	960	0.4	0.21	-0.21	0.13
	100+150	LY100	+	25	100	1180	1.5	0.73	-0.79	0.69
	400-200	SN400B	—	25	100	960	2	1.01	-0.99	0.82
	400-150	SN400B	—	25	100	960	1.5	0.78	-0.79	0.56
	235+150	LY225	+	16	100	470	4.3	2.11	-2.26	1.86
	235-150	LY225	—	28	100	470	4.5	2.21	-2.38	2.01
Shaking Table Test of Component	El Centro	SS400	—	22	130	1291	E.C. [a]	6.93	-3.10	0.33
Shaking Table Test BRB Frame	SS400-	SS400	—	16	60	1200	kb,hc [b]	6.55	-5.99	0.51
	LYP100	LY100	—	16	75	1200	kb,hc [b]	5.16	-5.47	0.30
	LYP235	LY225	—	16	75	600	kb,hc [b]	6.98	-5.96	0.59
Component Test under Random Amplitude Record	M SS400-	SS400	—	16	60	1200	kb,hc [b]	5.14	-5.46	0.49
	M LYP100	LY100	—	16	75	1200	kb,hc [b]	2.51	-5.30	0.28
	M LYP235	LY225	—	16	75	600	kb,hc [b]	7.04	-5.94	0.71
Test with Gradually Increasing Amplitude	TB-1	LY225	—	16	92	1370	Normal	4.40	-3.64	1.94
	TAS-1	LY225	—	16	92	1370	Normal	3.94	-3.93	2.04
	TAS-1'	LY225	—	16	92	1370	Near field	3.60	-5.16	1.89
	TAS-2	LY225	—	16	58	1610	Normal	3.15	-3.31	1.69
	TAS-2'	LY225	—	16	58	1610	Near field	4.01	-4.12	1.61

[a] El CentroNS [b] JMA Kobe NS, Hachinohe NS

For each of these tests the damage index at fracture was calculated using Miner's rule (Equation 5.1.7) and the proposed Coffin-Manson relationship for BRBs (Equations 5.1.4-6). As indicated in Figure 5.1.6, there is large variability in the accuracy of fracture for predicting damage indices of 0.29 to 1.68. Furthermore, Miner's rule is notably unconservative for the gradually random amplitude results, which also had a far larger average strain range (4%) as compared to the other tests (2%, refer Table 5.1.1). This is consistent with Nakagomi et al. (1995) [5.13], which found that fracture could occur at a predicted damage index of 0.05 to 1.2 when applying Miner's method to an element under large plastic strains.

Moreover, Miner's method requires analysis of individual amplitudes, a difficult task when considering standard response histories.

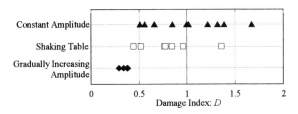

Figure 5.1.6 Accuracy of Miner's method

Fatigue capacity using skeletal ratio

An alternative to Miner's rule can be developed by separating the strains into skeletal and Bauschinger components. This decomposition is illustrated in Figure 5.1.7, with the skeletal parts defined as the first incursions at a given stress and Bauschinger contributions including everything else other than elastic unloading. Kato and Akiyama (Kato et al. 1973 [5.14]; [5.15]) have proposed that the deformation capacity is strongly related to the addition of the skeleton part that matches in the stress-strain curve of the tensile test.

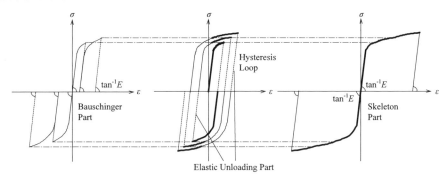

Figure 5.1.7 Decomposition of hysteretic loop

The distribution of skeletal and Bauschinger parts are shown in Figure 5.1.8 for each of the tests discussed earlier. The skeletal portion of cumulative plastic strain reaches 20% for the tests with gradually increasing amplitude, while it is less than 10% in all other tests. A similar difference is noted between the shaking table and constant amplitude test, indicating that a higher skeletal ratio apparently leads to a lower cumulative strain capacity.

94   Chapter 5. Cumulative Deformation Capacity

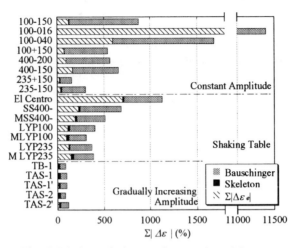

Fig. 5.1.8 Cumulative strain to point of fracture

Based on the above characteristics, a method is developed for estimating the cumulative strain capacity. By assuming that the hysteretic loop is expressed as a simple bilinear model (Figure 5.1.1) and the loop is repeated N_f times prior to the fatigue fracture, each part can be expressed as follows:

$$\chi = 4 \Delta\varepsilon_{ph} N_f \tag{5.1.8}$$

$$\chi_S = 3 \Delta\varepsilon_{ph} \tag{5.19}$$

$$\chi_B = \chi - \chi_S = 4 \Delta\varepsilon_{ph}(N_f - 0.75) \tag{5.1.10}$$

where χ = the cumulative plastic strain; χ_S = the skeleton part; χ_B = the Bauschinger part; and $\Delta\varepsilon_{ph}$ = half of the plastic strain range (average amplitude, Figure 5.1.1)

By substituting N_f obtained from Equation (5.1.8) into Equation (5.1.2), the cumulative plastic strain under a constant amplitude is given by

$$\Delta\varepsilon_{ph} = \frac{1}{2}\Delta\varepsilon_p = \frac{1}{2}C_2 \cdot N_f^{m_2} = C \cdot N_f^{m_2} \tag{5.1.11}$$

$$\ln \Delta\varepsilon_{ph} = \ln C + m_2 \ln \frac{\chi}{4\Delta\varepsilon_{ph}} \tag{5.1.12}$$

$$\chi = 4\left\{ \frac{C}{\Delta\varepsilon_{ph}^{(1+m_2)}} \right\}^{-\frac{1}{m_2}} \tag{5.1.13}$$

Chapter 5. Cumulative Deformation Capacity 95

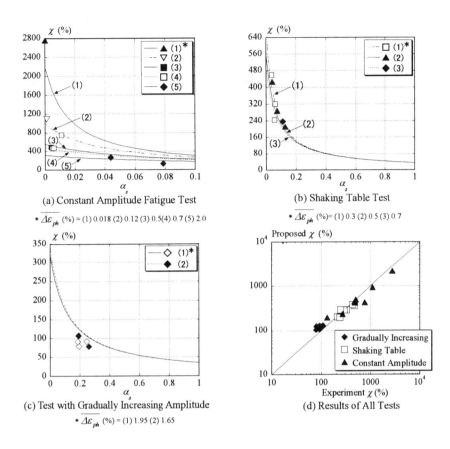

Figure 5.1.9 Comparison between experiment and proposed method
(Cumulative strain)

By assuming that the extent of damage in the skeleton part is a times that in the Bauschinger part, Equation (5.1.13) can be re-written as

$$\chi = a\chi_S + \chi_B = 4 \left\{ \frac{C}{\Delta\varepsilon_{ph}^{(1+m_2)}} \right\}^{-\frac{1}{m_2}} \tag{5.1.14}$$

When fatigue fracture occurs only due to the skeleton part without the Bauschinger part, the cumulative strain, denoted by χ_{SO}, is given by

$$a\chi_{SO} = 4 \left\{ \frac{C}{\left(\Delta\varepsilon_{ph}\right)^{(1+m_2)}} \right\}^{-\frac{1}{m_2}} \tag{5.1.15}$$

By substituting a obtained from Equation (5.1.15) into Equation (5.1.14), the fracture condition can be expressed as

Chapter 5. Cumulative Deformation Capacity

$$\frac{\chi_S}{\chi_{SO}} + \frac{\chi_B}{4} \left\{ \frac{\overline{\Delta\varepsilon_{ph}}^{(1+m_2)}}{C} \right\}^{-\frac{1}{m_2}} = 1.0 \tag{5.1.16}$$

With skeleton ratio α_s defined as the ratio of χ_s to χ

$$\alpha_s = \frac{\chi_S}{\chi} \tag{5.1.17}$$

and χ_B given by

$$\chi_B = (1 - \alpha_S)\chi \tag{5.1.18}$$

Equation (5.1.16) can be re-written:

$$\chi = \frac{1}{\dfrac{\alpha_S}{\chi_{SO}} + \dfrac{(1-\alpha_S)}{4} \left\{ \dfrac{\overline{\Delta\varepsilon_{ph}}^{-(1+m_2)}}{C} \right\}^{-\frac{1}{m_2}}} \tag{5.1.19}$$

where $\overline{\Delta\varepsilon_{ph}}$ = half of the average plastic strain range (average amplitude). In Equation (5.1.19), $\Delta\varepsilon_{ph}$ is replaced with $\overline{\Delta\varepsilon_{ph}}$ for applying it to the random amplitude response.

By using Equation (5.1.19), the cumulative strain capacity can be directly calculated. The constant C and m_2 are obtained from a constant amplitude fatigue test and these values for BRBs are determined as 27 and -0.71 respectively from Equation (5.1.6). Another constant χ_{so}, the cumulative plastic strain to the point of fatigue fracture especially brought only by the skeleton part, is regarded as a simple tensile test. Consequently, the constant χ_{so} can be defined as a minimum fracture elongation value in the past coupon tests and it is estimated as 35 (%) in the present study. These constants are substituted into Equation (5.1.19) and the following equation is obtained:

$$\chi(\%) = \frac{1}{\dfrac{\alpha_S}{35} + (1-\alpha_S) \left\{ \dfrac{\overline{\Delta\varepsilon_{ph}}^{-0.41}}{417.14} \right\}} \tag{5.1.20}$$

The value of $\overline{\Delta\varepsilon_{ph}}$ is calculated by the rain flow method. In Figure 5.1.9, the curves of the cumulative strain capacity obtained from Equation (5.1.20) are compared with the experimental results; (a) shows the results of a constant amplitude fatigue test; (b), those of a shaking table test; and (c), those of the test with a gradually increasing amplitude. In the figure, the proposed method is represented by the smooth lines with the marks indicate the results obtained experimentally. In (d), the results of the experiments and proposed method are compared for all three types of loading. Generally, the results calculated using Equation (5.1.20) can effectively predict the experimental results with the corresponding value of $\overline{\Delta\varepsilon_{ph}}$. The variance value for predicted results is calculated as 0.067 based on the experimental results, while that for Miner's method is 0.196. The accuracy of the proposed method is improved in comparison with Miner's method, especially for a range of large strains. In

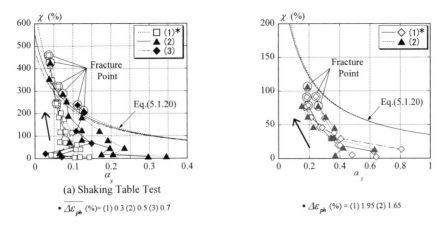

(a) Shaking Table Test

* $\overline{\Delta\varepsilon_{ph}}$ (%)= (1) 0.3 (2) 0.5 (3) 0.7

* $\overline{\Delta\varepsilon_{ph}}$ (%)= (1) 1.95 (2) 1.65

Figure 5.1.10 Shift of skeleton ratio to point of fracture

Figure 5.1.10, the process of strain accumulation is shown in each experiment. In the shaking table tests, the initial value of α_s is in the range of 0.05–0.35; then, it reduces slightly to around 0.05–0.15 and reaches the fracture lines defined by Equation (5.1.20). On the other hand, in the test with a gradually increasing amplitude, α_s is initially very high around 0.8; subsequently, it reduces to 0.2 and reaches the fracture line. Since the fracture lines shift downward at high values of α_s, a high initial value of α_s leads to a lower cumulative strain capacity. For prediction with the proposed method, only the key values of α_s and $\overline{\Delta\varepsilon_{ph}}$ are required. These values are related to the seismic response amplitude and the stiffness ratio of BRBs to the moment frames. They could be directly estimated from the maximum response of the structure as indicated by Akiyama (1999) [5.16]. Therefore, when these values are obtained, analyses of the individual amplitude of response vibrations, as in the case of Miner's method, are not required for estimating the cumulative strain capacity under random amplitudes.

As advocated by Akiyama (1985) [5.17], the seismic design method, which considers the seismic energy input and energy absorption capacity of the structure, has also gained popularity. It is important to accurately predict the capacity of BRBs to

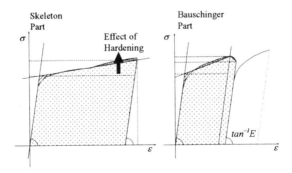

Figure 5.1.11 Calculation of absorbed energy

98   Chapter 5. Cumulative Deformation Capacity

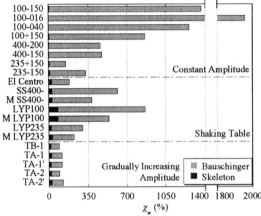 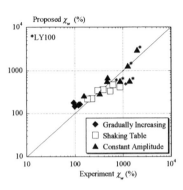

Figure 5.1.12 Cumulative absorbed energy

Figure 5.1.13 Comparison between experiment and proposed method (Cumulative absorbed energy)

act as energy dissipators. To this end, Equation (5.1.19) can also be used to estimate the energy absorption capacity. The absorbed energy value is calculated by the sum of closed areas of the hysteretic loop, and it is affected by the hardening stiffness after yielding (Figure 5.1.11). Figure 5.1.12 shows the absorbed energy of BRBs to the point of fracture in each experiment. It is evident that the energy absorption capacity of elasto-plastic dampers is not constant and is significantly affected by the strain amplitude and loading history, as in the case of the deformation capacity. For predicting the energy absorption capacity, the hardening stiffness ratio β is defined as the ratio of the additional areas due to the hardening stiffness to the areas without hardening; then, β is set to the right side of Equation (5.1.20). The value of β is generally in the range of 1.2–1.5 with an average of 1.37. The absorbed energy of BRBs to the point of fracture is calculated as follows:

$$\chi_w(\%) = \frac{\beta}{\dfrac{\alpha_S}{35} + (1-\alpha_S)\left\{\dfrac{\Delta\varepsilon_{ph}}{417.14}\right\}^{-0.41}} \qquad (5.1.21)$$

where χ_w = the normalized cumulative absorbed energy. This value is obtained by dividing the cumulative absorbed energy by the yield strength.

In Figure 5.1.13, the values of χ_w determined by Equation (5.1.21) are plotted along with those calculated from the hysteretic loops in each experiment. As in the case of the cumulative deformation, χ_w can be estimated effectively by the proposed method. Results obtained using LY100 (indicated by *) are on the conservative side. This is due to a remarkable increase in the yield strength of LY100 steel, which is not estimated by Equation (5.1.21). The mechanical property of LY100 is shown in Table 5.1.2. Even in this case, the accuracy of the proposed method has the variance value of 0.166, which is still considered to be acceptable.

Chapter 5. Cumulative Deformation Capacity

Table 5.1.2 Minimum specified values of mechanical properties for Japanese and comparable U.S. steel grades

Steel Grade	Steel Type	Minimum Specified Values of Mechanical Properties			
		f_y (MPa)	0.2 % f_y (MPa)	f_u (MPa)	ε_u (%)
Japanese Steel Grade: SS400 (JIS)	Carbon Steels for General Structure	245[a]	-	400-510	17[a]
Comparable U.S. Steel Grade: A36 (ASTM)	Carbon Steels for General Structure	250		400-550	20
Japanese Steel Grade: SN400B (JIS)	Carbon Steels for Building Structure	235-355[b]	-	400-510	22[b]
Comparable U.S. Steel Grade: A1043/A (ASTM)	Carbon Steels for Building Structure	250-360		400	23
Japanese Steel Grade: LY100[c]	Low-Yield-Strength Steel	-	80-120	200-300	50
Japanese Steel Grade: LY225[c]	Low-Yield-Strength Steel	215-245	-	300-400	40
Comparable U.S. Steel Grade: -	-	-	-	-	-

[a] Range of Thickness: 16 (mm) and under [b]: over 16(mm) and under 40 (mm) and 40 (mm) [c]: Ministerial Approved Standard

Equation (5.1.19) is derived by assuming that the hysteretic loop of BRB is expressed as a bilinear model and the cumulative plastic strain is given by Equation (5.1.8). In order to re-determine the relationship between $\overline{\Delta\varepsilon_{ph}}$ and N_f, Equation (5.1.8) is substituted into Equation (5.1.19) and the following equations are obtained; $\Delta\varepsilon_{ph}$ in Equation (5.1.8) is replaced with $\overline{\Delta\varepsilon_{ph}}$:

$$\overline{\Delta\varepsilon_{ph}} = \frac{\chi}{4N_f} = \frac{1}{\left\{\dfrac{4\alpha_S}{\chi_{SO}} + (1-\alpha_S)\left(\dfrac{\overline{\Delta\varepsilon_{ph}}}{C}\right)^{-(1+m_2)}\right\}^{-\frac{1}{m_2}} N_f} \tag{5.1.22}$$

$$N_f = \frac{1}{\dfrac{4\overline{\Delta\varepsilon_{ph}}\alpha_S}{\chi_{SO}} + (1-\alpha_S)\left(\dfrac{\overline{\Delta\varepsilon_{ph}}}{C}\right)^{-\frac{1}{m_2}}} \tag{5.1.23}$$

From Equations (5.1.8) and (5.1.9), α_s can be expressed as

$$\alpha_S = \frac{\chi_S}{\chi} = \frac{3}{4N_f} \tag{5.1.24}$$

By substituting Equation (5.1.23) into Equation (5.1.24), N_f is obtained as follows:

$$N_f = \left(1 - \frac{3\overline{\Delta\varepsilon_p}}{2\chi_{SO}}\right)\left(\frac{\overline{\Delta\varepsilon_p}}{C_2}\right)^{\frac{1}{m_2}} + 0.75 \tag{5.1.25}$$

where $\overline{\Delta\varepsilon_p}$ is the average plastic strain range ($\overline{\Delta\varepsilon_p} = 2\overline{\Delta\varepsilon_{ph}}$).

Hence, the fatigue curve of the large strain range is expressed by Equation (5.1.25). When α_s is estimated as 1, which implies that χ_{so} is equal to $3\overline{\Delta\varepsilon_p}/2$, N_f is calculated as 0.75. On the contrary, when N_f approaches infinity, which implies that $\overline{\Delta\varepsilon_p}$ approaches 0, Equation (5.1.25) is simplified as

$$N_f = \left(\frac{\overline{\Delta\varepsilon_p}}{C_2}\right)^{\frac{1}{m_2}} + 0.75 \tag{5.1.26}$$

Under this assumption, the second term is considered to be negligible. Therefore, Equation (5.1.26) can be expressed as

$$N_f = \left(\frac{\overline{\Delta\varepsilon_p}}{C_2}\right)^{\frac{1}{m_2}} \qquad (5.1.27)$$

This equation is the same as Equation (5.1.2) in which $\Delta\varepsilon_p$ is replaced with $\overline{\Delta\varepsilon_p}$. These properties are included in Equation (5.1.19). When N_f approaches infinity, Equation (5.1.27) approximates the Manson-Coffin equation, and when N_f is equal to 0.75, it converges on a certain strain range produced by the fracture of only the skeleton parts. The model of the fatigue curve is shown in Figure 5.1.14. In the range of N_f under 20, the plot diverges from the Manson-Coffin equation. Uneven distributions of large plastic strains are considered to be one of the reasons for this divergence [5.18].

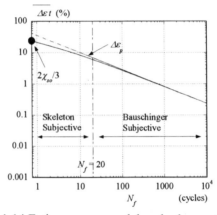

Figure 5.1.14 Fatigue curve model under large strain range

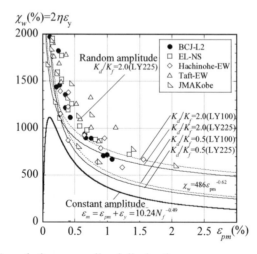

Figure 5.1.15 Cumulative normalized dissipating energy v.s. maximum strain

Figure 5.1.15 shows the cumulative normalized dissipating energy of BRBs distributed in various moment frames until fracture versus maximum experienced plastic strain. Because of the seismic response amplitudes working on BRBs in the frame are random, their dissipating energy is generally higher than the constant amplitudes with the same maximum amplitude. However, lower K_d/K_f layouts which means smaller amount of BRBs strength compared to those of elastic main frames yields to lower capacity, because of number of shaking cycles increases lead by the elastic response of the main frame.

From discussions above, it can be summarized that the evaluation of cumulative deformation capacity of BRB can be achieved by the flowing three methods.

  a) Evaluating cumulative plastic deformation capacity from the fatigue curve with the maximum plastic strain. – easy but conservative.
  b) Evaluating cumulative plastic deformation capacity from the fatigue curve with individual strain range with Miner rule (Equation5.1.7) – requires time history of each BRB strain, and rain flow treatments are required.
  c) Evaluating cumulative plastic deformation capacity from the fatigue curve with averaged plastic strain range with Equation 5.1.20 –time history of each BRB strain and rain flow treatments are not necessary.

5.2 EFFECT OF THE DEBONDING CLEARANCE

In Section 5.1, the following low cycle fatigue formula for the BRB as Equation (5.2.1).

$$\Delta\varepsilon_{eq}(\%) = 0.5 \cdot N_f^{-0.14} + 54.0 \cdot N_f^{-0.71} \tag{5.2.1}$$

Here, $\Delta\varepsilon_{eq}$ is the normalized deformation range, and N_f is the fracture cycle number. In addition, Takeuchi et al. (2006) [5.18] modified Equation (5.2.1) to obtain Equation (5.2.2) for a fracture cycle number of less than 20 (Equation (5.1.25).

$$N_f = \left(1 - \frac{3\Delta\varepsilon_{eq}}{70}\right) \cdot \left(\frac{\Delta\varepsilon_{eq}^{-1.41}}{3.63\times10^{-3}}\right) + 0.75 \tag{5.2.2}$$

This modification indicates that the concentration of the plastic strain at a zone in the core plate occurs when the stress exceeds the maximum value and the tangent modulus become negative. The fatigue formula for the BRB derived from Equation s. (5.2.1) and (5.2.2) is consistent with the results based on the experimental data from Nakamura et al. (2000) [5.2], as shown in Figure 5.2.1. In this figure, the fatigue performance of the BRB decreases from the fatigue performance of the steel material determined on the basis of the normalized deformation range given by Equation (5.2.3).

$$\begin{cases} \Delta\varepsilon_{eq}(\%) = 0.74N_f^{-0.11} + 35.0N_f^{-0.47} & \text{(SS400)} \\ \Delta\varepsilon_{eq}(\%) = 0.47N_f^{-0.087} + 33.0N_f^{-0.48} & \text{(LY100)} \\ \Delta\varepsilon_{eq}(\%) = 0.88N_f^{-0.14} + 72.0N_f^{-0.55} & \text{(LY225)} \end{cases} \tag{5.2.3}$$

Takeuchi et al. (2006) [5.19] have proposed an index of strain concentration ratio for circular tube braces, whereby the local strain at the point of plastic strain concentration is divided by the normalized deformation. The strain concentration ratio is defined by the specification of the braces. The definition does not involve large calculations such as those in the finite element method. Brace fracture is simply defined by the point at which the local strain value is equivalent to the fatigue formula for the steel material. Therefore, this method easily assesses brace fracture using macro-model of the braces. In this paper, the authors attempt to evaluate BRB fracture using a similar method.

In Matsui et al. (2010) [5.20], the BRB is constituted by a plane steel core plate restrained by a mortar filled steel tube, as shown in Table 5.2.1 and Figures 5.2.2 and 5.2.3. The mechanical property of SN400 is assumed to be same as that of SS400. Hypothetically, the core plate exhibits a high mode local buckling deformation continuously within the clearance between the core plate and the restrainer s under cyclic loading. In this case, the local buckling deformation y is calculated from the half lengths of the local buckling wavelength l_p as Equation (5.2.4).

$$\begin{cases} y = s \sin(\pi x/l_p) \\ s = s_0 + 0.5 v_p \varepsilon_{eqtm} t_c \end{cases} \quad (5.2.4)$$

Here, ε_{eqtm} is the maximum value of the normalized deformation, and s_0 is the initial value of the clearance between the core plate and the restrainer. Although local buckling occurs in the out-of-plane and in-plane, only the former is firstly considered. The half lengths of the local buckling wavelength l_p is calculated as Equation (5.2.5).

$$l_p = \pi t_c \sqrt{E_t/3\sigma_{cy}}/2 \quad (5.2.5)$$

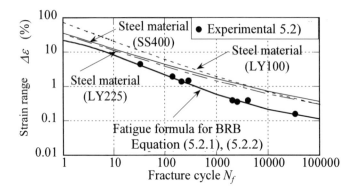

Figure 5.2.1 Low-cycle fatigue capacity for BRB and steel material

where t_c is the thickness of the core plate, σ_{cy} is the yield stress of the core plate, and E_t is the tangent modulus of the steel material. The stress–strain hysteresis curve can be modeled by the modified Menegotto–Pinto model proposed by Menegotto and Pinto (1973) [5.21]. The hysteresis curve calculated using the Menegotto–Pinto model is consistent with the experimental results obtained by Nakamura et al. (2000) [5.2] as shown in Figure 5.2.4. Here, ε_{eq} is the normalized deformation, and σ_{eq} is the equivalent stress calculated by dividing the axial force by the initial sectional area. The range of the normalized deformation $\Delta\varepsilon_{eq}$ is defined as Equation (5.2.6) as shown in Figure 5.2.5.

$$\Delta\varepsilon_{eq} = \varepsilon_{eqtm} - \varepsilon_{eq} \tag{5.2.6}$$

The tangent modulus E_t can be directly calculated using the proposed Menegotto–Pinto model. Here, for ease, the tangent modulus is approximated by the normalized deformation function as Equation (5.2.7), illustrated in Figure 5.2.6.

Table. 5.2.1 Mechanical Properties of BRB

Specimen	Steel	t_c (mm)	B_c (mm)	$\Delta\varepsilon$ (%)	N_f	Input strain amplitude
400-200	SN400B (SS400)	25	100	2	176	Constant (Nakamura et al. 2000)
400-150				1.5	140	
400-040				0.4	211	
100-150	LY100			1.5	287	
100-040				0.4	2041	
235-150	LY225	28		4.5	33	
235-016				0.16	2520	
-	SS400	12	50	3.2	19	Random (Takeuchi et al. 2010)

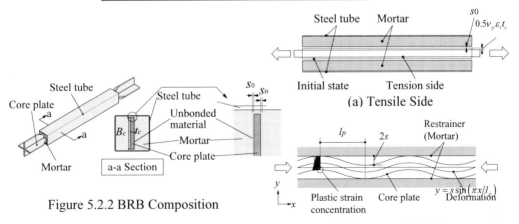

Figure 5.2.2 BRB Composition

(a) Tensile Side

(b) Compression Side
Figure 5.2.3 Core Plate Deformation

Chapter 5. Cumulative Deformation Capacity

$$E_t \atop (\text{N/mm}^2) = \begin{cases} \begin{cases} -3.68 \times 10^5 \cdot \Delta\varepsilon_{eq} + E & (\text{SS400}) \\ -1.12 \times 10^5 \cdot \Delta\varepsilon_{eq} + E & (\text{LY100}) \\ -4.84 \times 10^5 \cdot \Delta\varepsilon_{eq} + E & (\text{LY225}) \end{cases} & \left(0 \le \Delta\varepsilon_{eq} \le 2\varepsilon_y\right) \\ \begin{cases} 6.45 \times 10^3 \cdot \Delta\varepsilon_{eq}^{-2.04} + 500 & (\text{SS400}) \\ 1.27 \times 10^3 \cdot \Delta\varepsilon_{eq}^{-1.84} + 500 & (\text{LY100}) \\ 1.93 \times 10^3 \cdot \Delta\varepsilon_{eq}^{-2.65} + 500 & (\text{LY225}) \end{cases} & \left(2\varepsilon_y \le \Delta\varepsilon_{eq}\right) \end{cases} \quad (5.2.7)$$

The local buckling deformation gives the bending strain ε_b and the geometrical deformation ε_g additional to the normalized deformation ε_{eq}.

$$\begin{cases} \varepsilon_b = t_c/2\left(\pi/l_p\right)^2 s = 6s\sigma_{cy}/E_t t_c \\ \varepsilon_g = 1/4\left(\pi s/l_p\right)^2 = 3s^2 \sigma_{cy}/E_t t_c^2 \end{cases} \quad (5.2.8)$$

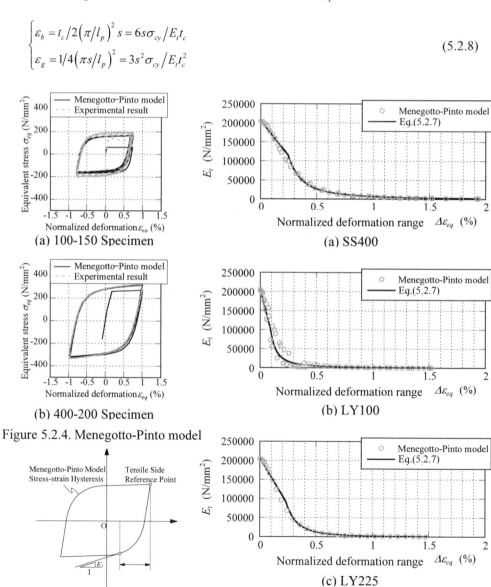

(a) 100-150 Specimen

(a) SS400

(b) 400-200 Specimen

(b) LY100

Figure 5.2.4. Menegotto-Pinto model

Figure 5.2.5 Normalized deformation

(c) LY225

Figure 5.2.6 Tangent modulus of core plate

Here, the normalized deformation range $\Delta\varepsilon_{eq}$ is calculated as Equation (5.2.9).

$$\Delta\varepsilon_{eq} = \varepsilon_{eqtm} - \varepsilon_{eq} \tag{5.2.9}$$

The local strain range $\Delta\varepsilon_h$ at the point at which the most concentrated plastic strain occurs in the core plate is calculated using Equation (5.2.10), and the strain concentration ratio α_c is defined by Equation (5.2.11).

$$\Delta\varepsilon_h = \Delta\varepsilon_{eq} + \varepsilon_b - \varepsilon_g \tag{5.2.10}$$

$$\alpha_c = \frac{\Delta\varepsilon_h}{\Delta\varepsilon_{eq}} = \frac{\Delta\varepsilon_{eq} + \varepsilon_b - \varepsilon_g}{\Delta\varepsilon_{eq}} \tag{5.2.11}$$

The local strain in-plane is also calculated using Equation (5.2.8) by substituting the thickness of the core plate t_c with the width of the core plate B_c. The local strain in-plane is generally 1/8th the local strain out-of-plane. In addition, the maximum values in- and out-of-plane do not consistently agree. Therefore, the effect of the local buckling in-plane generally does not significantly affect the cumulative deformation capacity of the BRB and out-of-plane strain is considered as dominant.

The BRB undergoes fracture at the point at which the local strain calculated from the normalized deformation ε_{eq} and multiplied by the strain concentration ratio α_c is consistent with the fatigue formula given in Equation (5.2.3). Using this evaluation method, the BRB fatigue formula is assessed, as shown in Figure 5.2.7. The plots in this figure show the experimental results derived from Nakamura et al. (2000) [5.2] and Takeuchi et al. (2010) [5.22]. The fatigue formula is consistent with the experimental results. Here, the strain range of the experimental results with random amplitude is assessed as the average plastic strain range by the rainflow method, and the fracture cycle is equivalent to the average plastic strain range. The initial clearance between the core plate and the restrainer s_0 is set at 1 mm in Nakamura et al. (2000) [5.2] and 2 mm in Takeuchi et al. (2010) [5.22]. Figure 5.2.7 shows that the performance given by the BRB fatigue formula decreases as the clearance s between the core plate and the restrainer increases. Therefore, the strain concentration ratio α_c of the BRB can be described as a function of the clearance s. For example, the strain

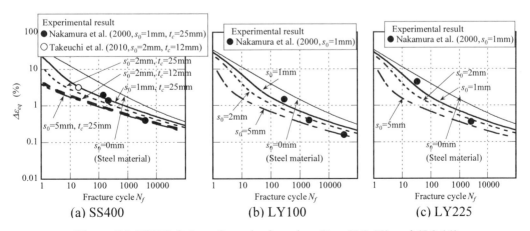

Figure 5.2.7 BRB fatigue formulas based on Eqs. (5.2.10) and (5.2.11)

concentration ratio α_c is approximated as Equations (5.2.12) and (5.2.13) by the least squares method as shown in Figure 5.2.8, whereby ε_y is the yield strain and $\Delta\varepsilon_{eq}$ is the strain amplitude when the fracture cycle number is 20.

$$\alpha_c = \frac{\Delta\varepsilon_h}{\Delta\varepsilon_{eq}} = \begin{cases} 1 & (\Delta\varepsilon_{eq} \leq 2\varepsilon_y) \\ 1+25\frac{s}{t_c}f(\Delta\varepsilon_{eq}) & (2\varepsilon_y \leq \Delta\varepsilon_{eq} \leq \Delta\varepsilon_{low}) \\ 1+25\frac{s}{t_c}\beta & (\Delta\varepsilon_{low} \leq \Delta\varepsilon_{eq}) \end{cases} \quad (5.2.12)$$

$$\begin{cases} f(\Delta\varepsilon_{eq}) = \begin{cases} 1.90\Delta\varepsilon_{eq}^{-0.62} & (SS400) \\ 1.51\Delta\varepsilon_{eq}^{0.64} & (LY100) \\ 2.82\Delta\varepsilon_{eq}^{-0.35} & (LY225) \end{cases} \\ \beta = \begin{cases} 0.5 & (SS400) \\ 0.5 & (LY100) \\ 1.5 & (LY225) \end{cases} \end{cases} \quad (5.2.13)$$

The proposed Equations. (5.2.12) and (5.2.13) are compared with the restrainers in

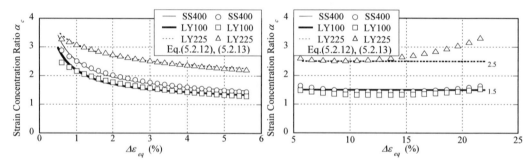

Figure 5.2.8 Strain coefficient ratio

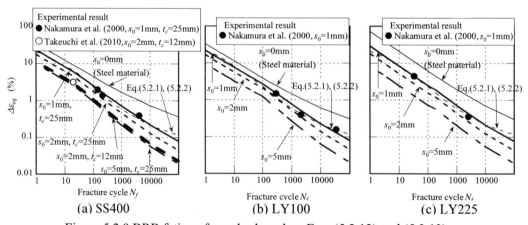

(a) SS400   (b) LY100   (c) LY225

Figure 5.2.9 BRB fatigue formulas based on Eqs. (5.2.12) and (5.2.13)

Figure 5.2.9, which generally consistent with the test results.

The fatigue evaluation of the BRB is originally based on constant stress amplitudes. Conversely, the amplitude of the response of the member subjected to seismic input is random. In such case, the stress range distribution is generally determined by the rainflow method.

As one method to apply the fatigue formula as Equation (5.2.3) to a random amplitude, Miner (1945) [5.11] defined a fatigue condition based on Equation (5.2.14), which is explained in 5.1. Under this condition, when the cumulative damage factor of individual amplitudes reaches 1.0, the element exhibits fatigue failure.

$$D = \sum_{i=1}^{m} D_i = \sum_{i=1}^{m} \frac{n_i}{N_{fi}} \qquad (5.2.14)$$

Here, D is the damage factor, n_i is the number of cycles for the strain range, and N_{fi} is the number of failure cycles for the strain range. Besides Takeuchi et al. (2008) [5.1] proposed a method whereby the average plastic strain range is applied to the fatigue failure condition, and this method was used in the evaluation in the previous section. In the following, the difference between Miner's rule and the average plastic strain range is discussed. The number of fracture cycles for the average plastic strain range

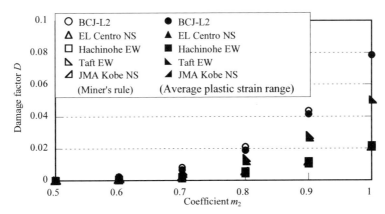

Figure 5.2.11 Difference between evaluation by Miner's rule evaluation using average plastic strain range

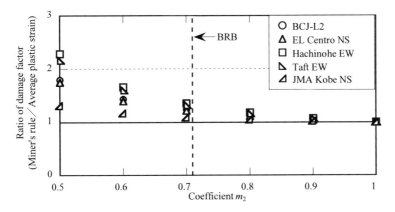

Figure 5.2.12 Ratio of damage factor

is defined as Equation (5.2.15).

$$\overline{N_f} = \left(\frac{\overline{\Delta \varepsilon_p}}{C_2} \right)^{-\frac{1}{m_2}}$$

(5.2.15)

Here, $\overline{\Delta \varepsilon_p}$ is the average plastic strain range, and C_2 and m_2 are the exponential values of the fatigue formula in the range of the plastic region. The cumulative plastic strain is calculated as Eq. (5.2.16).

$$\sum \overline{\Delta \varepsilon_p} = 2 \cdot \overline{N_f} \cdot \overline{\Delta \varepsilon_p} = \frac{2 \cdot \overline{\Delta \varepsilon_p}^{\frac{m_2-1}{m_2}}}{C_2^{-m_2}}$$

(5.2.16)

Conversely, the cumulative plastic strain calculated by Miner's rule is as Equation (5.2.17)

$$\begin{cases} \sum \overline{\Delta \varepsilon_p} = 2 \sum_{i=1}^{m} n_i \Delta \varepsilon_p \\ \sum_{i=1}^{m} \frac{n_i}{N_{fi}} = 1 \end{cases}$$

(5.2.17)

When the exponential value $m_2 = 1.0$, Equation (5.2.16) is identical to Equation (5.2.17), and both evaluations are perfectly consistent. Thus, the difference between these evaluations relies on the exponential value m_2.

To investigate the influence of the exponential value m_2, seismic response analysis results obtained by Takeuchi et al. (2006) [5.23] are used. The analysis model was a 15-story rigid BRB frame. For the seismic wave input, BCJ-L2, El Centro NS, Hachinohe EW, Taft EW, and JMA Kobe NS were applied. The maximum velocities of these seismic wave inputs were normalized to 75 cm/s. The ratio of the stiffness of the frame to that of the BRB was 1.0. The material of the core plate of the BRB was LY225.Figure 5.2.11 shows the damage factor calculated using Miner's rule and the average plastic strain range; Figure 5.2.12 shows their ratio. These figures show that the damage factor increases as the exponential value m_2 decreases from 1.0. From Equation (5.2.1), the exponential value m_2 is 0.71, and the damage factor calculated using Miner's rule is approximately 1.2 times that calculated using the average plastic strain range. Takeuchi et al. (2008) [5.1] reported that the damage factor calculated using the average plastic strain range gives enough accuracy better than that calculated using Miner's rule, and easier to evaluate because it does not require the individual amplitudes. As results of these studies, the authors used the average plastic strain range as the index for evaluating cumulative deformation capacities of BRBs under random amplitudes strain, instead of Miner's method.

5.3 EFFECT OF THE PLASTIC CORE LENGTH

Uneven waveform and plastic strain distribution along the very long brace are also considered to decrease the low-cycle fatigue performance. Although there are very few cyclic loading tests have been carried out on large scale BRBs, the tests carried out for 4.2m long BRB (L_p=2.5m) and 7.5m BRB (L_p=6.2m) by Nishimoto et al. [5.24] as shown in Figure 5.3.1. It is reported that the longer BRB has less cumulative strain than ordinary size BRBs even their cumulative strain exceed 80% or more.

Therefore, the engineers are required to take this effect into consideration when using the large scale BRBs.

Figure 5.3.1 Large scale BRB test

Referemces

[5.1] Takeuchi T, Ida M, Yamada S, Suzuki K: Estimation of Cumulative Deformation Capacity of Buckling Restrained Braces. *ASCE Journal of Structural Engineering*, 2008; **134**(5):822-831.

[5.2] Nakamura H, Takeuchi T, Maeda Y, Nakata Y, Sasaki T, Iwata M, Wada A: Fatigue Propertoes of Practical-Scale Unbonded Braces. *Nippon steel Technical Report*, 2000; (82):51-57.

[5.3] Hasegawa H, Takeuchi T, Iwata M, Yamada S, Akiyama H: Dynamic Performances of Unbonded Braces. *AIJ Technical Report*, 1999; (9):103-106. (*in Japanese*)

[5.4] Yamaguchi M, Yamada S, Matsumoto Y, Tanigawa K, Ono M, Takeuchi T, Ogawa N, Akiyama H: Shaking Table Test of Damage Controlled Frame with Buckling Restrained Braces. *AIJ J. Struct. Constr. Eng.,* 2002; (558), 189-196. (*in Japanese*)

[5.5] Yamaguchi M, Yamada Y, Takeuchi T, Wada A: Seismic Performance of Buckling Resistant Brace within a Steel Frame in the Case of Ultimate Earthquake. *J. Constr. Steel,* 2004; **12**, 207-210 (*in Japanese*).

[5.6] Ookouchi Y, Takeuchi T, Uchiyama T, Suzuki K, Sugiyama T, Ogawa T, Kato S: Experimental Studies of Tower Structures with Hysteretic Dampers. *IASS J. of Int. Assoc. for Shell and Spatial Structures*, 2006; **47**(3).

[5.7] Manson SS. Behavior of Materials under Conditions of Thermal Stress. *NACA-TR-1170*, 1954.

[5.8] Tavernelli JF, Coffin LF, Jr: Experimental Support for Generalized Equation Predicting Low Cycle Fatigue. *ASME J. of Basic Engineering,* 1962; **84**(4):533-537.

[5.9] Maeda Y, Nakata Y, Iwata M, Wada A: Fatigue Properties of Axial-Yield Type Hysteresis Dampers. *AIJ J. of Struct. Constr. Eng.*, 1998; (503):109-115. (*in Japanese*)

[5.10] Nakagomi T, Iwamoto T, Kamura H, Shimokawa H, Harayama K: Experimental Study on Fatigue Characteristic of Flat-Bar Brace with Low

110   Chapter 5. Cumulative Deformation Capacity

Yield Stress Steel Stiffened by Square Steel Tube. *AIJ J. Struct. Constr. Eng.*, 2000; (530):155-161. (*in Japanese*)

[5.11]   Saeki, E, Sugisawa M, Yamaguchi T, Mochizuki H, Wada A: A Study on Low Cycle Fatigue Characteristics of Low Yield Strength Steel. *AIJ J. Struct. Constr. Eng.*, 1995; (472):139-147. (*in Japanese*)

[5.12]   Miner, MA: Cumulative Damage in Fatigue. *ASME J. of Applied Mech.*, 1945; **12**, A159-164.

[5.13]   Nakagomi T, Lee K. Experimental Study on Fatigue Characteristic of SM490 by Repeated Load. *AIJ J. Struct. Constr. Eng.*, 1995; (469):127-136. (*in Japanese*)

[5.14]   Kato B, Akiyama H, and Yamanouchi Y: Predictable Properties of Material under Incremental Cyclic Loading. *IABSE Report of the Working Commission*, 1973; **13**.

[5.15]   Kato B. Akiyama H: Theoretical Prediction of the Load-Deflexion Relationship of Steel Members and Frames. *IABSE Report of the Working Commissions*, 1973; **13**.

[5.16]   Akiyama H: Earthquake-Resistant Design Method for Buildings Based on Energy Balance. *Gihodo Press.*, Tokyo, 1999. (*in Japanese*)

[5.17]   Akiyama H: Earthquake Resistant Limit-State Design for Building. *Univ. Tokyo Press*, Tokyo, 1985.

[5.18]   Takeuchi T, Shirabe H, Yamada S, Kishiki S, Suzuki K, Saeki E, Wada A: Cumulative Deformation Capacity and Damage Evaluation for Elasto-plastic Dampers at Beam Ends. *AIJ J. Struct. Constr. Eng.*, 2006; **(600)**: 115-122. (*in Japanese*)

[5.19]   Takeuchi T, Matsui R: Cumulative Cyclic Deformation Capacity of Circular Tubular Braces under Local Buckling. *ASCE Journal of Structural Engineering*, 2008; **137**(11):1311-1318.

[5.20]   Matsui R, Takeuchi T: Cumulative Deformation Capacity of Buckling Restrained Braces Taking Local Buckling of Core Plates into Account. *Proc. 15th World Conference on Earthquake Engineering (Lisbon)*, 2012.

[5.21]   Menegotto M, Pinto PE: Method of Analysis for Cyclically Loaded R.C. Plane Frames Including Changes in Geometry and Non-Elastic Behaviour of Elements under Combined Normal Force and Bending. *IABSE Report of the Working Commissions*, 1973; **13**.

[5.22]   Takeuchi T, Ohyama T, Ishihara T: Cumulative Cyclic Deformation Capacity of High Strength Steel Frames with Energy Dissipation Braces (Part 1). *AIJ J. Struct. Constr. Eng.*, 2010; **75**(655):1671-1679. (*in Japanese*)

[5.23]   Takeuchi T, Miyazaki K: Estimation of Cumulative Deformation Capacity for Buckling Restrained Braces Placed in Frames. *AIJ J. Struct. Constr. Eng.*, 2006; (603):155-162. (*in Japanese*)

[5.24]   Nishimoto K, Nakata Y, Kimura I, Aiken I, Yamada S, Wada A: Sub-assembly testing of large Buckling-restrained Unbonded Braces, *13WCEE*, No. 1133.

Chapter 6

PERFORMACE TEST SPECIFICATION FOR BRB

CHAPTER CONTENTS

6.1 TEST CONFIGURATIONS

6.2 TEST REGIME AND LOADING PROTOCOL

6.3 QUALIFICATION REQUIREMENTS

6.4 POST EARTHQUAKE INSPECTION

6.1 TEST CONFIGURATIONS

Although the axial yielding mechanism of BRBs is conceptually simple, the performance depends on the precise detailing of the debonding mechanism and restrainer, and is sensitive to fabrication quality. To ensure that a BRB will perform as intended, most jurisdictions require physical testing either as part of supplier prequalification or on a project-specific basis. It is important that the test specimens be fabricated by the appointed manufacturer, and be of similar proportions and use the same details as those used in design. A variety of test configurations are suitable for this purpose, with common setups adopted in previous research and qualification testing categorized as follows.

1) Uniaxial test

The uniaxial test is the simplest and can be conducted using a standard compression/tension test machine as shown in Figure 6.1.1. In the most basic form only general characteristics of the buckling-restraining system are determined, although the test setup can be modified to impose the rotational demands that exist in real frames. This is achieved by including an initial eccentricity or constant imposed rotation, with some examples depicted in Figure 6.1.2.

Two types of rotations should be considered: in-plane rotation affecting the cumulative inelastic deformation capacity, and out-of-plane drift to assess BRB stability, as discussed in Chapter 4. Recall that the critical inelastic mode shape may be anti-symmetric and this is not necessarily observable unless out-of-plane drift is included to enforce the critical imperfection pattern. Care must be taken in selecting representative connection details, with stiff, short gussets conservative for in-plane rotations, but long, flexible gussets conservative for stability tests.

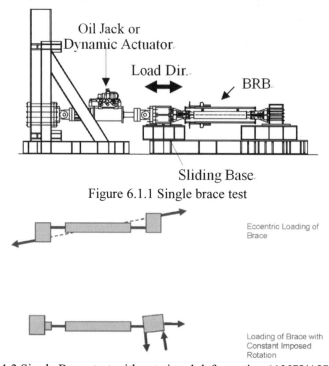

Figure 6.1.1 Single brace test

Figure 6.1.2 Single Brace test with rotational deformation (ANSI/AISC 341-05)

2) Inclined test

An alternative test configuration is to install the BRB diagonally with an oil jack or actuator attached horizontally to a sliding table or pinned column, as shown in Figure 6.1.3. This configuration imposes cyclic rotational deformations equal to story drift, which is conservative relative to the actual frame action.

Additionally, a combination of cyclic in-plane rotation with initial out-of-plane drift can be introduced for stability tests by offsetting one end, as shown in Figure 6.1.4.

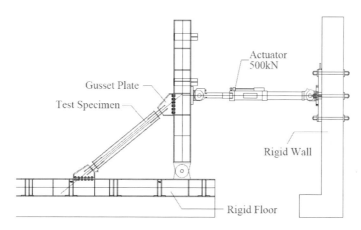

Figure 6.1.3 Inclined layout with column

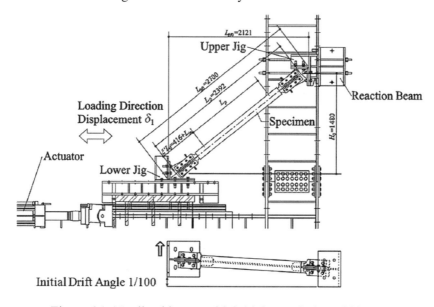

Figure 6.1.4 Inclined layout with initial out-of-plane drift [6.3]

3) In-frame test

The most realistic test configuration is the in-frame test, consisting of BRBs installed in the column-beam frame and realistic story drift imposed, as shown in Figure 6.1.5. This test provides the best insight into the actual system behavior, but is more expensive than a uniaxial or inclined test, and is not particularly suitable for parametric tests. Important limitations in BRBF system performance have previously been identified in full frame tests, and so these play an important role in validation.

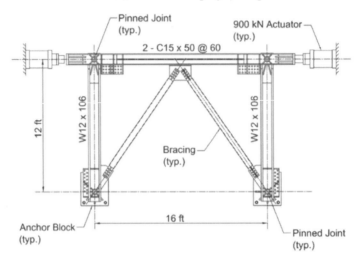

Figure 6.1.5 Frame test with BRBs [6.1]

6.2 TEST REGIME AND LOADING PROTOCOL

In jurisdictions where BRBs are well established, a specific testing protocol may be required by the local authorities. Numerous parameters can affect performance besides the yield force, including core plate thickness, fabrication tolerances, debonding gap variations, the proportions and shape of the restrainer and core, steel material and mortar strength, not to mention the connection geometry, restrainer end details and overall dimensions. Therefore, testing is typically required on a supplier-by-supplier basis for each type of BRB, with the following aims:

1) Demonstrate stability under design deformations

2) Determine brace overstrength and fatigue properties

3) Validate workmanship and quality control of fabricator

The testing regimes used in Japan and the US are representative of the two main qualification systems, with testing conducted as part of supplier prequalification and on a project basis, respectively.

The US code AISC 341-16[6.1] specifies a minimum loading protocol developed to ensure satisfactory performance for a near fault west coast US event. While specified as a project-by-project requirement, in practice most suppliers have an extensive catalogue of previous test results that can be used to justify most typical designs. Similitude to previous tests is demonstrated by brace yield strength ($0.3 \sim 1.2 N_y$), core proportioning and orientation, debonding mechanism and connection details. Two tests are required, with at least one required to be a subassembly test meant to

Chapter 6. Performance Test Specification for BRB   115

demonstrate in-frame performance. This may be satisfied by using either a uniaxial test with imposed rotations (Figure 6.1.2), inclined (Figure 6.1.3-6.1.4) or in-frame test configuration (Figure 6.1.5). A gradually increasing loading protocol indexed against the design drift is specified, and a cumulative ductility of $\eta \geq 200$ (defined as cumulative plastic deformation / yield deformation) must be achieved without instability or non-ductile failure mechanisms (Table 6.2.1 (a)). The code does not require the BRB to remain stable until core fracture, nor does it require constant amplitude fatigue testing.

In Japan, BRBs are used as hysteretic dampers, with devices prequalified and subjected to approval by the Building Center of Japan (BCJ) [6.2]. While prequalification testing requirements are demanding, these have only recently been codified. Test specimens are to be provided from the same manufacturer using the same fabrication procedure as will be used for actual projects and may be no less than 1/2 of the actual size. The testing protocol consists of a series of tests to confirm the basic response characteristics, stability and cumulative energy dissipation capacity, including:

1) Gradually increasing cyclic loading test:
    The standard test used for BRB prequalification is a cyclic regime with progressively increasing amplitudes, as shown in Table 6.2.1 (b). In Japan, the most popular protocol consists of core strains (axial deformation divided by yielding length) of $\varepsilon = 0.5\%$, 1.0%, 2.0%, and 3.0%, with 2 or 3 cycles at each amplitude to confirm that no cyclic degradation occurs. This is then followed by fatigue testing at 2.0% or 3.0% strain until fracture.
    The basis of this protocol comes from typical Japanese design practice and suppliers have previously been qualified for strains in the range of 1.5~2.5% under a Level 2 (1/500yr) event. The cumulative plastic strain from this protocol roughly corresponds to the expected maximum demand from a single event, although recent focus on extremely long duration or multiple events has demonstrated that this may be insufficient.

2) Gradually increasing cyclic loading test with initial out-of-plane drift:
    At least one of the gradually increasing cyclic loading tests should include initial out-of-plane drift to confirm the out-of-plane stability, as discussed in Chapter 4. An initial out-of-plane story drift of 1.0% rad is recommended, corresponding to the typical criteria for design level earthquakes. In Japan, BRB gussets are typically provisioned with full-depth edge or center stiffeners and fixed end transverse beams provided, making it easy to conservatively capture these boundary conditions in the test rig.

3) Constant amplitude cyclic loading test:
    At least 3 constant amplitude tests should be conducted to failure, with the amplitudes set as the maximum qualification strain, a lower value (determined by the practicalities of testing time), and a medium amplitude. These are required to obtain the low cycle fatigue curve and hence cumulative energy dissipation capacity.

In none of these tests should any form of unintended instability or non-ductile failure be observed, ensuring that the device is properly capacity-designed and will perform reliably in actual conditions. This can be observed by monitoring the axial hysteresis, checking that no in-cyclic or cycle-to-cycle degradation occurs at a given strain amplitude. Additionally, for the stability test it is preferable to monitor the out-of-plane displacements at the end the neck just outside of the restrainer end to detect incipient instabilities and confirm that a sufficient margin of safety is provided. The target failure mechanism should be core fatigue-induced fracture, but recognizing that the low cycle fatigue capacity will be lower than an equivalent coupon test due to higher-mode or local buckling. Prohibited non-ductile mechanisms include, among others, local bulging as defined in Chapter 3, and overall instability as discussed in Chapter 4. Bolt slippage is acceptable, but the maximum compression-to-tension overstrength factor (β) must be kept less than 1.2.

Strain vs drift index

Note that the US loading protocol defines the amplitudes by design story drift, Δ_{bm}, reflecting the emphasis on project based qualification, while the Japanese prequalification system uses the core axial strain ε. In practice, the maximum strains used for testing are similar under both systems. From Equations (2.3.2) and (2.3.4), the relationship between yield drift Δ_y, design drift Δ_{bm} and core strain ε can be described as follows.

$$\varepsilon = \frac{L_0}{L_p} \cdot \frac{\Delta}{\cos\theta \sin\theta} \qquad (6.1)$$

For ε_y=0.05~0.2%, θ = 20~45°, L_p/L_0 = 0.3~0.7 and A_c/A_e = 0.4~0.5, Δ_{by} = 0.13~0.25% and Δ_{bm} =0.5~2.0%. Where, L_p/L_0 is the plastic length ratio and θ the BRB angle from the horizontal. The yield drift specified in ANSI/ASCE 341-05 (Δ_{by}) depends not only on the plastic length ratio L_p/L_0, but also the ratio of the elastic region's cross section area to that of the yielding core, typically with Δ_{by}=0.13~0.25%.

The US and Japanese testing requirements also index the cumulative energy dissipation capacity differently. While cumulative ductility η gives an approximate indication of the cumulative energy dissipation capacity, the cumulative plastic strain is directly related to the low cycle fatigue strength, independent of yield strength.

As in Figure 6.2.1, the cumulative total or plastic strain (%) is more reliable index than yield ratio, which is significantly affected by yield strain for each steel material.

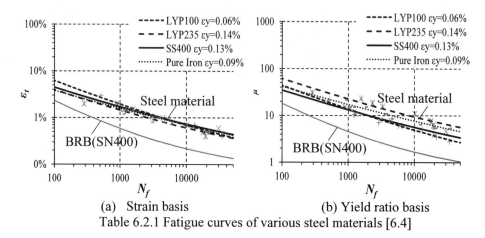

(a) Strain basis   (b) Yield ratio basis

Table 6.2.1 Fatigue curves of various steel materials [6.4]

Target cumulative demand

While a BRB that successfully suppresses instabilities and non-ductile mechanisms through to fracture will significantly exceed both of the above loading protocols, it is worthwhile to reflect on the basis and fitness-for-purpose of the minimum acceptance criteria. If yield drift is assumed to be Δ_{by}=0.2% and the design story drift Δ_{bm}=1.0%, the minimum cumulative plastic strain defined in ANSI/AISC 341-16 is around $\sum \varepsilon_p$ = 47%, but only 24% if Δ_{by}=0.1%. However, the typical Japanese protocol requires a minimum cumulative plastic strain of $\sum \Delta \varepsilon_p$ = 66%.

Both of these cumulative demands are representative of an expected single event. The AISC protocol is based on a study by Sabelli [6.5], which subjected 3 and 6-story buildings to short duration near-fault records compiled for Los Angeles as part of the SAC project, reporting cumulative plastic demands of $140\Delta_{by}$~$200\Delta_{by}$ (≈20%). As mentioned previously, the Japanese protocol is based on a maximum strain used in design of ε = 2.5%.

Several situations may justify a loading protocol with an increased cumulative demand, including where there is an expectation of multiple events occurring over the building's lifetime, and where there is potential for a particularly long duration event. One particularly challenging long duration event is the expected Nankai-trough event in Japan, which can impose exceptional cumulative demands [6.6]. As part of an extensive retrofit program, Matsui et al. [6.7] found that a 21-story building model reached cumulative plastic strain of 80~100% (η≈800~1000), significantly exceeding the current requirement.

Table 6.2.1 Example BRB testing protocol

(a) ANSI/AISC 341-16 and US practice

Cycle (Story drift angle)	Plastic deformation ($\Delta_{bm} = 4\Delta_{by}$)	Cumulative strain ($\Delta_{by} = 0.20\%$)	Cumulative plastic strain
$\Delta_{bm} \times 2$	$= 2 \times 4 \times (\Delta_{by} - \Delta_{by}) = 0\Delta_{by}$	$= 2 \times 4 \times 0.2 = 1.6\%$	$= 2 \times 4 \times 0 = 0\%$
$0.5\Delta_{bm} \times 2$	$= 2 \times 4 \times (2\Delta_{by} - \Delta_{by}) = 8\Delta_{by}$	$= 2 \times 4 \times 0.4 = 3.2\%$	$= 2 \times 4 \times 0.2 = 1.6\%$
$1.0\Delta_{bm} \times 2$	$= 2 \times 4 \times (4\Delta_{by} - \Delta_{by}) = 24\Delta_{by}$	$= 2 \times 4 \times 0.8 = 6.4\%$	$= 2 \times 4 \times 0.6 = 4.8\%$
$1.5\Delta_{bm} \times 2$	$= 2 \times 4 \times (6\Delta_{by} - \Delta_{by}) = 40\Delta_{by}$	$= 2 \times 4 \times 1.2 = 9.6\%$	$= 2 \times 4 \times 1.0 = 8.0\%$
$2.0\Delta_{bm} \times 2$	$= 2 \times 4 \times (8\Delta_{by} - \Delta_{by}) = 56\Delta_{by}$	$= 2 \times 4 \times 1.6 = 12.8\%$	$= 2 \times 4 \times 1.6 = 11.2\%$
$1.5\Delta_{bm} \times 4$	$= 4 \times 4 \times (6\Delta_{by} - \Delta_{by}) = 80\Delta_{by}$	$= 4 \times 4 \times 1.2 = 19.2\%$	$= 4 \times 4 \times 1.2 = 16.0\%$
($1.5\Delta_{bm}$ until fracture)			
Total	$= 208\Delta_{by}$	=52.8%	=47%

(b) BCJ and Japanese practice

Cycle (Plastic length strain)	Plastic deformation ($\Delta_{by} = 0.25\%$)	Cumulative strain ($\Delta_{by} = 0.25\%$)	Cumulative plastic strain
$\Delta_{by} \times 3$	$= 3 \times 4 \times (\Delta_{by} - \Delta_{by}) = 0\Delta_{by}$	$= 3 \times 4 \times 0.25 = 3\%$	$= 3 \times 4 \times 0 = 0\%$
$0.5\% \times 3$	$= 3 \times 4 \times (2\Delta_{by} - \Delta_{by}) = 8\Delta_{by}$	$= 3 \times 4 \times 0.5 = 6\%$	$= 3 \times 4 \times 0.25 = 3\%$
$1.0\% \times 3$	$= 3 \times 4 \times (4\Delta_{by} - \Delta_{by}) = 36\Delta_{by}$	$= 3 \times 4 \times 1.0 = 12\%$	$= 3 \times 4 \times 0.75 = 9\%$
$2.0\% \times 3$	$= 3 \times 4 \times (8\Delta_{by} - \Delta_{by}) = 84\Delta_{by}$	$= 3 \times 4 \times 2.0 = 24\%$	$= 3 \times 4 \times 1.75 = 21\%$
$3.0\% \times 3$	$= 3 \times 4 \times (12\Delta_{by} - \Delta_{by}) = 132\Delta_{by}$	$= 3 \times 4 \times 3.0 = 36\%$	$= 2 \times 4 \times 2.75 = 33\%$
(3.0% until fracture)			
Total	$= 264\Delta_{by}$	=81%	=66%

Additionally, clients (or building tenants), may expect BRBs to have sufficient capacity to not require replacement following a major event. Direct inspection is often challenging, if not impossible, as the yielding core is typically permanently encased, and cumulative deformation monitors are only occasionally installed. In anticipation of such a situation, it may be prudent to conduct constant amplitude fatigue testing to construct the low cycle fatigue curves, if not already required as part of the prequalification test regime.

6.3 QUALIFICATION REQUIREMENTS

In summary, the recommended prequalification test regime consists of the following:

1) Gradually increasing cyclic loading tests with and without out-of-plane drift. The hysteretic loop must be stable without cyclic degradation, with the exception of pin or bolt slippage. The ratio of maximum compressive-to-tensile strength (β) should be smaller than 1.2.

2) In all tests, the connections are to remain stable, no restrainer bulging is to be observed, and the BRB is to retain load bearing capacity until the fatigue-induced fracture.

3) Stable fatigue curves should be obtained from constant amplitude cyclic loading tests at a minimum of three different plastic axial strain amplitudes for each type of BRB. This curve is used to construct the fatigue curve and confirm the remaining cumulative cyclic deformation capacity throughout the life of the structure.

6.4 POST EARTHQUAKE INSPECTION

Though BRBs are increasingly popular and have been tested extensively in lab settings, few have been subjected to significant plastic excursions in an actual earthquake. It is possible that future events will provide learning opportunities and potentially expose weaknesses with current practice. However, the expectation is that well-designed BRBs will show few signs of damage and should be able to be withstand multiple design level events due to the anticipated reserve capacity.

The level of inspection and analysis required will depend on the intensity of the earthquake. A visual inspection should generally be conducted after any event where yielding would be expected to confirm that no premature failure mechanisms have developed. Following a major earthquake it may be necessary to calculate the residual capacity to justify leaving the BRBs in place.

A two part inspection procedure is suggested:

Stage 1 (Visual): inspect for signs of any premature failure mechanisms

Stage 2 (Desktop study): analyze the residual fatigue capacity (major earthquake only)

Before discussing these procedures in detail, it is useful to review the performance of BRBs during the 2011 Tohoku Earthquake.

6.4.1 BRBs in the 2011 Tohoku Earthquake

To the author's knowledge, the 2011 Tohoku Earthquake was the first to subject BRBs to significant inelastic demands. Though relatively few records are publically available, the known response of several structures provides valuable learning points.

A detailed survey of 38 passively controlled structures fitted with accelerometers was conducted by JSSI, focusing on midrise and tall buildings in Tokyo. BRBs were used in four of these buildings, ranging in height from 5 to 40 stories. In each case the demand was less than the BRB yield strength.

Significant yielding was recorded at Koriyama Big-Eye (Section 7.2.5), a 24-story, 133m building complete in 2001 in Fukushima Prefecture (234km from epicenter) and shown in Figure 6.4.1. The structure consists of a moment frame designed to remain elastic under a Level 2 event, LY235 BRBs with short plastic lengths (L_p/L=0.25~0.3) are installed over the lower third, viscoelastic dampers in the middle third and normal braces in the top. Cumulative (1 no.) and peak deformation (5 no.) recording devices were installed (Figure 6.4.2), although it was later found that some of the peak deformation devices were not functioning correctly. A nearby K-Net station (FKS018) recorded 1.1g PGA, but a spectral acceleration of just 0.08g (T=3s, h=5%). The cumulative deformation measurements and earthquake record were used to calibrate a finite element model, determine the strain time history and estimate the residual cumulative damage index.

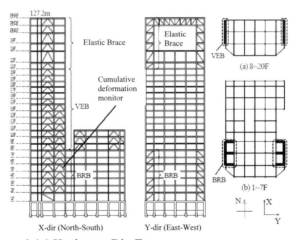

Figure 6.4.1 Koriyama Big Eye

Though the initial visual inspection suggested only a possibility of nominal yielding, a desktop study benchmarked against the deformation readings indicated a peak ductility demand of $\mu \approx 3.8$ and a cumulative plastic strain of $\Sigma\varepsilon_p \approx 22\%$ ($\Sigma\varepsilon_p/\varepsilon_y \approx 200$) in the Y direction [6.8]. During prequalification testing the supplier had conducted constant amplitude tests to derive the fatigue curve. This was used to confirm that the actual damage index from this event was less than 6% of the cumulative capacity, leaving plenty of residual capacity for expected future strong ground motions and justifying the decision to leave all BRBs in place.

Figure 6.4.2 Deformation monitoring devices

This experience indicates several key learning points for post-earthquake inspection:

1. Visual inspection is an unreliable indicator of peak or cumulative ductility demand
2. Displacement monitoring devices are invaluable and the only reliable means to confirm the ductility demand and reserve capacity absent of direct access to the core. It is important to ensure that the monitoring devices are accessible, the building maintenance staff are familiar with the function and operation of the devices, and that periodic inspection and records are maintained, including after all large earthquakes.
3. Site acceleration records and BRB-specific fatigue curves are can be used to provide quantitative justification of the residual capacity.
4. Well-designed BRBs can withstand multiple severe earthquakes, and replacement is not necessarily required, even following significant yielding.

6.4.2 Visual inspection

Currently, no BRB-specific guidance exists for post-earthquake inspection. While visual inspection may give a rough indication of significant deformation and yielding, it is not a reliable indicator of demand or residual capacity. However, it is primarily useful to confirm that the no premature failure mechanisms are present. It

Unlike most other ductile systems, the yielding component is typically not directly visible, and the engineer must observe the behavior indirectly. Some signs of movement or minor damage do not affect performance and can be ignored, while others might be of concern.

The following are some of the checks that should be conducted.

1) Whether the BRB has yielded

Large deformations are typically associated with residual deformation, dislodged debonding material and mortar discharge. This is expected and acceptable. Eventually once the cumulative deformation capacity is consumed the BRB will fracture, but this is not expected in any single event.

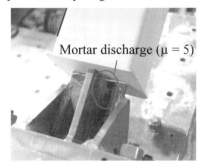

Figure 6.4.3 Expected signs of yielding

2) Signs of bulging

Bulging (Chapter 3) is typically only a concern for rectangular cores encased in rectangular restrainers, which can be identified from the design drawings. It may be necessary to inspect the restrainer from the side or use a flat edge. This is not expected in well-designed BRBs and if observed, would likely require the brace to be replaced.

Axial view   Side view

Figure 6.4.6 Restrainer bulging (not expected)

3) Signs of out-of-plane buckling

Out-of-plane buckling (Chapter 4) is a progressive failure initiated by plastic hinges forming at the gusset, neck and/or restrainer, and is sometimes associated with damage of the adjacent beam. If yielding or lateral displacements are observed either retrofit or replacement will likely be required.

Restrainer end deformation   Gusset yielding
Figure 6.4.7 Out-of-plane buckling (not expected)

6.4.3 Desktop study

Following particularly severe earthquakes, a desktop study may be required to confirm the residual capacity and determine if the BRBs should be replaced. The procedures discussed in Chapter 5 may be employed to estimate the cumulative fatigue damage, using supplier-specific fatigue curves (Section 6.2). Note that this requires an appropriate ground motion record, fatigue curve, structural analysis model, and if available, deformation measurements.

References

[6.1]   ANSI/AISC 341-16, *Seismic Provisions for Structural Steel Buildings*, 2016

[6.2]   Building Center of Japan: *Specifications for BRB certification*, 2016 (*in Japanese*)

[6.3]   Takeuchi T, Ozaki H, Matsui R, Sutcu F: Out-of-plane Stability of Buckling-Restrained Braces including Moment Transfer Capacity. *Earthquake Engineering & Structural Dynamics*, 2014; **43**(6):851–869, DOI:10.1002/eqe.2376.

[6.4]   Saeki E, Sugisawa M, Yamaguchi T, Mochizuki H, Wada A: A Study on Low Cycle Fatigue Characteristics of Low Yield Strength Steel, *AIJ J. of Struct. Constr. Eng.*, 1995; (472):139-147 (*in Japanese*)

[6.5]   Sabelli R: Research on Improving the Design and Analysis of Earthquake-resistant Steel-Braced Frames, *The 2000 NEHRP Professional Fellowship Report*.

[6.6]   Ministry of Land Infrastructure and Transportation: *Tentative plan for measures against long-period ground motion in high-rise buildings*, 2017.

[6.7]   Matsui R, Inaba Y, Takeuchi T: A Screening Method to Examine Beam-End Damage of Steel Braced Frame Including Brace Fracture, *Proceedings of 16WCEE, Santiago*, 2017.

[6.8]   Inaba Y, Morimoto S, Tsuruta S, Takeuchi T, Matsui R. Damage record of buckling restrained braces that received actual ground motion. *AIJ Kanto Branch Research Report Collection* 2017, (*in Japanese*)

Chapter 7

BRBF APPLICATIONS

CHAPTER CONTENTS

7.1 DAMAGE TOLERANT CONCEPT

7.2 RESPONSE EVALUATION OF BRBF

7.3 SEISMIC RETROFIT WITH BRBS

7.4 RESPONSE EVALUATION OF BRBS FOR RETROFIT OF RC FRAMES

7.5 DIRECT CONNECTIONS TO RC FRAMES

7.6 APPLICATIONS TO TRUSS AND SPATIAL STRUCTURES

7.7 SPINE FRAME CONCEPTS

7.1 DAMAGE TOLERANT CONCEPT

7.1.1 Damage Tolerant Concepts

Buildings have significantly increased in scale and value over the past century, particularly with the introduction of important building contents such as electronic equipment and information crucial for business continuity. There are ongoing arguments on the extent of plastic deformation in a structure that will potentially damage these contents and interrupt business or continuous occupancy in large earthquakes. Particularly in urban environments, the broader costs to society of long downtimes for repair or rebuild associated with traditional ductile design can be devastating. Construction activities impose severe demands on the environment by requiring the production of construction materials. This could be mitigated by extending the building life span. All of these problems could be addressed in part by designing large buildings that are usable after severe earthquakes.

In 1992 Wada et. al [7.1.1] proposed the concept of "Damage Tolerance Structures" where energy dissipation is concentrated in special members designated as "Damage Fuses" and the main structure is kept safe to carry gravity loads. After particularly severe earthquakes the energy dissipating devices (called as "dampers" hereafter) designed as the damage fuses may be replaced as needed, but ideally are designed to withstand multiple events expected throughout the building life. This concept is theoretically based on Prof. Connor's "Performance based design" methodology [7.1.2] which suggests that a more rational design could be achieved if each structural component individually corresponds to each design requirement. In Figure 7.1.1, the elastic moment frame is provided to carry gravity loads, suppress demands from concentrating in a single story and limit residual drifts, while input earthquake energy is dissipated by special seismic members. This concept is called a "Damage Tolerant Structure", because damage is concentrated in specially designated, easily repairable seismic element protecting the main structure and not impairing the function of the building. Similar design philosophies have been proposed elsewhere afterwards, including "Structural Fuse Concept" in the US [7.1.3] and "Low Damage Design" in New Zealand [7.1.4].

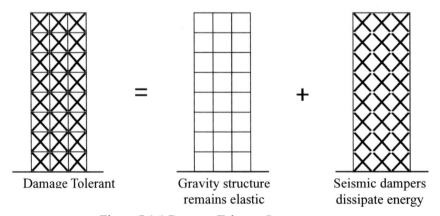

Figure 7.1.1 Damage Tolerant Structure concept

In Japan, construction of buildings over 60m tall requires special permission from the Governmental body in charge of construction. The basic design criteria (Table 7.1.1) was initially established by Prof K. Muto during construction of the 36-story Kasumigaseki building, the first in Japan taller than 100m. Elastic design was required under a Level 1 (serviceability) event, while no more than 1% drift and story ductility of 2.0 was permitted for a Level 2 event (design level). This was intended to control PΔ effects, and ensure comfortable living while limiting damage to secondary members such as external walls, windows, partitions and mechanical equipment. Prof Akiyama's suggestion of designing according to the "total earthquake input energy" further influenced Japanese seismic design philosophy. The special design procedures required for tall buildings, energy based design philosophy and consequence of tall building damage in mega-cities such as Tokyo has traditionally led to widespread use of high performance damping systems, satisfying demanding performance targets.

With the development of high strength and ductile steel materials engineers are now able to use BRBs as hysteretic dampers to economically achieve immediate occupancy performance level. Since the initial proposal for the Damage Tolerant Structure in 1992, steels with yield strengths of up to 800MPa (e.g. SM490, HT590, HT780) have become common in the elastic main frame, while other high strength wires and structural steels of up to 1000MPa have introduced new possibilities for novel structural topologies. With highly ductile low yield steels such as LY100 and LY225 is possible to admit plastic deformation of specially designated fuse members for Level 1 events. So it can be said that "New materials drives new type of structures ".

Table 7.1.1 Earthquake ground motion and seismic design in Japan

	Level 1	Level 2
	Likely earthquake ground motion during building life span	Possible largest earthquake ground motion
Static Design	Static lateral force for elastic design defined on the code. Allowable stress design. Interstory drift angle ≤1/200	No criteria for high-rise steel buildings. For reinforced concrete high-rise buildings, 1.5 times lateral shear capacity to the elastic design force around 1/100 interstory drift angle
Dynamic Design	Maximum Velocity of Ground Motion =25cm/sec Interstory Drift Angle ≤ 1/200 Ductility Factor ≤ 1.0	Maximum Velocity of Ground Motion =50cm/sec Interstory Drift Angle ≤ 1/100 Ductility Factor ≤ 2.0

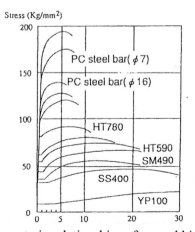

Figure 7.1.2 Stress strain relationships of several kinds of steel

The basic concept is to select a high strength material for the beams and columns, proportioning the main frame to remain elastic at the design drift. Conversely, the energy dissipation members are designed to yield under small drifts and control the response. To ensure that the moment frame remains elastic, we need to consider the column and beam demands, which are determined according to the stiffness distribution indicated by Table 7.1.2. The portion of drift associated with overall bending may be neglected, as this imposes axial column deformation rather than beam end flexure. At lower stories shear deformation is an increasingly large proportion of drift, but the proportion changes not only by vertical position, but also with the building's aspect ratio, frame dimensions, and cross section shapes of the beams and columns.

Interstory drift at midheight of typical tall buildings can conservatively be assumed to be composed of 70-90% shear deformation. Columns contribute less to drift as they are generally shorter than beams and have larger sections to limit potential plasticity to the beam end. Beam deformation can be taken as 60-70% of the total shear deformation, or 42-63% of the overall drift. Assuming that flexure accounts for 70-90% of the beam contribution, bending deformation is 30-60% of the story drift. As the beam yields in a structure with strong columns and weak beams this proportion increases up to about 80%.

Under a Level 1 earthquake event with up to 1/200 story drift, the beam must remain elastic for demands corresponding to a 3/1000 beam bending angle (60% of 1/200 story drift). For a Damage Tolerant Structure, the beam should remain elastic under a Level 2 earthquake, corresponding to a 6/1000 beam rotation (60% of 1/100 story drift). If the beam yields, rotations of up to 8/1000 are expected (80% of 1/100 story drift). Alternatively, if the frame bending contribution were neglected, these rotational demands would increase to 4/1000, 7/1000 and 8/1000 for Level 1 (elastic), Level 2 (elastic) and Level 2 (plastic) earthquakes, respectively.

Table 7.1.2 Five components of frame shear deformation

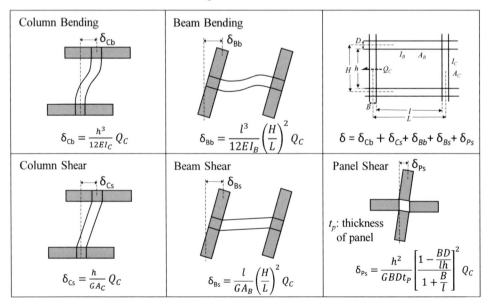

Chapter 7. Applications for BRBF   127

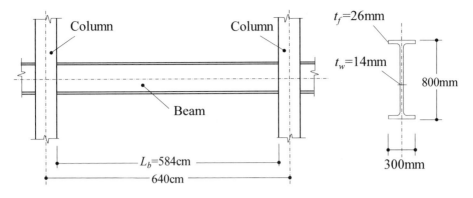

Figure 7.1.3 Typical steel building frame

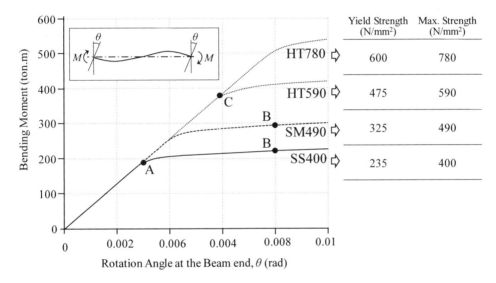

Figure 7.1.4 Relationships of bending moment vs. rotation angle at beam end

For the example as Figure 7.1.3, the required beam flexural demands are achievable with some of the high strength steels listed in Figure 7.1.4. SS400 and SM490 are common in building structures, while HT590 and HT780 are used for special industrial structures. Use of HT780 may be limited due to the low ductility and associated weldability issues. The moment-rotation of a typical beam (H-800 x 300 x 14 x 26, 5.8 m clear span) is shown in Figure 7.1.4, with curvature integrated to determine the end flexural rotation and strain determined from the maximum curvature demand and neutral axis depth. It is apparent that the beam can be designed to remain elastic under a Level 1 earthquake (Point A, 1/200 drift) for all steel grades. If high strength steel is used (HT590 or HT780) an elastic response can be achieved under a Level 2 earthquake (Point C, 1/100 drift), although yielding is expected for the normal steel grades (Points B, 1/100 drift).

The extent of yielding under a Level 2 event is indicated by Figure 7.1.5. Keeping the main structure elastic for the Level 2 earthquake has further advantages: the elastic stiffness provides restoring force; damage concentration is avoided and the whole building can be designed to deform smoothly.

It is entirely possible to achieve a Damage Tolerant Structure using beams with SN490B (f_y = 325MPa). This steel grade was used in both example projects presented at the end of section 7.2 (Koriyama Big-eye and Environmental Energy Innovation Building). Interestingly, the initial design of the later building using a ductile moment frame proved more expensive than the final design using BRBs. The BRBs reduced the seismic demands and enabled smaller beams, which in return increased the main frame's yield drift.

Without energy dissipation of dampers, the elastically responding main frame will likely have an unacceptable response. Energy dissipating members can be installed in the structure either in a series, or parallel configuration, as shown in Figure 7.1.6. Series configurations are suitable if the main frame is stiff and brittle, with deformation efficiently concentrated in the dampers and additional protection provided by the period lengthening effect. However, if the main structure is flexible and has a large elastic range, the parallel configuration is more suitable and is adopted here. In the parallel system, the initial stiffness is a sum of the damper (K_d) and frame (K_f) stiffness, and the dampers should be arranged to directly transmit the structural deformation. BRBs are suitable for use as elasto-plastic dampers within this system, as they are characterized by a large cumulative deformation capacity, large plastic strain range and stable hysteresis.

This Damage Tolerant Structure concept has been widely adopted in Japan, where bidirectional steel moment frames are commonly used with dampers to control drift.

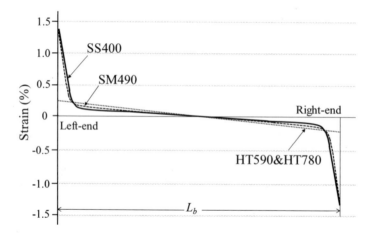

Figure 7.1.5 Strain distribution along the flange of each beam at point B and C in Fig. 7.1.4

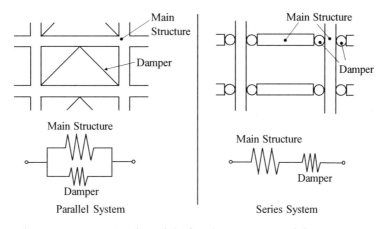

Figure 7.1.6 Structural model of main structure and damper

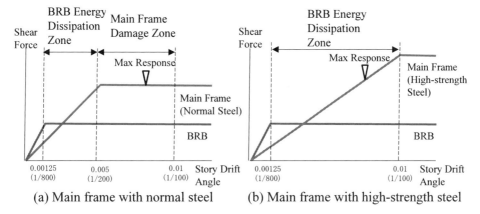

(a) Main frame with normal steel (b) Main frame with high-strength steel

Figure 7.1.7 Shear force-story drift relationship of Damage Tolerant Structure

The efficiency of the system is sensitive to the damper-to-frame stiffness ratio (K_d/K_f), which is typically in the range of $K_d/K_f = 0.5\sim3.0$ for a relatively stiff moment frame. Following an initial frame design, pushover analysis is used to confirm that the frame remains elastic up to design drift (0.5-1.0%). Increasing the main frame steel grade permits a larger elastic drift (Figure 7.1.7). BRBs are then added to meet the drift limit under the design level earthquake, and to patch any soft stories in the main frame. By keeping the main frame elastic and limiting the damper stiffness to $K_d/K_f \leq 3.0$, the structure will effectively return to its original shape with negligible residual drift.

7.1.2 Project Application

An early example of a Damage Tolerant Structure is the Triton Square Project, a 40 story (180 m) office building located in Tokyo. A typical floor plan is shown in Figure 7.1.8 and the frame is shown in Figure 7.1.9, consisting of HT780 columns, HT590 beams and LY100 BRBs on all four sides. While the BRB layout introduces some inefficiencies due to the indirect connection, the low yield strength ensured a sufficient yield drift angle. Results of a nonlinear analysis (Figure 7.1.10-11) confirmed that the BRBs yield at 1/400 drift, while the beams remain elastic until 1/100 drift.

130   Chapter 7. Applications for BRBF

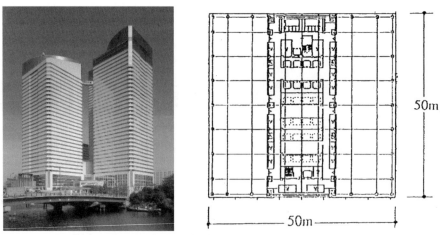

Figure 7.1.8 View and plan of Triton Square Project

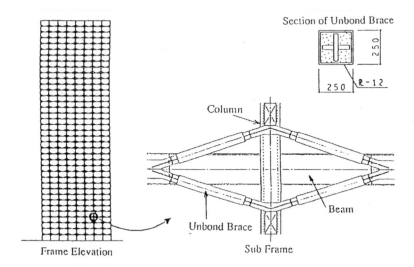

Figure 7.1.9 Frame system proposed for Triton Square Project

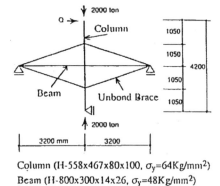

Column (H-558x467x80x100, σ_y=64Kg/mm^2)
Beam (H-800x300x14x26, σ_y=48Kg/mm^2)
Unbond Brace (Pl-35.2x200, σ_y=10Kg/mm^2).

Figure 7.1.10 Analysis model of sub frame

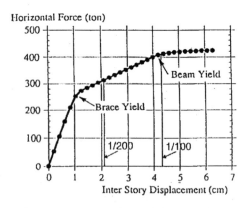

Figure 7.1.11 Horizontal force and inter-story displacement relationship

The numerical results were confirmed with a 1/2.3 scale subassembly test, with 1/100 drift applied cyclically by the testing apparatus shown in Figure 7.1.12(a). Test specimens are shown in Table 7.1.3, including 4 moment frames (Figure 7.1.12(b)) with varying steel grades, and one complete subassembly including the BRBs (Figure 7.1.13). The components of story drift were determined for the moment frame (Table 7.1.4), and the ratio of beam bending deformation was confirmed as 53%.

The horizontal force-displacement relationships are shown in Figure 7.1.14. The frames with HT780/HT590 steel (No.1 and 2) remained elastic through 1/100 drift, while the frames with SM490/SS400 steel (No.3 and 4) yielded at 1/200 drift. For the final specimen, the BRB yielded at 1/1000 drift, while the main frame remained elastic through 1/100 drift, confirming the Damage Tolerant Design.

Table 7.1.3 List of specimens

Number	Frame Type	Steel used for Columns	Steel used for Beams
No.1	Pure Frame	HT780 ($\sigma_y = 72$ kg/mm^2)	HT780 ($\sigma_y = 72$ kg/mm^2)
No.2	Pure Frame	HT780 ($\sigma_y = 72$ kg/mm^2)	HT590 ($\sigma_y = 54$ kg/mm^2)
No.3	Pure Frame	SM490 ($\sigma_y = 36$ kg/mm^2)	SM490 ($\sigma_y = 36$ kg/mm^2)
No.4	Pure Frame	SM490 ($\sigma_y = 36$ kg/mm^2)	SS400 ($\sigma_y = 26$ kg/mm^2)
No.5	With Braces*	HT780 ($\sigma_y = 72$ kg/mm^2)	HT590 ($\sigma_y = 54$ kg/mm^2)

*Unbond Braces using YP10 for core plate ($\sigma_y = 10$ kg/mm^2)

Table 7.1.4 Components of elastic frame story drift

	Bending	Shear
Column	12.7%	5.9%
Beam	53.2%	9.4%
Panel	—	18.8%

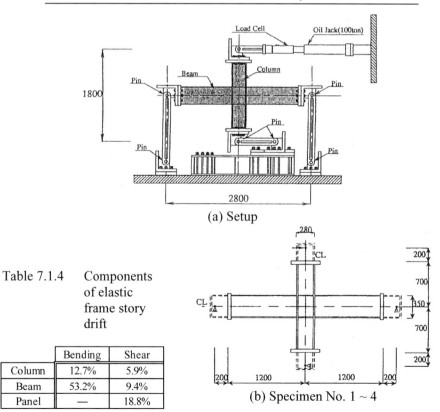

Figure 7.1.12 Test setup and specimen

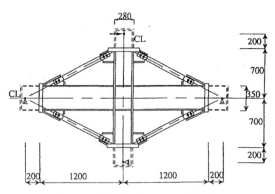

Figure 7.1.13 Specimen No. 5

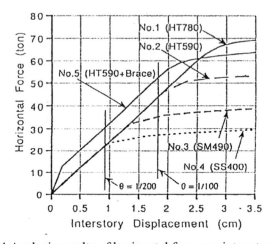

Figure 7.1.14 Analysis results of horizontal force vs. inter story displacement

References

[7.1.1] Wada A, Connor J, Kawai H, Iwata M, Watanabe A: Damage Tolerant Structure, *ATC-15-4, Proc. 5th US-Japan WS on the Imprement of Building Structural Design and Construction Practices,* 1992

[7.1.2] Conner J, Wada A: Performance Based Design methodology for structures, *International workshop fon recent developments in base-isolation techniques for buildings*, Tokyo, 1992.

[7.1.3] Vargas R, Bruneau M: Analytical investigation of the Structural Fuse Concept, *MCEER-06-0004*, 2006.

[7.1.4] MacRae G, Clifton C: Low Damage Design of Steel Structures, Steel Innovations 2013 Workshop, Christchurch, 2013.

7.2 RESPONSE EVALUATION OF BRBF

7.2.1 Equivalent Linearization Method

Together with the concept of Damage Tolerant Design, the idea of passive vibration-control using BRBs is gaining popularity. Frequently, dynamic time history analysis using a set of ground motion records is required to confirm adequate performance. However, initial sizing of the BRBs requires a simple analytical theory to provide insight into the relationship between the seismic input, main frame and damper design, and response parameters. This section introduces a simplified evaluation method for elasto-plastic energy dissipation systems such as BRBs based on the equivalent linearization method and the accuracy is validated by time history analyses [7.2.1].

The general model of a passively controlled building is shown in the left-side of Figure 7.2.1. Various types of energy dissipation devices (dampers) can be incorporated within a moment frame, with their properties listed in Table 7.2.1 and the frame story shear stiffness denoted as K_{fi}. The damper efficiency is sensitive to the connection stiffness between the damper and frame, which is denoted as K_{bi} in Figure 7.2.2. The combined stiffness of the damper K_{di} and connections K_{bi} is then denoted as K_{ai} and the system is converted into an equivalent single degree of freedom (SDOF) model shown on the right side of Figure 7.2.1, where parameters in Table 7.2.1 are set as constant and assuming proportional damping. The overall structural response can be then studied, setting $K_{di} = K_d$, $K_{bi} = K_b$, and $K_{fi} = K_f$, and assuming the main frame remains elastic.

From Figure 7.2.3, the equivalent secant stiffness of a structure, including the response of elasto-plastic dampers such as BRBs is expressed as follows.

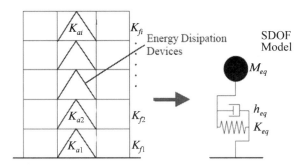
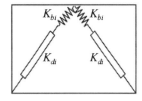

Fig.7.2.2 Influence of connection member stiffness

Figure 7.2.1 Simplification of passively-controlled building

Table 7.2.1 Parameters for energy-dissipation devices building

Type of Energy Dissipation Devises	Main Parameters	Index	Parameter to Control	
Elast-plastic (Hysteresis)	Damper stiffness	K_a	K_{ai}/K_{fi}	K_{bi}/K_{di}
	Yield drift	θ_{dy}	θ_{dyi}	
Visco-elastic	Damper stiffness	K_a	K_{ai}/K_{fi}	K_{bi}/K_{di}
	Loss factor	η_d	η_d	
Viscous	Damping factor	C_d	$C_{di}\omega/K_{fi}$	$K_{bi}/C_{di}\omega$

$$K_{eq} = (K_a + \mu K_f)/\mu = K_f + K_a/\mu, \text{ where } K_a = 1/(1/K_d + 1/K_b) \quad (7.2.1)$$

The increased stiffness relative to the bare frame (K_f) is given by,

$$\frac{K_{eq}}{K_f} = 1 + \frac{K_a}{K_f \mu} = 1 + \frac{K_d}{K_f \mu (1 + K_d/K_b)} \quad (7.2.2)$$

From the area enclosed in the hysteresis curve shown in Figure 7.2.3, the equivalent damping ratio for a single cycle can be expressed as a function of μ and K_a/K_f. The achieved single cycle equivalent damping is illustrated in Figure 7.2.4.

$$h_{eq}' = \frac{E_d}{2\pi K_{eq} \mu^2} = \frac{2(\mu-1)K_a/K_f}{\pi \mu(\mu + K_a/K_f)} \quad (7.2.3)$$

For random excitation, the effective damping ratio is less than Equation (7.2.3), as each cycle has a different ductility demand. From the Newmark-Rosenblueth rule, this can be estimated from the average integrated response across all amplitudes [7.2.2, 7.2.3], where, h_0 is damping ratio of the main structure. Equation (7.2.4) reduces the equivalent damping to approximately 80% of the single cycle damping (Figure 7.2.4).

$$h_{eq} = h_0 + \frac{1}{\mu}\int_1^\mu h_{eq}' d\mu = h_0 + \frac{2(1+K_a/K_f)}{\pi \mu} \ln \frac{\mu + K_a/K_f}{(1+K_a/K_f)\mu^{\frac{1}{1+K_a/K_f}}} \quad (7.2.4)$$

As presented by Kasai et.al [7.2.2], [7.2.4], the effect of passive energy dissipation devices includes the combined effect of period shift and increased damping.

1) Effect of decreasing fundamental period; As dampers are added, the stiffness of the structure increases by K_{eq}/K_f and the fundamental period decreases from T_0 to $T_{eq} = T_0\sqrt{K_f/K_{eq}}$. In the constant-velocity portion of the response spectrum (i.e. $T > 0.6$ sec in design spectrum), this period shift will increase accelerations by T_0/T_{eq} and decrease displacements by T_{eq}/T_0.
2) Effect of additional Damping; The effect of increasing equivalent damping from h_0 to h_{eq} reduces both the acceleration and displacement response. While many equations have been proposed to evaluate the effect of damping on the seismic response, a formula developed by Kasai (Equation (7.2.7)) is used in this study.

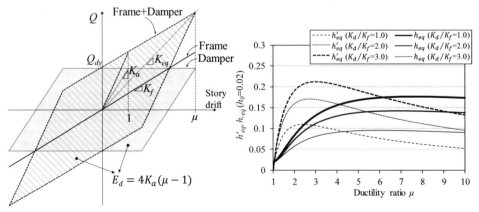

Figure 7.2.3 Elasto-plastic device model   Figure 7.2.4 Effect of μ on equivalent damping

Combining both effects, the reduced response of total force (regarding acceleration a_{eq}/a_f) and displacement (δ_{eq}/δ_f) in the constant velocity region is given by the following equations. Note that these are response modification factors and they are evaluated with respect to the moment frame before adding damper, rather than the combined elastic system.

Acceleration reduction: $\dfrac{a_{eq}}{a_f} = F_h \sqrt{\dfrac{K_{eq}}{K_f}}$ (7.2.5)

Displacement reduction: $\dfrac{\delta_{eq}}{\delta_f} = F_h \sqrt{\dfrac{K_f}{K_{eq}}}$ (7.2.6)

Where, F_h is the response reduction coefficient as a result of the damping and obtained by the following Equation [7.2.4].

$F_h = \sqrt{\dfrac{1+ah_0}{1+ah}}$ (recorded wave: a=25, artificial wave: a=75, Artificial wave with standard deviation: a=40) (7.2.7)

The relationship between a_{eq}/a_f, δ_{eq}/δ_f, K_d/K_f, and μ can be depicted graphically as performance curves, as shown in Figure 7.2.5. Note that this chart is used to preliminarily select "how much BRB to add in the moment frame."

Using these performance curves, the maximum response of a single degree of freedom structure with energy dissipation devices can be evaluated by the following steps.

1) Calculating the first natural period of the structure, T_0 without damper (BRBs).
2) Evaluating the shear force and displacement response of the structure (a_f, δ_f) without damper from the response spectrum of acceleration and displacement, respectively.

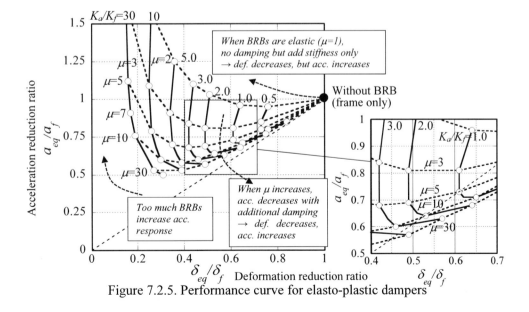

Figure 7.2.5. Performance curve for elasto-plastic dampers

136   Chapter 7. Applications for BRBF

3) Evaluating the reduction effects of damper on shear force and displacement response from Figures 7.2.5. The response with damper (a_{eq}, δ_{eq}) can be calculated using Equations (7.2.2)-(7.2.7).

4) For elasto-plastic dampers including μ or u_0 in reduction functions, iterating the steps 2 and 3 until stable value is obtained. From the graphs of reduction effects, the following characteristics of each damper are also observed. The displacement reduction effect of elasto-plastic dampers mainly relies on the damper-to-frame stiffness K_d/K_f, and the shear force reduction effect mainly relies on the ductility μ. Overly stiff dampers and low ductility μ eliminates the shear force reduction effect, as shown in Figure 7.2.5.

7.2.2 Simple Example Evaluation

The above equivalent linearization approach is explained with an example structure as follows.

1) Response evaluation

A 15 story building as shown in Figure 7.2.6 is used for a sample calculation. The mass and stiffness of each floor as indicated in Table 7.2.2. This model is modified from an actual office building build in the suburbs of Tokyo, adjusted to have the first natural period of 2.0 sec without BRBs.

The initial design is based on the equivalent static force distribution. For structures less than 60m in Japan the equivalent lateral load distribution is given by A_i shear

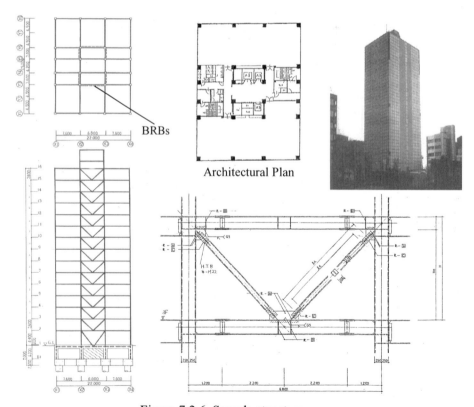

Figure 7.2.6. Sample structure

Table 7.2.2

(a) Mass and stiffness without damper

Story	M(t)	K_f(kN/mm)
15	581	250
14	430	273
13	430	302
12	430	311
11	430	328
10	430	342
9	434	352
8	438	372
7	438	408
6	438	410
5	438	442
4	438	454
3	438	487
2	480	546
1	480	581

(b) Natural periods without damper

Frequency	Own Period
$f_1 = 0.5$	$T_1 = 2.00$
$f_2 = 1.39$	$T_2 = 0.72$
$f_3 = 2.28$	$T_3 = 0.44$

force distribution, a combination of uniform, linear and parabolic distributions that becomes increasingly nonlinear at longer periods. A_i represents the story shear coefficient, with the equivalent static force for level i calculated by multiplying A_i by the seismic weight at that level and above.

$$A_i = 1 + \left[\left(\frac{1}{\sqrt{\alpha_i}} - \alpha_i \right) \right] \frac{2T}{1+3T}, \quad \text{where,} \quad \alpha_i = \sum_{j=i}^{N} m_j \Big/ \sum_{j=1}^{N} m_j \qquad (7.2.8)$$

T is the natural period of the first vibration mode which can be assumed as $0.03H$ for steel structure, $0.02H$ for RC buildings (H: total height in m). Defining $u_i^{(0)}$ and B_i as absolute displacement and shear force ratio for each story under A_i distribution and base shear ratio C_B respectively, the equivalent mass M_{eq}, height H_{eq} and natural period T_{eq} for the equivalent SDOF model can be evaluated by the following equations.

$$M_{eq}^{(0)} = \frac{\left(\sum_{i=1}^{N} m_i \cdot u_i^{(0)} \right)^2}{\sum_{i=1}^{N} m_i \cdot u_i^{(0)2}} = \frac{\left(\sum_{i=1}^{N} m_i \sum_{j=1}^{i} \frac{B_j}{K_{fj}} \right)^2}{\sum_{i=1}^{N} m_i \left(\sum_{j=1}^{i} \frac{B_j}{K_{fj}} \right)^2} \qquad B_i = \frac{Q_i^{(0)}}{Q_B^{(0)}} = \frac{C_B A_i \sum_{j=i}^{N} m_j}{C_B \sum_{j=1}^{N} m_j} \qquad (7.2.9)$$

$$H_{eq} = \frac{\sum_{i=1}^{N} m_i \cdot u_i^{(0)} \cdot H_i}{\sum_{i=1}^{N} m_i \cdot u_i^{(0)}} = \frac{\sum_{i=1}^{N} m_i \cdot H_i \sum_{j=1}^{i} \frac{B_j}{K_{fi}}}{\sum_{i=1}^{N} m_i \sum_{j=1}^{i} \frac{B_j}{K_{fi}}} \qquad (7.2.10)$$

$$T_{eq}^{(0)} = 2\pi \sqrt{ \sum_{i=1}^{N} \left[m_i \frac{u_i^{(0)}}{Q_B^{(0)}} \right] } = 2\pi \sqrt{ \sum_{i=1}^{N} \left[m_i \sum_{j=1}^{i} \frac{B_j}{K_{fi}} \right] } \qquad (7.2.11)$$

138   Chapter 7. Applications for BRBF

Equation (7.2.11) gives T_{eq} = 2.0sec for the example building, which is identical with eigenvalue analysis results. This is equivalent to $0.036H$ (H = 55m), slightly less stiff than ordinary buildings.

Although the precise equivalent mass and height can be obtained from Equations (7.2.9) and (7.2.10), a reasonable approximation is to take the equivalent mass as 80% of the total mass, and equivalent height as 2/3(67%) of total height.

Equivalent Mass: M_{eq} = 6753 t$\times$0.8 = 5402 t

Equivalent Height: H_{eq} = 55m$\times$0.67 = 37 m

From the equivalent mass and period, the equivalent shear spring stiffness for the SDOF system is obtained as;

$K_f = M_{eq}\times(2\pi/T)^2 = 53.2\times10^3$kN/m = 53.2 kN/mm

For a design response spectrum for Japanese Level-2 earthquake (500ys return period) defined in the constant velocity region by S_D=0.825T/π(m), S_V=1.65(m/s), and S_A=3.3π/T (m/s^2) for h=0.02 damping, the bare structure response is:

Response acceleration for SDOF: $a^{(0)} = 3.3\pi/T = 5.18$ m/s

Base shear force: $Q^{(0)} = M_{eq}\, a^{(0)} = 27982$ kN

Likewise, the maximum response displacement at the equivalent height of the SDOF model is:

Maximum response displacement $u^{(0)} = Q^{(0)}/K_f = 526$mm ($=0.825T/\pi$)

Maximum story drift angle: $\theta^{(0)} = u^{(0)}/H_{eq} = 0.014 = 1/70$

(Story drift at actual floor is 3600/70=53mm)

When elasto-plastic dampers (BRBs) with K_d/K_f = 2.0, K_b/K_d = 2.5 are provided, equivalent stiffness of the system becomes:

$$\frac{K_a}{K_f} = \frac{1}{K_f/K_d + K_f/K_b} = \frac{1}{1/2.0 + 1/5.0} = 1.43$$

Equivalent damper stiffness: $K_a = K_f\times 1.43 = 76$ kN/mm

For the yield drift angle of BRB is 1/750, the yield ratio corresponding to $u^{(0)}$ is then:

$\mu^{(0)} = 750/70 = 10.7$

Equivalent stiffness and equivalent damping are calculated as (h_0=0.02):

$$K_{eq}^{(1)} = K_f + \frac{K_a}{\mu^{(0)}} = 53.2 + \frac{76}{10.7} = 60.3\,\text{kN/mm}$$

$$h_{eq}^{(1)} = h_0 + \frac{2(1+K_a/K_f)}{\pi\mu^{(0)}}\ln\frac{\mu^{(0)}+K_a/K_f}{(1+K_a/K_f)\mu^{(0)^{\frac{1}{1+K_a/K_f}}}} = 0.111$$

Response reduction ratio by damping is (a =75 for artificial spectrally matched wave):

$$F_h^{(1)} = \sqrt{\frac{1+75h_0}{1+75h_{eq}^{(1)}}} = \sqrt{\frac{1+75\times0.02}{1+75\times0.111}} = 0.517$$

Response displacement with the dampers is:

$$u^{(1)} = u^{(0)} F_h \sqrt{\frac{K_f}{K_{eq}^{(1)}}} = 525 \times 0.517 \times \sqrt{\frac{53.2}{60.3}} = 255 \text{ mm}$$

Story drift angle is $\theta^{(1)} = u^{(1)}/H_{eq} = 0.0069 = 1/145$
Because the previous yield ratio $\mu^{(1)}$ is for $\theta^{(0)}$. The new yield ratio against $\theta^{(1)}$ is:

$\mu^{(1)} = 750/145 = 5.17$

Then the new equivalent stiffness and damping ratio are:

$K_{eq}^{(2)} = 68 \text{kN/mm}$, $h_{eq}^{(2)} = 0.117$, $F_h^{(2)} = 0.506$, $u^{(2)} = 236$ mm, $\theta^{(2)} = 0.0063 = 1/157$

(Story drift at actual floor is 3600/157 = 22.9 mm)

As the system has converged, ($u^{(3)} \approx u^{(2)}$) no further iterations are required. The base shear ratio is;

$$Q^{(2)} = Q^{(2)} F_h^{(2)} \sqrt{\frac{K_{eq}}{K_f}} = 27982 \times 0.506 \times \sqrt{\frac{68}{53.2}} = 16007 \text{kN} = 0.30 M_{eq}$$

(Base shear ratio against total mass = 0.24)

7.2.3 Damper Distribution

Once the SDOF response has been obtained, the dampers can be distributed according to one of several rules. A simple distribution is to maintain a constant K_d/K_f ratio among all stories. The obtained response displacement and shear forces using A$_i$ distribution are compared with time-history analysis using the BCJ-L2 wave [7.2.5], an artificial wave matching the response spectra used for design. Good agreement is achieved, as shown in Figure 7.2.7. As this method distributes dampers with proportional damping, the story ratios of shear forces and story drifts are reduced by the same proportion, and the phase of vibration is kept unchanged.

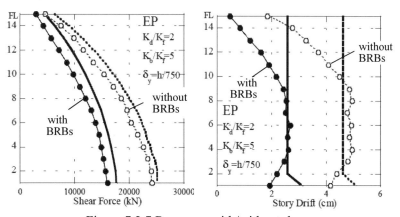

Figure 7.2.7 Response with/without damper

140   Chapter 7. Applications for BRBF

This method can also be applied to uneven damper distributions, for instance with dissipation energy set proportional to the elastic strain energy [7.2.6]. Assuming an initial equivalent damping ratio at each story as $h_{eqi}^{(1)}$, and the equivalent damping for whole SDOF model can be evaluated using the following formula.

$$h_{eq}^{(1)} = \frac{\sum_{i=1}^{N} h_{eqi}^{(1)} \cdot W_i^{(1)}}{\sum_{i=1}^{N} W_i^{(1)}}, \qquad W_i^{(1)} = \frac{1}{2} K_{eqi}^{(1)} \Delta u_i^{(1)2} = \frac{(B_i Q_B^{(0)})^2}{2 K_{eqi}^{(1)}} \qquad (7.2.12a,b)$$

The modified natural period and equivalent mass of SDOF is as follows;

$$T_{eq}^{(1)} = 2\pi \sqrt{\sum_{i=1}^{N} \left[m_i \frac{u_i^{(1)}}{Q_B^{(0)}} \right]} = 2\pi \sqrt{\sum_{i=1}^{N} \left[m_i \sum_{j=1}^{i} \frac{B_j}{K_{eqj}^{(1)}} \right]}, \qquad (7.2.13a)$$

$$M_{eq}^{(1)} = \frac{\left(\sum_{i=1}^{N} m_i \cdot u_i^{(1)} \right)^2}{\sum_{i=1}^{N} m_i \cdot u_i^{(1)2}} = \frac{\left(\sum_{i=1}^{N} m_i \sum_{j=1}^{i} \frac{B_j}{K_{eqj}^{(1)}} \right)^2}{\sum_{i=1}^{N} m_i \left(\sum_{j=1}^{i} \frac{B_j}{K_{eqj}^{(1)}} \right)^2} \qquad (7.2.13b)$$

Iterate the ductility ratio using $F_h^{(n)}$ (Equation (7.2.7)) until convergence is achieved:

$$\mu_i^{(n)} = \mu_i^{(0)} \cdot F_h^{(n)} \frac{T^{(n)}}{T^{(0)}} \qquad (7.2.14)$$

Once a stable yield ratio $\mu_i^{(n)}$ is obtained, the final base shear $Q_B^{(n)}$ can be evaluated as follows, and with shear forces in each story given by $B_i Q_B^{(n)}$;

$$Q_B^{(n)} = Q_B^{(0)} \cdot F_h^{(n)} \frac{T^{(0)}}{T^{(n)}} \frac{M_{eq}^{(n)}}{M_{eq}^{(0)}} \qquad (7.2.15)$$

Finally, the drift in each story $\Delta u_i^{(n)}$ can be obtained from the following;

$$\Delta u_i^{(n)} = (B_i Q_B^{(n)} - K_{ai} \Delta u_{yi}) / K_{fi} \qquad (7.2.16)$$

The above evaluation procedure is applied to the uneven damper distributions as shown in Figure 7.2.8, with comparisons to time history analyses presented in the accompanying plots. The uneven story drift caused by the eccentric damper distributions is captured and demonstrates the validity of this method. However, such partial damper distributions as (U) or (G)should be avoided in actual structural design.

Chapter 7. Applications for BRBF 141

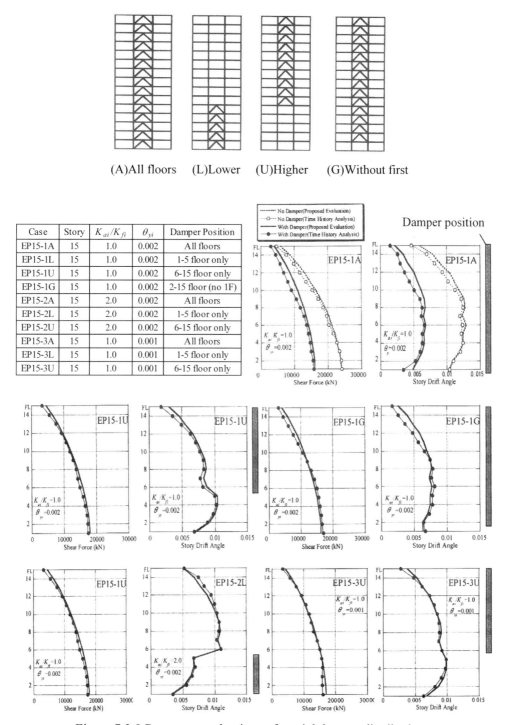

Figure 7.2.8 Response evaluations of partial damper distribution

7.2.4 Optimal damper distribution

Although the response evaluation for a given damper distribution requires iterative calculations, the overall required damper stiffness to achieve a target drift can be simply obtained by setting the yield drift and hence μ_i. For example, the target drift angle in the first example is give as $\theta = u / H_{eq} = 0.0067 = 1/150$,

Target response displacement: $\quad u = H_{eq} \cdot \theta = 37000/150 = 247$ mm

Target yield ratio: $\quad \mu = \theta/\theta_{yield} = 750/150 = 5.0$

Target displacement reduction ratio: $\delta_{eq}/\delta_f = \theta / \theta^{(0)} = 70/150 = 0.47$

From the performance curves in Figure 7.2.5, the required stiffness of the added components is $K_a/K_f=2.5$. The ratio of connection-to-damper stiffness is estimated as $K_{bi}/K_{di} = 5.0$, or alternatively this can be stated in terms of connection-to-full brace stiffness, with $K_{bi}/K_{ai} = 1 + K_{bi}/K_{di} = 6.0$. The required damper-to-frame stiffness in each story is then obtained as:

$$\frac{K_{di}}{K_{fi}} = \frac{K_a}{K_f}\left(1+\frac{K_{di}}{K_{bi}}\right) = 2.5\left(1+\frac{1}{5.0}\right) = 3.0$$

If the bare frame has a soft story or uneven drift response, as in Figure 7.2.9 (b) and (c), the dampers can be used to obtain a uniform interstory drift response distribution. The optimal damper distribution to achieve a uniform interstory drift target can be obtained by the following equations, as proposed by Kasai et al [7.2.6].

$$K_{ai} = \frac{Q_i}{\Delta H_i}\frac{\sum_{i=1}^{n}(K_{fi}\Delta H_i^2)}{\sum_{i=1}^{n}(Q_i\Delta H_i)}\left(\mu+\frac{K_a}{K_f}\right) - \mu K_{fi} \geq 0, \quad \Delta H_i: \text{height of } i\text{-th story} \qquad (7.2.17)$$

This method is based on the assumption of 1) a constant target story drift θ_i and yield ratio μ_i, 2) equivalent static force distribution (e.g. A_i distribution) given by shear forces Q_i, and 3) total hysteretic to strain energy ratio of multistory system is same as that of equivalent SDOF system. The last condition means that the total damping ratio is the same as the SDOF system. The combined stiffness distribution $K_{fi} + K_{ai}$ is selected to follow the A_i distribution achieving a constant interstory drift response as shown in Figure 7.2.9.

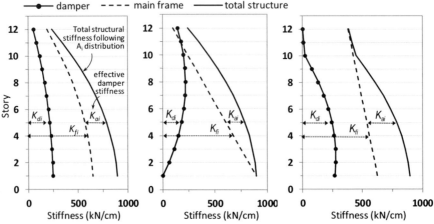

(a) Normal drift distribution (b) Large drift at upper (c) Large drift at bottom

Figure 7.2.9 Optimal damper distribution for constant story drift target

7.2.5 Application Examples

Several representative examples of steel structures using BRBs are introduced in this section, including one structure that experienced strong ground motion. With modern computing capabilities, time history analysis is typically used as a final performance verification. However, the Damage Tolerant Structure concept introduced in Section 7.1 and Equivalent Linearization method described earlier in Section 7.2 are still widely used to design BRBs to achieve higher performance targets.

The first example is a Damage Tolerant Structure that was subjected to design level ground motions during the 2011 Tohoku Earthquake, achieving immediate Occupancy performance level. Figure 7.2.10 shows the Koriyama Big-eye building, a 24-story, 132.6m high structure located in Fukushima, Japan and completed in 2001 [7.2.7]. Moment frames consisting of square hollow section columns and I-section beams are provided in both directions, designed with a story yield drift of approximately 1%. The beams used SM490B material and were tapered to be wider at the column face, with typical sections at midheight H-600 x 500 ~ 300 x 12 x 16 with 8 m spans. The damper system includes BRBs in the lower stories to control the seismic response with visco-elastic dampers provided in the upper stories both for seismic and wind vibration. A BRB yield of just 0.13~0.16% story drift was achieved by using a low yield steel (LY225) and short plastic length ($L_p/L_0 = 0.25$~0.3). The energy dissipation system is effective in keeping the main frame elastic under a Level 2 earthquake and reduced the steel tonnage from ordinary ductile design.

An early international project was the retrofit of Federal Building in Salt Lake City, US, shown in Figure 7.2.11. The existing 8-story structure was constructed in early 1960's and was retrofitted according to FEMA 273/356, by installing 344 BRBs along the perimeter with the yield strengths of up to 1900 kips (8455kN).

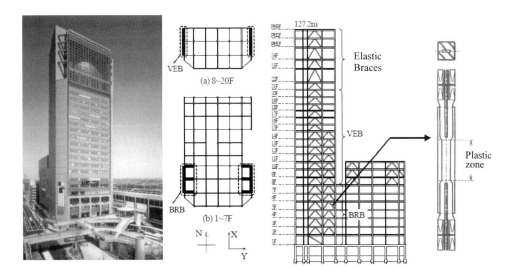

Figure 7.2.10 Koriyama Big-eye Building

Figure 7.2.11 Bennett Federal Building, Salt Lake City

Figure 7.2.12 Typical BRBF application in Tokyo (Gran Tokyo North)

Figure 7.2.13 Erection of large BRBF

Another example of a Damage Tolerant Design is the Grand Tokyo (Figure 7.2.12), a 205 m high, 43-story building in Tokyo, Japan completed in 2007. This building is a typical example of BRB application in high-rises build in major cities in Japan, and many other 200m-class buildings are constructed in a similar manner. BRBs reaching 10000kN or more strength (Figure 7.2.13) are used for those structures.

A recent example for low-rise building is the Environmental Energy Innovation Building at Tokyo Institute of Technology, which was completed in 2012 and is shown in Figure 7.2.14(a). Covered by 4650 solar cell panels, this building is designed as self-electricity-providing building in sunny days [7.2.8]. BRBs with LY225 cores are distributed along the perimeter, achieving a BRB-to-frame stiffness ratio of $K_d/K_f = 1.0$ and first story shear strength of 10,000kN, approximately 1/8 of the main frame shear strength (Figure 7.2.14(b)). As shown in Figure 7.2.14(c), the BRBs start yielding at 1/700 story drift angle, which corresponds to a base shear ratio of 0.15, reducing maximum story angle to less than half. While the ordinary structure without BRBs cause serious beam end yield and fracture under a Level-2 earthquake (Figure 7.1.14(d)), additional BRBs are sufficient to keep the main structure elastic and reduce maximum story drift angle within immediate occupancy level. Typical beams are H-450 × 250 × 12 × 25 (SM490) sections with 4 m spans, and do not yield until 1.1~1.2% drift.

Chapter 7. Applications for BRBF 145

(a) Building view from South

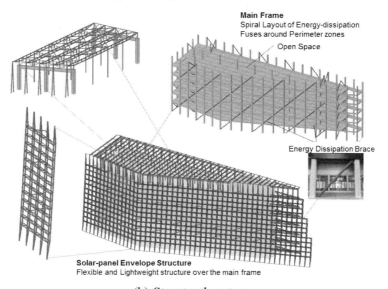

(b) Structural system

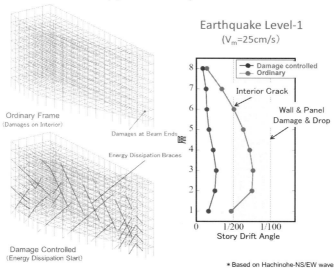

(c) Damage and drift at L-1 earthquake

Figure 7.2.14 Environmental Energy Innovation Building, Tokyo Tech -1

146 Chapter 7. Applications for BRBF

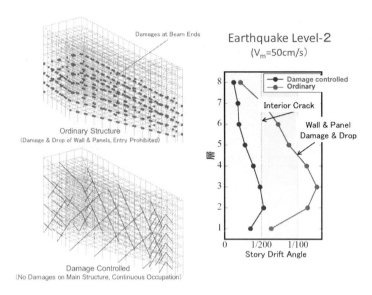

(d) Damage and drift at L-2 earthquake

Figure 7.2.14 Environmental Energy Innovation Building, Tokyo Tech -2

References

[7.2.1] Takeuchi T, Kasai K, Ohara K, Nakajima H, Kimura Y: Performance evaluation and design of passively controlled buildings using equivalent linearization, *Structural Engineers World Congress*, 2002, 263

[7.2.2] Kasai K, Fu Y, Watanabe A: Two types of passive control systems for seismic damage mitigation, *Journal of Structural Engineering, ASCE*, 1998

[7.2.3] Newmark N.M, Rousenblueth E: *Fundamentals of earthquake engineering*, Prentice-Hall Inc., 1971

[7.2.4] Fu Y, Kasai K: Comparative study of frames using viscoelastic and viscous dampers, *Journal of Structural Engineering, ASCE*, 1998; **124**(5)

[7.2.5] Building Research Institute, Building Center of Japan: *Recommendation for artificial earthquake wave for design*, 1992 (*in Japanese*)

[7.2.6] Japan Society of Seismic Isolation: *Passive response control design manual, 2nd edition*, 2005 (*in Japanese and Chinese*)

[7.2.7] Sugiyama M, Morimoto S, Koizumi M: Design of Koriyama west city redevelopment, *The Structural Technology,* 1999.8, 28-33 (*in Japanese*)

[7.2.8] Takeuchi T: Structural design with seismic energy-dissipation concept, *Proc. IABSE 2015*, 2015:SK-1.

7.3 SEISMIC RETROFIT WITH BRBS

7.3.1 Damage Tolerant Structure Concept Applied to Retrofit

Although the seismic performance of older buildings is variable, it usually depends on the effective design code at the time of construction. Codes have typically been updated in response to damages observed during major earthquakes, revising structural design or detailing practice to suppress non ductile failure modes, or in some cases increasing the seismic demands regarding design. For example, in Japan, RC buildings constructed prior to 1971 tend to have insufficient stirrups in columns, and have a high risk of shear failure in the case of a severe earthquake. As the building stock includes a large volume of such vulnerable buildings, retrofit to improve strength, stiffness or ductility is often required.

BRBs have several desirable characteristics that frequently receive attention for retrofit projects. In brace configurations BRBs are relatively stiff and can be designed to yield at small drifts, providing substantial energy dissipation. As the compressive and tensile strengths are nearly equal, connection overstrength demands are minimized, reducing the amount of local strengthening required. It is also possible to insert BRBs strategically to act as fuses, protecting particular members.

Both the Damage Tolerant concept introduced in Section 7.1 and the equivalent linearization method discussed in Section 7.2 can be directly applied to retrofit design. In the case of an existing non-ductile moment frame, BRBs with shortened plastic lengths can be installed in a brace configuration while utilizing the existing frame's elastic stiffness. Furthermore, soft stories can be upgraded by tuning the BRB cores according to the optimal stiffness distribution discussed in Section 7.2.4. A variety of retrofit concepts are depicted below.

7.3.1 Concept of Integrated Facade Engineering

One of the typical retrofit strategies for non-ductile moment frames is to install BRBs as bracing elements along the perimeter, either as an external frame or in-plane with the existing frame. However, such retrofits are often difficult to implement while maintaining continuous occupation and frequently will have a negative effect on the building's aesthetics. At this point it should be recognized that façades have various functions; they are not only a suitable location for seismic reinforcement, but also affect energy efficiency and architectural appearance. To resolve these competing functions, the concept of "Integrated Façade" can be employed, treating structural retrofit, façade design and environmental design combined together, including improvements on seismic performances using seismic energy dissipation devices. (Takeuchi et.al [7.3.1], [7.3.2]).

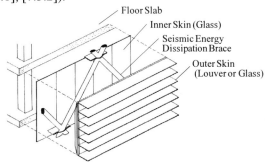

Figure 7.3.1. Concept of integrated façade

148   Chapter 7. Applications for BRBF

An example of an Integrated Façade is shown in Figure 7.3.1. The existing structure is retained to support gravity loads and provide elastic stiffness, while Buckling Restrained Braces (BRB) are introduced outside of the glass façade, serving both as seismic energy dissipation members and as attachment points for an additional outer skin of louvers or glass.

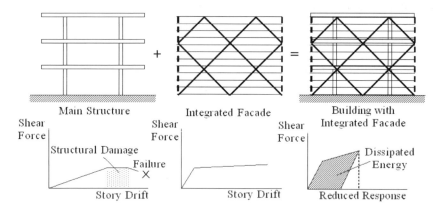

Figure 7.3.2 Concept of structural design

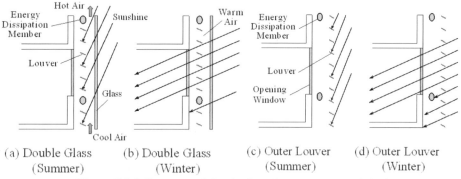

Figure 7.3.3 Concept of physical environment control design

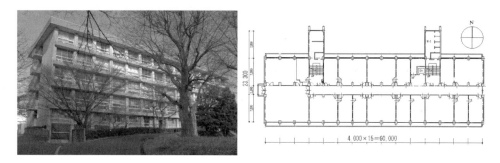

Figure 7.3.4 Building view before retrofit   Figure 7.3.5 Building plan

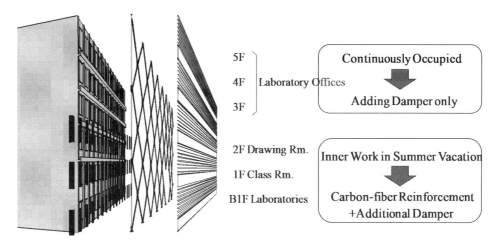

Figure 7.3.6. Retrofit concept

It is important that the façade is not designed as a pure structural member or architectural element, but integrated together. Structurally, either BRBs or other dampers could be used for the brace elements, dissipating energy, reducing the response and protecting the main structure, as shown in Figure 7.3.2. Environmentally, the double skin is provided to improve energy efficiency, with the glass concept Figures 7.3.3 (a) and (b) which is popular in Europe. However, its effects are focused on winter, and require air ventilation system in summer. In subtropical area such as Japan, outer skin systems composed of louvers as shown in Figures 7.3.3 (c) and (d) are proposed.

7.3.2 Application to existing aged building

Integrated façade concept was applied to an existing building. The Midorigaoka-1st building at Tokyo Institute of Technology is a 6-story RC building designed in 1966, prior to the revision of the Building Code of Japan in 1971. The elevation and plan of the building are shown in Figure 7.3.4 and 7.3.5. The building has 23.3m x 60m rectangular plan with cores for stairs and restrooms. Horizontal stability for the N-S direction is secured by strong RC walls; however, the structural system for the E-W direction is composed of moment frames with fragile columns and beams with 4-m spans. Values of the seismic index I_S (JDPA(1989) [7.3.3]), which indicates the capacity relative to current standards, in the E-W direction are much less than target value of 0.7. With a minimum value of 0.27 in 2nd floor there is a high risk of a soft story collapse.

The retrofit concept is shown in Figure 7.3.6. The lower floors (BF-2F) of the building are classrooms, which are not used in summer season and replacement of window frames and column reinforcement are possible. Columns in these floors are reinforced by carbon fiber sheets, preventing shear failure and improving deformation capacities. To achieve the target strength, additional BRBs with louvers are attached to the façades. These braces are designed to yield at required minimum strength, and then start dissipating energy as hysteretic dampers. A standard BRB design with circular restrainers and cast pin connections were used, as shown in Figure 7.3.7, but a special adjustable detail was also installed to improve permissible site tolerances.

150   Chapter 7. Applications for BRBF

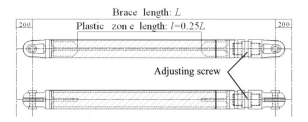

BRB	Mark	Size	Strength (kN)	No.	Position
	RB1	PL-19×152 (LY225)	650	15	4F
	RB3	PL-32×153 (LY225)	1102	13	3-4F
	RB4	PL-40×159 (LY225)	1431	80	B1-3F

Figure 7.3.7 Applied BRB members

7.3.3 Structural Experiment and Analysis

For evaluating seismic performance of the retrofit, three types of BRB with plastic zone length ratio of L_p/L =0.7, 0.4, 0.25, and ordinary H-section braces with buckling strengths equivalent to the BRB yield strength are studied adding on the shear force - story drift relationship of the RC main frame. For evaluating the hysteresis of the main frame, following three types of ultimate strength indexes on E-W direction are compared.

(A) Ultimate story strength determined from the seismic index Is, which is calculated for each column and wall member at each story according to Japanese retrofit design recommendation for RC frames [7.3.3]. The corresponding displacements are determined according the member ductility, with the critical member in this case achieving the ultimate capacity at a story drift angle of 1/250 ($F = 1.0$).

(B) Summation of the column and wall cracking and ultimate shear strengths according to the AIJ RC design recommendations [7.3.4]. The initial and cracked stiffness is also provided, giving the total story strength and displacements.

(C) 3D pushover analysis, with member cracking and ultimate strengths determined from (B), but including column axial and beam flexural deformations.

Obtained shear force-deflection curves for 2nd floor before retrofit according to each method are shown in Fig. 7.3.8(a)

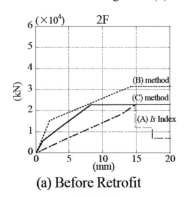
(a) Before Retrofit

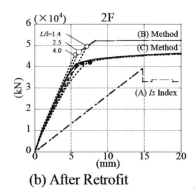
(b) After Retrofit

7.3.8 Shear force-story drift relationship at 2nd Floor

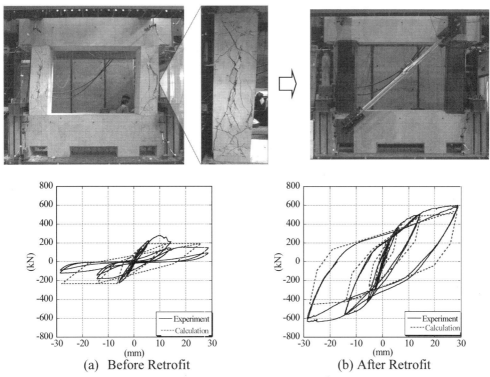

Figure 7.3.9 Reduced mock-up test for 2nd floor frame

Method (B) neglects column axial deformations and produces a higher shear strength than Method (C), while Methods (C) and (A) converge at the ultimate shear strength. While the *Is* indexes (A) from the Japanese retrofit design recommendations capture the strength degradation, Method (C) provides the best stiffness estimate up until the ultimate strength. Therefore, actual shear force – story drift relationship is assumed to follow the line (C) until 15 mm (0.4% story drift angle), then deteriorate along the line (A) in this design. The improved shear force-deflection curves after retrofit in 2nd floor calculated by the method (A)-(C) are shown in Figure 7.3.8 (b). The relationship between calculation methods are similar to Figure 7.3.8(a), however, the ultimate strengths are increased by almost twice. The effect of plastic zone length of BRB is observed on the difference of yield drifts.

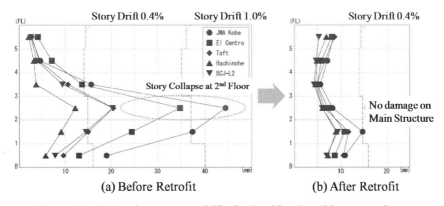

Figure 7.3.10 Maximum story drift obtained by time-history analyses

For verifying the evaluated hysteretic characteristics of frames, reduced mock-ups for 2nd floor frame before and after retrofit are fabricated, and cyclic loading tests are carried out up to 1/50 story drift angle. The test results are shown in Figure 7.3.9. The 1/2.5 scale specimens model the 2nd floor column, with axial force introduced by post-tensioning bars. Obtained hysteretic loops are shown in Figure 7.3.9 (a), (b). Frame before retrofit started shear failure at 0.4% story drift angle ($\delta = 10$mm), then horizontal capacity drastically degraded by each cycle (Figure 7.3.9 (a)). On contrary, frame after retrofit, which is reinforced by carbon fiber and BRB did not present shear failure, showed stable hysteretic loops up to cycles of 2% story drift angle (Figure 7.3.9 (b)).

Time-history analyses are carried out with the hysteretic loop models shown with dashed lines under the condition of $L_p/L = 0.25$. Seismic waves of El Centro NS, Taft EW, Hachinohe NS, and JMA Kobe NS with PGV scaled to 50 cm/s (Level-2), and the design artificial wave BCJ-L2 are used for the 3-D analytical models of the building. Figure 7.3.10 (a) shows the response of the building before retrofit, whose maximum drift exceeds 0.1%. Considering the results of the mock-up test, the building is expected to collapse with the shear failure at the 2nd floor columns in real situation. Figure 7.3.10 (b) shows the response with BRB with plastic zone lengths ratio of $L_p/L = 0.25$ satisfies maximum story drift being less than 0.4%, which means almost no damage on the main structure.

7.3.4 Design of Connection and Outer facade

The connection between the BRBs and existing building transfers a horizontal force of up to 2800 kN, and was detailed to avoid obstructing the building functionality. A typical detail is shown in Figure 7.3.11. First, chemical anchors are drilled into the perimeter beams from the outside. Next, steel beams with shear-studs are inserted in eaves, and fixed to perimeter beams by injecting mortar. Finally, the BRBs are connected to brackets attached to the outer face of the shear transfer beams.

The thermal performance of the new façade (Figure 7.3.12-14) was also investigated using CFD analysis, with the louvers proving effective in providing shade from the summer sun, while acting as light shelves to improve daylighting and as double skin to improve energy efficiency in the winter. Furthermore, durability of the BRBs may be improved as the louvers shield the rain.

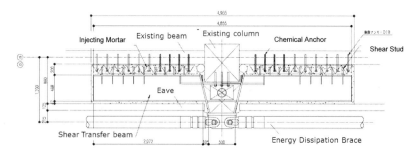

Figure 7.3.11 Detail of the connection between frame and BRB

Chapter 7. Applications for BRBF   153

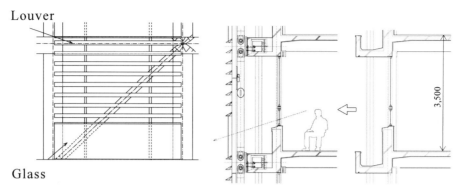

Figure 7.3.12 Detail of the outer skin

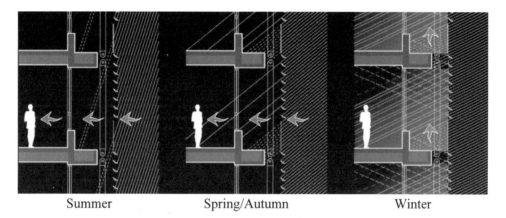

Figure 7.3.13. Environmental effect of outer skin

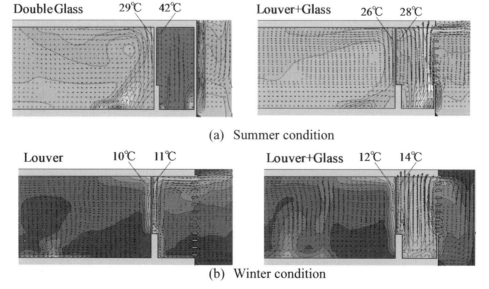

(a) Summer condition

(b) Winter condition

Figure 7.3.14 Thermal distribution around perimeter zone
(Tokyo, south, noon)

154   Chapter 7. Applications for BRBF

(a) Original eave (b) Setting steel beam (c) Attachment of BRB   (d) Louver & Glass
Figure 7.3.15 Perimeter work process

Figure 7.3.16 Carbon fiber reinforcement

Figure 7.3.17 BRB Attachment

Figure 7.3.18 Building façade after retrofit

(a) Exterior appearance   (b) Interior view
Figure 7.3.19 Concept of diagonal louver BRBs (Mock-up)

The construction sequence is shown in Figures 7.3.15 to 7.3.18, starting in July 2005 and completing the following March. Louder construction activities were carried out the second month during university holiday, with minimal disturbance to occupants. In Figure 7.3.15, process of retrofit works at the perimeter zone is shown. (a) is the original eave, and (b) shows the setting of the connection beams in the eave. (c) shows the attachment of BRBs, and (d) shows after attachment of outer skin on BRBs. Prior to the brace attachment (Figure 7.3.17), carbon fiber reinforcement for the columns has been completed (Figure 7.3.16). Figure 7.3.18 shows the building elevation after the completion, which represents a completely renewed appearance. The retrofit work was carried out within ordinary retrofit cost range and schedule even with the outer skin, because of no additional piles were required.

7.3.5 BRBs designed as diagonal louvers

The concept of "Integrated Façade Engineering" can be developed for various other configurations. Figure 7.3.19 shows the concept of using slender BRBs as diagonal louvers. Each louver functions as a BRB with 300 kN yield strength, providing a horizontal yield strength of around 2000 kN along each span. Diagonal louvers are considered to be effective for sunshine control in west and east facades. This concept is applied for the seismic retrofit of administration building in Tokyo Tech in 2008, as shown in Figure 7.3.20.

(a) Exterior appearance   (b) Interior view
Figure 7.3.20 Seismic retrofit application (Administration Build. Tokyo Tech)

References

[7.3.1] Takeuchi T, Yasuda K, Iwata M: Studies on Integrated Building Façade Engineering with High-Performance Structural Elements, *IABSE 2006 (Budapest)*, 442-443 2006

[7.3.2] Takeuchi T, Yasuda K, Iwata M: Seismic Retrofitting using Energy Dissipation Façades, *ATC-SEI09 (San Francisco)*, 2009

[7.3.3] Kenchiku Bosai: *Seismic evaluation and retrofit*, English Version, 2001.

[7.3.4] Architectural Institute of Japan: *AIJ Standard for structural calculation of reinforced concrete structures*. 2010. (*in Japanese*)

7.4 RESPONSE EVALUATION OF BRBS RETROFIT FOR RC FRAMES

As shown in Section 7.3, installing BRBs is an effective retrofit for non-ductile RC frames. While it may be desirable to design the BRBs to ensure that the existing frame remains elastic, cracking or yielding may be permitted under a design level event. For simplified retrofit design, the equivalent linearization method from Section 7.2 can be extended to nonlinear frames, as well [7.4.1], [7.4.2]. This section presents a simplified design method for RC frames retrofitted with BRBs attached via elastic steel frames (SFs), as shown in Figure 7.4.1.

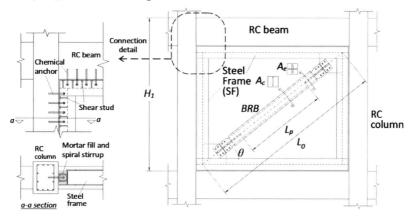

Figure 7.4.1. Layout of BRB retrofit application on an RC frame with connection details

Proposed subassembly addresses two common challenges encountered when retrofitting older RC structures over the world. First, it is common for the existing beams or columns to be relatively small in cross-section or lacking strength especially in RC frames outside of Japan, requiring additional strengthening for the structural members. Secondly, it is a challenging task to sort out an in-plane attachment of BRBs on an existing RC frame in a practical manner. Here, the steel frame properties can be tuned to provide the required stiffness and strength, while simplifying the connection to the existing frame and distributing the local transfer forces. This is achieved by attaching post-fixed chemical anchors to the RC frame and welded shear studs to the steel frame, with mortar infill and stirrups to establish continuity. The Japanese Standard for Seismic Diagnosis of Existing Reinforced Concrete Structures [7.4.3] recommends this connection be designed for the combined strength of the steel frame and BRB.

The proposed design method is based on the equivalent linearization method, but extended to include the hysteretic and strain energy contribution from the following three components:

- Existing RC frame: trilinear Takeda model
- New BRBs: elastic-perfectly plastic
- New steel frame (SF): elastic

The design steps are as follows.

1) Step 1: Evaluating structural behavior of the existing RC frame:

First, the cracking and yielding points of the existing building is evaluated using non-linear pushover analysis. For simplicity the yield displacement of each story δ_{fyi} canbe assumed as equal.

2) Step 2: Defining an equivalent SDOF model:

Next, an equivalent SDOF system shown in Figure 7.4.2 is defined, using the initial elastic stiffness K_{fi} from step 1, as well as the story mass m_i and height H_i of each story. The initial period T_f, as well as the equivalent mass M_{eq} (Equation 7.2.9) and height H_{eq} (Equation (7.2.10)) is determined.

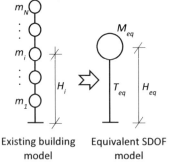

Figure 7.4.2. Equivalent SDOF system

3) Step 3: Evaluating the hysteretic energy dissipated by the RC frame

Following the results of step 1, the RC frame with bending collapse mechanism is idealized as a degrading trilinear Takeda model [7.4.4], as shown in Figure 7.4.3.

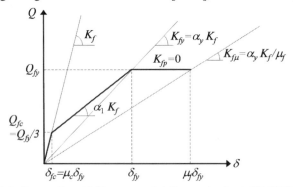

Figure 7.4.3. Degrading tri-linear model for equivalent SDOF RC frame.

In this figure, the yield base shear Q_{fy}, the cracking shear Q_{fc}, the yield displacement δ_{fy} and the cracking displacement δ_{fc} for the RC frameis shown. Note that the displacements are determined by scaling the typical story yielding or cracking displacement by the ratio of the equivalent height to individual story heights H_{eq}/H_1.

Several assumptions are needed to simplify the calculation of equivalent damping h_{eq} in later steps. Taking $Q_{fc} \approx Q_{fy}/3$ and the ductility at cracking $\mu_c = \delta_{fc}/\delta_{fy} = 1/10$, the post-crack stiffness factors become $\alpha_1 = 0.22$ and $\alpha_y = 0.3$. Additionally, while concrete structures typically undergo hardening following yielding, the post-yield behavior is assumed as perfectly plastic.

The initial elastic stiffness K_f is calculated from Equation 7.4.1, and is related to the tangent crack stiffness by α_1, and to the secant stiffness at yield by α_y. The subsequent secant stiffness at a given ductility μ_f is given by $K_{f\mu} = K_f \alpha_y / \mu_f$, or in general at any given ductility by Equation (7.4.2 a-c). $\mu_f \delta_{fy}$ is usually set as target drift.

$$K_f = M_{eq}\left(\frac{2\pi}{T_f}\right)^2 \tag{7.4.1}$$

$$K_{f\mu} = pK_f, \quad T_{f\mu} = T_f / \sqrt{p} \tag{7.4.2.a}$$

$$p = \frac{\alpha_1(\mu_f - \mu_c) + \mu_c}{\mu_f} \quad (\mu_c < \mu_f \le 1) \tag{7.4.2b}$$

$$p = \frac{\alpha_y}{\mu_f} \quad (\mu_f > 1) \tag{7.4.2c}$$

As the RC frame exhibits a pinching effect, the hysteretic energy of the RC frame and BRB are calculated separately. Figure 7.4.4 depicts the hysteretic energy E_f that is dissipated by the RC frame after cracking in pre-yielding and post-yielding stages.

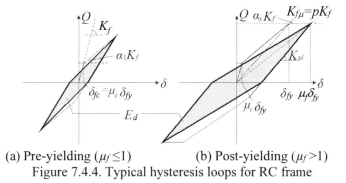

(a) Pre-yielding ($\mu_f \le 1$)   (b) Post-yielding ($\mu_f > 1$)
Figure 7.4.4. Typical hysteresis loops for RC frame

Evaluation of hysteretic energy requires the unloading stiffness K_{ul}, which is defined for each stage by the Takeda model [7.4.4] as follows:

$$K_{ul} = \frac{Q_{fc} + Q_{fy}}{\delta_{fc} + \mu_f \delta_{fy}} = K_f \frac{2\mu_c + \alpha_1(\mu_f - \mu_c)}{\mu_f + \mu_c} \quad (\mu_c < \mu_f \le 1) \tag{7.4.3a}$$

$$K_{ul} = \frac{Q_{fc} + Q_{fy}}{\delta_{fc} + \delta_{fy}} \frac{1}{\mu_f^\lambda} = K_f \frac{\alpha_y + \mu_c}{(1+\mu_c)\mu_f^\lambda} \quad (\mu_f > 1) \tag{7.4.3b}$$

where λ is the unloading stiffness degrading parameter (in this study it is assumed: $\lambda = 0.4$). Therefore the hysteretic energy dissipated by the RC frame may be obtained from Equation (7.4.4 a,b):

$$E_f = \begin{cases} 2K_f\left(\mu_f \delta_{fy}\right)^2 \dfrac{p\mu_c(1-p)}{\mu_c + p\mu_f} & (\mu_c < \mu_f \le 1) \\[2ex] 2K_f\left(\mu_f \delta_{fy}\right)^2 \left[p - \dfrac{p^2(1+\mu_c)\mu_f^\lambda}{\mu_c + p\mu_f}\right] & (\mu_f > 1) \end{cases} \tag{7.4.4a} \tag{7.4.4b}$$

4) Step 4: Evaluating the hysteretic energy dissipated by BRBs and effect of the elastic SF

The BRB yield displacement can be estimated from Section 2.3, and typically falls between 1/400 ~ 1/1000.

Similar to the RC frame, the post-yielding stiffness is neglected for simplicity, with the BRB assumed to be elastic-perfectly plastic, as shown in Figure 7.4.5. The hysteretic energy E_d dissipated by BRBs is then given by Equation (7.4.5).

$$E_d = 4 K_d (\mu_d - 1)(\delta_{dy})^2, \quad \mu_d > 1 \tag{7.4.5}$$

where μ_d is the ductility ratio of the BRB ($\mu_d = \mu_f \delta_{fy}/\delta_{dy}$). In this section the BRB connections are assumed to be infinitely stiff for simplicity. If this assumption is not valid, K_a should be used instead of K_d.

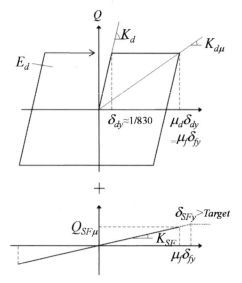

Figure 7.4.5. BRB and SF force-displacement relations

Furthermore, the secant stiffness for a given ductility ratio $K_{d\mu}$ is given by:

$$K_{d\mu} = K_d / \mu_d \tag{7.4.6}$$

The efficiency of the system is sensitive to the damper-to-frame stiffness ratio K_d/K_f, which is typically in the range of $K_d/K_f = 1\sim3$ when retrofitting RC moment frames with dampers. Similarly, the steel frame-to-BRB stiffness is typically in the range of $\gamma_s = K_{SF}/K_d = 0.04\sim0.10$. ($\gamma_s \geq 0.05$ is recommended [7.4.2]) For the proposed retrofit method it is also important to design this steel frame to remain elastic within target displacement range.

The Japanese Manual for Design and Construction of Passively-Controlled Buildings [7.4.5] recommends that the shear strength of additional dampers in a structure should correspond to a base shear coefficient of approximately 30%. Following this recommendation, initial value of K_d/K_f ratio can be assumed with the following equation:

$$\frac{K_d}{K_f} = \frac{C_B M_{eq} g}{K_f (\delta_{dy} + \gamma_s \mu_{tar} \delta_{fy})} \tag{7.4.7}$$

Where C_B is the base shear coefficient recommended by the relevant code, μ_{tar} is the target ductility of the retrofitting project, and $\gamma_s = K_{SF}/K_d$.

5) Step 5: Evaluating equivalent damping ratio before and after the retrofit

The estimated monotonic loading curve of the retrofitted structure (RC+BRB+SF) is shown in Figure 7.4.6, with the total secant stiffness at a given ductility denoted by $K_{\Sigma\mu}$:

$$K_{\Sigma\mu} = K_{f\mu} + K_d + K_{SF} \quad (\mu_d \leq 1) \tag{7.4.8.a}$$

$$K_{\Sigma\mu} = K_{f\mu} + K_{d\mu} + K_{SF} \quad (1 < \mu_d) \tag{7.4.8.b}$$

The equivalent potential energy $E_{\Sigma e}$ is then given by:

$$E_{\Sigma e} = \frac{1}{2} K_{\Sigma\mu} (\mu_f \delta_{fy})^2 \tag{7.4.9}$$

Considering the hysteretic energy dissipated by the BRBs and RC frame, the total equivalent damping $h'_{eq}=h_f+h_d$ for a single cycle is calculated by Equation (7.4.10) [7.4.6]

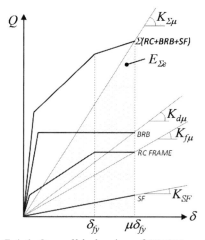

Figure 7.4.6. Overall behavior of SDOF model with BRB

$$h'_{eq} = \frac{E_f + E_d}{4\pi E_{\Sigma e}} \tag{7.4.10}$$

As discussed in Section 7.2, because a structure exhibits a large number of hysteresis loops with diverse amplitudes during a random excitation such as an earthquake, an average damping h_{eq} for a range from zero to maximum amplitude is evaluated here. [7.4.7].

$$h_{eq} = h_0 + \frac{1}{\mu_m} \int_1^{\mu_m} h'_{eq} d\mu \tag{7.4.11}$$

For simplicity, the average equivalent damping h_{eq} can be estimated from the equivalent damping of the peak cycle h_Σ and a typical damping reduction factor R, with the structural inherent damping assumed as $h_0 = 0.03$. While for typical BRBs $R \approx 0.8$, Figure 7.4.7(b) indicates that $R \approx 0.6$ is more appropriate for this particular application. By substituting Equations (7.4.4), (7.4.5) into (7.4.10), the equivalent damping h_{eq} can be expressed as follows

Chapter 7. Applications for BRBF

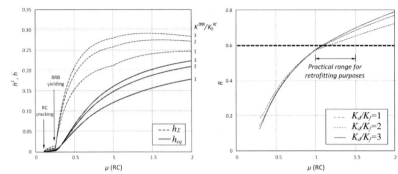

(a) Total damping and average damping   (b) Damping reduction factor R
Figure 7.4.7 Reduced Damping Evaluation

$$h_{eq} = h_0 + Rh'_{eq} = h_0 + \frac{p\dfrac{p\mu_f + \mu_c - p\mu_f^\lambda(1+\mu_c)}{p\mu_f + \mu_c} + \dfrac{2}{\mu_d}\dfrac{K_d}{K_f}\left(1-\dfrac{1}{\mu_d}\right)}{\pi\left[p + \dfrac{K_d}{K_f}\left(\gamma_s + \dfrac{1}{\mu_d}\right)\right]} R \quad (7.4.12)$$

Meanwhile, equivalent damping ratio of RC frame before retrofit can be estimated as following.

$$h_{f\mu} = h_0 + Rh'_{f\mu} = h_0 + \frac{R}{\pi}\frac{p\mu_f + \mu_c - p\mu_f^\lambda(1+\mu_c)}{p\mu_f + \mu_c} \quad (7.4.13)$$

Maximum story drift angle before retrofit $\theta_{f\mu} = \delta_{f\mu}/H_{eq}$ can be obtained from displacement response spectrum using natural period $T_{f\mu}$ from Equation (7.4.2a) and damping $h_{f\mu}$ from Equation (7.4.13). Please note this response is on the assumption that $T_{f\mu}$ and $h_{f\mu}$ are kept constant for any amplitude. Next, the efficient amount of BRB and SF for reducing the maximum story drift angle to the target $\theta_{\Sigma tar}$ is determided.

6) Step 6: Evaluate response reduction and required BRB capacity
As shown in Section 7.2, acceleration and displacement responses are affected by both the increased equivalent damping and stiffness. The response displacement reduction coefficient F_h is given by Equation (7.4.14) [7.4.5], with $a=25$ adopted considering the unstable response of RC structures compared to steel structures:

$$\frac{\theta_{\Sigma tar}}{\theta_{f\mu}} = \frac{T_{\Sigma\mu}}{T_{f\mu}}\sqrt{\frac{1+ah_{f\mu}}{1+ah_{eq}}} \quad (7.4.14)$$

The stiffening effect is calculated from the secant period at the target displacement of the existing frame $T_{f\mu}$ and retrofitted frame $T_{\Sigma\mu}$, by Equation 7.4.15.

$$\frac{T_{\Sigma\mu}}{T_{f\mu}} = \sqrt{\frac{K_{f\mu}}{K_{\Sigma\mu}}} = \sqrt{p\bigg/\left(p + \frac{K_d}{K_f}\left(\gamma_s + \frac{1}{\mu_d}\right)\right)} \quad (7.4.15)$$

The damper stiffness required to satisfy the target displacement can be directly determined, as well. First, Equation (7.4.14) is substituted into Equation (7.4.13).

$$p(1+ah_{f\mu})\left(\frac{\theta_{f\mu}}{\theta_{\Sigma tar}}\right)^2 = \left(p + \frac{K_d}{K_f}\left(\gamma_s + \frac{1}{\mu_d}\right)\right)(1+ah_{eq}) \quad (7.4.16)$$

Evaluating Equation (7.4.12,13), substituting it into Equation (7.4.16) and solving for the damper to frame stiffness ratio $r_d = K_d/K_f$ leads to the following closed form expression:

$$r_d = \frac{K_d}{K_f} = \frac{p\left(\left(\dfrac{\theta_{f\mu}}{\theta_{\Sigma tar}}\right)^2 - 1\right)\left(1 + a\left(h_0 + \dfrac{R}{\pi} \cdot \dfrac{p\mu_f + \mu_c - p\mu_f^{\lambda}\left(1 + \mu_c\right)}{p\mu_f + \mu_c}\right)\right)}{\left(1 + ah_0\right)\left(\gamma_s + \dfrac{1}{\mu_d}\right) + \dfrac{2aR}{\pi\mu_d}\left(1 - \dfrac{1}{\mu_d}\right)} \tag{7.4.17}$$

Recall that μ_f, μ_d and μ_c are the ductilities of the frame, damper and cracking of frame, α_1 and α_y denote the ratio of cracked tangent and post-yield secant stiffness to the initial frame stiffness, and γ_s is the ratio of the steel frame to damper stiffness.

7) Step 7: Distribute BRB

BRBs may be distributed along the height of the building by targeting a constant peak story drift [7.4.5].

a) The equivalent damping for the full structural system is constant
b) Under the Ai shear force distribution defined in Equation (7.2.8), the peak story drift for each story is equal to the target drift $\theta_{\Sigma tar}$.
c) The damper ductility μ_{di}, RC frame ductility μ_i, and steel frame to damper stiffness ratio γ_{si} is equal for all stories.

Considering condition a), Equation (7.4.18) is obtained.

$$\frac{\sum_{i=1}^{N} E_{di}}{\sum_{i=1}^{N}\left(E_{fei} + E_{dei}\right)} = \frac{E_d}{E_{fe} + E_{de}} \tag{7.4.18}$$

Substituting in the strain energy and each hysteretic energy term leads to Equation (7.4.19).

$$\frac{\sum_{i=1}^{N}\left[K_{di}\left(\mu_{di} - 1\right)\left(\theta_i \Delta H_i / \mu_{di}\right)^2\right]}{\sum_{i=1}^{N}\left[\left(K_{f\mu i} + K_{di}/\mu_{di} + \gamma_{si}K_{di}\right)\left(\theta_i \Delta H_i\right)^2\right]} = \frac{K_d\left(\mu_d - 1\right)}{\left(K_{f\mu} + K_d/\mu_d + \gamma_s K_d\right)\mu_d^2} \tag{7.4.19}$$

This reduces to Equation (7.4.20) by considering that the story parameters are constant from conditions b) and c), with $\theta_i = \theta$, $\mu_{di} = \mu_d$ and $\mu_{fi} = \mu_f$.

$$\sum_{i=1}^{N}\left(K_{di}\Delta H_i^2\right) \bigg/ \sum_{i=1}^{N}\left(K_{f\mu i}\Delta H_i^2\right) = K_d/K_{f\mu} \tag{7.4.20}$$

Applying the Ai distribution, the story drift becomes equal to:

$$\theta_{\Sigma tar} = \frac{Q_i \Delta H_i}{\left(K_{f\mu i} + \left(\gamma_s + 1/\mu_d\right)K_{di}\right)\Delta H_i^2} = \frac{\sum_{i=1}^{N}\left(Q_i \Delta H_i\right)}{\sum_{i=1}^{N}\left\{\left(K_{f\mu i} + \left(\gamma_s + 1/\mu_d\right)K_{di}\right)\Delta H_i^2\right\}} \tag{7.4.21}$$

Finally, the required damper stiffness K_{di} for an individual story is determined from Equation (7.4.22), which is obtained by substituting Equation (7.4.21) into Equation (7.4.20).

$$K_{di} = \frac{Q_i}{\Delta H_i} \frac{\sum_{i=1}^{N}\left(K_{f\mu i}\Delta H_i^2\right)}{\sum_{i=1}^{N}(Q_i \Delta H_i)}\left(\frac{1}{\gamma_s + 1/\mu_d} + \frac{\mu_f}{\alpha_y} \cdot r_d\right) - \frac{K_{f\mu i}}{\gamma_s + 1/\mu_d} \geq 0 \qquad (7.4.22)$$

When $\mu_f/\alpha_y=1$ and $\gamma_s=0$, above equation yields to Equation (7.2.17).

The design can be shortened starting with evaluating response before retrofit from response spectrum $S_d(T_{f\mu}, h_{f\mu})$ using Equations (7.4.2a), (7.4.13), then providing efficient BRBs and SFs following Equations (7.4.17) and (7.4.22).

To demonstrate the validity of this method, a BRB retrofit scheme for a typical five-story RC school building in Turkey is represented. The building shown in Figure 7.4.8 was constructed in 1992 in Istanbul, which is a high-risk seismic zone. Neither the structural member sizes nor reinforcement complies with current code provisions, where the longitudinal frame is weaker than the transverse direction.

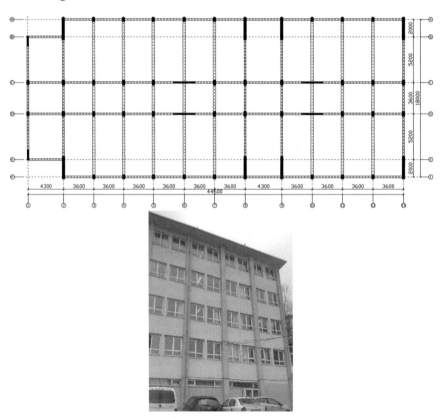

Figure 7.4.8. Typical RC school building in Turkey

Target story drift for a retrofit project is specified in various codes. In NEHRP Commentary on the Guidelines for Rehabilitation of Buildings (FEMA 273) [7.4.8], as well as FEMA 356 [7.4.9] and ATC-40 [7.4.10], the maximum story drift angle to achieve immediate occupancy is limited to 1/100. However, the Japanese Standard for

Seismic Diagnosis of Existing Reinforced Concrete Structures [7.4.3] recommends 1/150 rad which is also used in this example.

Push-over analysis of the existing RC frame is shown in Figure 7.4.9(a), where it is idealized as a trilinear model shown in Figure 7.4.9(b), with the yield point based on equivalent energy. Further simplification is shown in Figure 7.4.9(c) and Table 7.4.1 which is achieved by assuming identical story yield displacement and a perfectly plastic post-yielding phase. Eigenvalue analysis indicates an initial period of $T_0 = 0.7$ sec, with the equivalent mass $M_{eq} = 4433.5$ tons (Equation (7.2.9)) and height $H_{eq} = 10.5$ m (Equation 7.2.10). From Equation (7.4.1), the initial equivalent stiffness is $K_f = 356.8$ kN/mm. The frame ductility at the target story drift of 1/150 is obtained as $\mu_f = 1.42$.

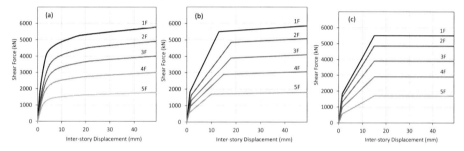

Figure 7.4.9. (a) Push-over curves for the model building (b) Substitute degrading tri-linear behavior (c) Simplified tri-linear behavior.

Table 7.4.1. Simplified tri-linear behavior values for model building.

	H_i (m)	$m_i g$ (kN)	K_f (kN/mm)	δ_{fc} (mm)	Q_{fc} (kN)	δ_{fy} (mm)	Q_{fy} (kN)
5F	16.0	5403	377.8	1.5	556.7	15	1700.0
4F	12.8	11779	644.4	1.5	966.7	15	2900.0
3F	9.6	11779	866.7	1.5	1300.0	15	3900.0
2F	6.4	11779	1077.8	1.5	1616.7	15	4850.0
1F	3.2	11779	1222.2	1.5	1833.3	15	5500.0

BRBs were selected with a core area of $A_c=55.5$cm^2, yield strength of $\sigma_y = 225$N/mm^2, plastic length ratio of $L_p/L_0=0.5$ and elastic area ratio of $A_e/A_c = 2.5$. The BRBs are installed at an angle of $\theta = 36.4°$ in a steel frame consisting of W10×10×49 (H-250×250×9×14) steel column and beam sections with a yield strength of $\sigma_{ySF} = 325$N/mm^2, producing a steel frame to BRB stiffness of $\gamma_s = 0.047$. The damper to frame stiffness is calculated from Equation (7.4.7) as $K_d/K_f = 2.25$, corresponding to the BRBs and the steel frame resisting 30% of the base shear. The equivalent damping of the retrofitted system is then calculated as $h_{eq} = 0.22$, with an equivalent period of $T_{\Sigma\mu} = 0.81$sec.

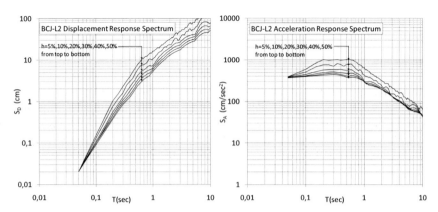

Figure 7.4.10. BCJ-L2 acceleration and displacement response spectrum
(h=5%, 10%, 20%, 30%, 40%, 50%)

The design spectrum is shown in Figure 7.4.10, with the retrofitted frame resulting in a spectral displacement of 6.69 cm, corresponding to a 1/157 story drift and achieving the target story drift. The number of BRBs installed at each level n_{di} is then calculated from Equation (7.4.24).

$$n_{di} = \frac{K_{di} \cdot \delta_{dyi}}{Q_{dy1}} \qquad (7.4.24)$$

Where Q_{dy1} is the yield force of a single BRB and δ_{dyi} the yield displacement, which can be evaluated by scaling from SDOF model by $\delta_{dyi} = (H_1/H_{eq})\,\delta_{dy}$.

For comparison, a retrofit alternative employing conventional braces (CBs) was also assessed. Brace sizes are summarized in Table 7.4.2 and use the same material as the BRBs. Time history analysis of lumped mass models was then conducted for the bare RC frame, BRBs without the steel frame and two retrofit schemes, with the CBs modeled using the Shibata-Wakabayashi buckling model [7.4.11].

Table 7.4.2. Number of BRBs and CBs applied per floor

	BRB cross-section	K_{di} (kN/mm)	Number of BRBs	CB cross-section	Number of CBs
5F	Plastic core 222mm×26mm A_p=5550mm²	850	4	W8×8×35 A=6540mm²	4
4F		1450	6		6
3F		1950	8		8
2F		2425	9		9
1F		2750	11		11

The maximum story drift obtained by the BCJ-L2 wave are shown in Figure 7.4.11. The bare RC frame greatly exceeds the target drift, while the BRB retrofit controls the response to within acceptable limits of 1/150. However, when the steel frame is excluded, damage concentrates at the second story and drift at this floor is obtained slightly over the target displacement. Due to the unbalanced behavior of the CBs in compression and tension, damage tends to concentrate on the first story once buckling is initiated.

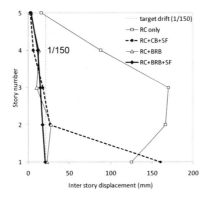

Figure 7.4.11. Maximum inter-story displacement distribution

In addition, the BRB retrofit scheme was analyzed for the set of records shown in Table 7.4.3 and Figure 7.4.12, which were scaled by BCJ-L2 wave at the target period of $T_{\Sigma\mu} = 0.81$s.

Table 7.4.3. Ground motion records used for dynamic time-history analysis

Input Motion	PGA (cm/sec^2)	S_A at T_μ^Σ =0.81sec (cm/sec^2)	Scaling factor (%)
Kobe - JMA (N-S)	817.85	1868.91	40.1
El Centro (N-S)	341.78	537.55	139.6
Miyagi Oki 1978 (N-S)	206.40	555.33	135.1
Taft – Kent County (E-W)	174.42	297.92	251.9
Northridge –Sylmar (N-S)	826.80	431.82	173.8
Hachinohe – Tokachi (E-W)	176.58	618.21	121.4
BCJ-L2	355.66	750.33	100.0

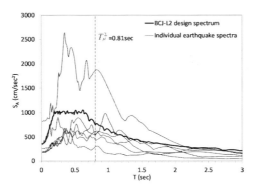

Figure 7.4.12. BCJ-L2 design spectra and unscaled records

The peak story drifts of the retrofitted model for each record are shown in Figure 7.4.13, with the mean response achieving the target drift.

168 Chapter 7. Applications for BRBF

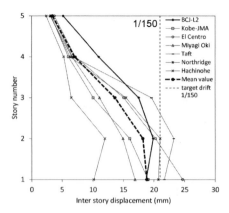

Figure 7.4.13. Maximum inter-story displacement distribution for selected earthquakes and mean inter-story displacement

Residual drift is another key criteria used in post-earthquake damage assessment [7.4.12]. A residual drift of less than approximately 1/200 is typically required for continued use of the building. This was confirmed by McCormick et al. [7.4.13], who studied the sensitivity of occupants due to residual deformations and found that occupants reported significant discomfort for residual inclinations greater than 1/125.

In the proposed retrofit, the steel frame is intended to remain elastic, providing significant restoring force and reducing residual displacements. The displacement time history is shown in Figure 7.4.14 for the bare and retrofitted frames, both with and without the supplementary steel frame. In general, the BRBs are effective in controlling the response, but only when the steel frame is included residual drifts are eliminated.

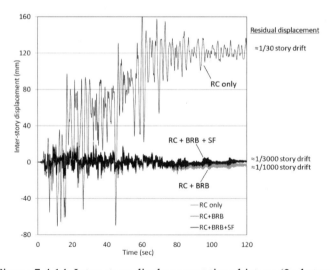

Figure 7.4.14. Inter-story displacement time-history (2nd story)

The robustness of the proposed retrofit method was also analyzed using incremental dynamic analysis (IDA) [7.4.14], with the spectral acceleration and peak story drift selected as the intensity and demand measures, respectively. As shown in Figure 7.4.15 (a), both the BRB and CB retrofits give similar and stable results up to 0.2g, at which point the CBs start to buckle.

The model retrofitted with BRBs exhibits a stable behavior even for intensities larger than 1g, which is the design intensity of this BRB. Figure 7.4.15(b) shows the IDA curves for maximum residual displacement, indicating that residual displacement attained by the RC building retrofitted with CBs exceeds acceptable values for input intensities larger than 0.6g. Even at 1g level of input motion the RC+BRB +SF model attains less than 1/2000 rad residual drift, which is a negligible value.

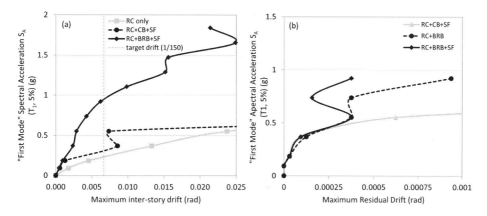

(a) maximum inter-story drift angle (b) maximum residual drift angle
Figure 7.4.15. IDA curves

Finally, the retrofit subassembly was tested at full scale in Istanbul Technical University to validate the composite response and connection details, as shown in Figure 7.4.16 [7.4.2]. The stiffness and strength was increased from the evaluated hysteresis due to composite connection between the steel and RC frame, but generally the proposed subassembly performed as intended. The hysteretic response and equivalent damping for cyclic loads of up to 0.67% drift (1/150) is shown in Figures 7.4.17 and 7.4.18, indicating stable energy dissipation corresponding to approximately 15% equivalent damping.

While R-model for RC frame and RS-model for RC+SF stays around 5% damping, RSB-model for RC+SF+BRB reaches 15% damping at 0.67% story drift.

7.4.16 Cyclic loading test for RC retrofit with BRB+SF

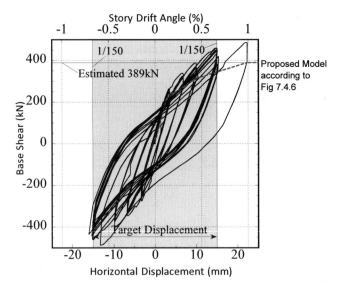

7.4.17 Obtained hysteresis compared with the proposed model

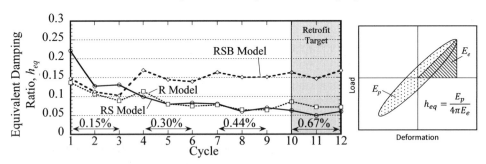

7.4.18 Equivalent damping ratio along the amplitudes and cycles

References

[7.4.1] Sutcu F, Takeuchi T, Matsui R: Seismic retrofit design method for RC buildings using buckling-restrained braces and steel frames. *Journal of Constructional Steel Research*, 2014; **101**:304-313.

[7.4.2] Fujishita K, Sutcu F, Matsui R, Takeuchi T: Damage Distribution based Energy-dissipation Retrofit Method for Multi-story RC Building in Turkey, *Proc. IABSE*, 2015

[7.4.3] Kenchiku Bosai: *Seismic evaluation and retrofit*. English Version, 2001.

[7.4.4] Takeda T, Sozen MA, Nielsen NN: Reinforced concrete response to simulated earthquakes. *J Struct Div ASCE*, 1970; **96**(12):2557–2573.

[7.4.5] Japan Society of Seismic Isolation: *Passive response control design manual, 2nd edition*, 2005. (*in Japanese and Chinese*)

[7.4.6] Jacobsen LS: Damping in composite structures. *Proc. of 2nd World Conference on Earthquake Engineering*, Japan; 1960, 1029-1044.

[7.4.7] Newmark NM, Rosenblueth E: *Fundamentals of earthquake engineering*.

New Jersey: Prentice-Hall Inc., 1971.

[7.4.8] Federal emergency management agency: *NEHRP guidelines for the seismic rehabilitation of buildings, FEMA 273.* 1997.

[7.4.9] Federal emergency management agency: *Prestandard and commentary for the seismic rehabilitation of buildings, FEMA 356.* 2000.

[7.4.10] Applied Technology Council: *Seismic Evaluation and Retrofit of Concrete Buildings, ATC 40 Report.* 1996.

[7.4.11] Shibata M, Wakabayashi M: Mathematical expression of hysteretic behavior of braces—part 2 application of dynamic response analysis. *Trans AIJ* 1982, (320), 29–35. (*In Japanese*)

[7.4.12] Yazgan U, Dazio A: Post-earthquake damage assessment using residual displacements. *Earthquake Engineering & Strucural Dynamics*, 2012; (41), 1257-1276.

[7.4.13] McCormick J, Aburano H, Ikenaga M, Nakashima M: Permissible Residual Deformation Levels for Building Structures Considering Both Safety and Human Elements. *14th World Conference on Earthquake Engineering, Beijing, China*; 2008

[7.4.14] Vamvatsikos D, Cornell CA: Incremental dynamic analysis. *Earthquake Engneering and Structural Dynamics* 2002; **31**(3):491–514.

7.5 DIRECT CONNECTIONS TO RC FRAMES

7.5.1 Conventional applications and major problems

As described in Section 7.4, Buckling restrained braces (BRBs) have been increasingly used in reinforced concrete (RC) structures during the past decades over the world in either existing buildings [7.5.1]-[7.5.3] or in new projects [7.5.4]. Although RC moment-resisting frames exhibit higher lateral stiffness than steel frames do, the effectiveness of using BRBs to mitigate the seismic damage to RC frames has been demonstrated through both numerical analyses and experimental tests [7.5.5]-[7.5.7]. It can be simply understood by comparing the yield deformation of BRBs and RC frames. As proposed by Priestley et al. [7.5.6], the yield story drift ratio, R_y, of frame buildings can be empirically estimated as $R_y = 0.5\varepsilon_y L_B/h_B$ for RC frames and $R_y = 0.65\varepsilon_y L_B/h_B$ for steel frames, where ε_y is the yield strain of longitudinal reinforcing bars or structural steel, L_B and h_B are the span and depth of beams, respectively. Assuming $\varepsilon_y = 0.002$ and $L_B/h_B = 15$ as a practical case, the yield drift ratio is 1/67 for RC frames and 1/50 for steel frames. In a buckling restrained braced frame (BRBF), these drift ratios are much greater than the drift ratio at which the BRBs yield, which is usually less than 1/400 in the design practice in Japan. In other words, the braced frame structural system, no matter the frame is an RC or a steel one, can take great advantage of the plastic deformation of BRBs to dissipate earthquake energy and thus mitigate structural responses before the frame yields.

Similar to applications in steel structures, the bracing configurations in Figure 7.5.1 are among the most commonly used ones for RC structures with BRBs. Nevertheless, there remain several challenges when combining steel braces with concrete frames. A significant challenge is to transfer the brace tension force to concrete members which are inherently weak in tension. Conventional solutions include attaching or inserting steel braced frames instead of separate braces to RC frames by extensive anchor bolts, as explained in 7.3. This practice is widely used in Japan for seismic retrofit of existing RC frames and efforts have been made to reduce the number of anchor bolts to lower the cost and environmental impact [7.5.7]-[7.5.9].

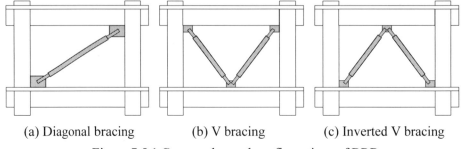

(a) Diagonal bracing (b) V bracing (c) Inverted V bracing

Figure 7.5.1 Commonly-used configurations of BRBs

For new constructions, an intuitive solution is to embed some steel parts in concrete members to receive the brace gusset connections. Ogawa et al. [7.5.9] reported their test on V and inverted-V BRB RC frames. A considerable amount of wide flange steel was embedded in the concrete members, primarily in the beams and the beam-to-column joints, to receive the BRB gusset plates (Figure 7.5.2). Gu et al. [7.5.10] also attempted to apply BRBs in newly-built RC frame buildings. Following the connection details recommended by [7.5.11]- [7.5.13], steel cages consisting of top

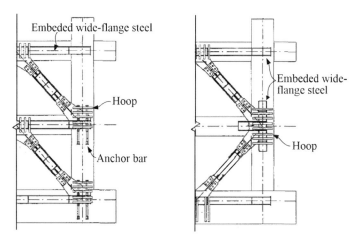

Figure 7.5.2 BRB connections by embedded wide-flange steel (Ogawa et al. 2004)

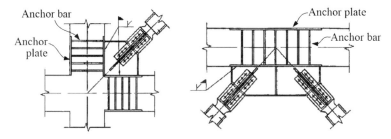

Figure 7.5.3 BRB connections by embedded anchor plate and anchor bars

and bottom anchor plates that were connected by anchor bars, were embedded at the end of beams and columns to receive BRB gusset plates (Figure 7.5.3).

Another problem comes from the detrimental interaction between gusset plates and frame members, which is usually referred to as the 'frame action' (Figure 7.5.4). Kishiki et al. [7.5.14] investigated the stress concentration at the toes of corner gussets in steel braced frames because of the frame action. Tsai et al. [7.5.15] showed through a full scale pseudo dynamic test that such concentrated stress may lead to premature fracture of gusset plates. Chou et al. [7.5.16] demonstrated in their experimental test that corner gusset plates could buckle at much lower story drift than expected when free-edge stiffeners were absent. Numerical analysis showed that the force in gusset plates resulting from the frame action was on the same order as the brace axial force.

In addition to its detrimental effect on gusset plates, the frame action may also result in considerable over-strength in RC frames and sometimes unfavorable shear failure of adjoining concrete columns [7.5.17] by reducing their effective lengths (Figure 7.5.5). It is impractical to include such complicated behavior of gusset connections in structural modelling for routine design purposes. Instead, braces are usually assumed to be pin-connected to the frame and truss elements are used to simulate braces, such as those conducted by [7.5.18] and [7.5.19].

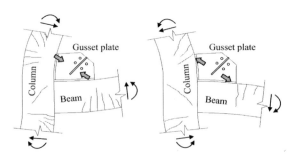

Figure 7.5.4 Frame action in RC frames with BRBs when (a) frame pinches and (b) frame opens

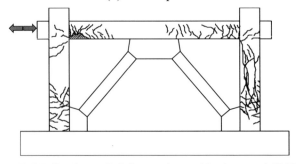

Figure 7.5.5 Cracks on RC frames braced by inverted-V BRBs under static cyclic loading (reproduced based on [7.5.17])

While specific design methods can be developed to address the effect of frame action in corner gussets [7.5.20], new corner gusset configurations were proposed to avoid frame action. Ishii et al. [7.5.21] anchored the gusset plates of BRBs to the side surfaces of RC beam ends by post-tensioned steel rods. As observed in their test, the damage to the underneath concrete would considerably impair the effectiveness of the connection and thus reduce the energy dissipation of BRBs when such a connection is placed at the beam end, where plastic hinges are expected.

In the following sections, a variety of innovative applications of BRBs in RC frames are introduced.

7.5.2 Unconstrained gusset connection for BRBs in RC frames

Berman and Bruneau [7.5.22] proposed an unconstrained gusset connection for steel constructions, in which the gusset plate is separated with the column by an intended gap and bolted to the beam end. This idea can also be applied for BRBs in RC frames. Qu et al. [7.5.23] proposed two different connection details for unconstrained gusset plate in RC structures. One uses post-tensioned steel rods to fasten gusset plates on top surfaces of beams (denoted as PT type hereinafter, Figure 7.5.6 (a)) and in the other case, extensions of gusset plates are embedded within the underneath concrete beam (denoted as EB type hereinafter, Figure 7.5.6 (b)). The unconstrained gusset connection features an intended gap that separates the gusset plate from the column to prevent it from touching the column surface even if the structure sustains large lateral drift.

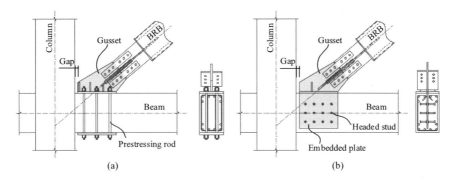

Figure 7.5.6 Unconstrained gusset connections: (a) post-tensioned (PT) type and (b) embedded plate (EB) type [7.5.23]

For PT type, high-strength steel rods go through the beam and are post-tensioned to fasten the base plate of the gusset on the beam. The shear force on the gusset plate is resisted by the friction between the base plate and the concrete surface, while the tensile force is resisted by post-tensioning of the steel rods. Because both friction action and post-tensioned rods exhibits very high stiffness, such a connection is expected to be very stiff.

For EB type, the gusset plate extends into the beam and is anchored there by headed stud groups on both sides of the embedded plate. The embedment does not go into the beam- column joint to ease the load transfer as well as to avoid hindrance to the joint reinforcement. Rather than making holes on the embedded plate to give way to closed stirrups, open stirrups with 135° hooks are used for easier construction. Since the embedded plate can contribute a lot to the shear strength of the concrete beam within the embedment region, the amount of stirrups in this segment are not a critical issue.

To address the aforementioned problems reported by Ishii et al. [7.5.21], local 'damage control' is necessary for the connection region in which the RC beam end that receives the unconstrained BRB gusset is preferred to remain free of damage even if the structure is subjected to major earthquakes. In particular, the potential plastic hinge that usually occurs at the RC beam end is preferred to be relocated to outside the gusset connection region (i.e., forward to the center of the span). This shares the same concept as the reduced beam sections (RBS) in steel moment-resisting frames [7.5.24].

The intended location of beam plastic hinges can be controlled by re-arranging the beam longitudinal rebars to adjust the flexural strength of different beam segments. As shown in Figure 7.5.7, a braced beam without such 'damage control' (DC) (Figure 7.5.7(b)) has the same longitudinal reinforcement as a bare frame beam (Figure 7.5.7(a)), which is expected to yield at the end (i.e., Section I) under major earthquakes. In this case, the beam yield force, V_{By}, of the braced beam is likely to be less than that of the bare frame beam, V_{B0}, because the flexural strength at Section I is reduced from M_{I0} to M_{Iy} by the effect of tensile force, F_N, of the brace.

The plastic hinge can be moved to Section II if the amount of rebars there is reduced and that at Section I is increased so that the flexural strength $M_{IIy} = M_{II0}$ and $M_{Iy} > M_{I0}$, where M_{II0} is the moment at Section II when M_{I0} is reached at Section I (Figure 7.5.7(c)). Section II is offset by L_h outside the gusset connection region. In such a manner, the beam yield force, V_{By}, remains equal to V_{B0}. More importantly, the beam

176   Chapter 7. Applications for BRBF

segment between Section I and II would keep essentially elastic and free of damage so that the brace can work well with the rest of the system even if the beam segment outside the gusset connection is heavily damaged.

Full-scale half-span cantilever beams with brace gusset connections were subjected to static cyclic loading to examine the behavior of unconstrained gusset connection with local damage control schemes. To simplify the loading setup, the cantilever beams were rotated 90° and cast into RC stubs at the bottom, which were fastened to the lab's strong floor through six post-tensioned steel rods and were blocked by a pair of steel shear keys on both sides (Figure 7.5.8).

The main dimensions of the specimens are shown in Figure 7.5.7 and Figure 7.5.8. In particular, the base plate of the gusset plate was 440 mm long and placed 10 mm away from the stub surface to keep the gusset plate away from the stub surface even if the beam sustains as large as 10% chord rotation. The beam free end (i.e. the upper end in the test setup) was driven by two 200 kN displacement-controlled actuators in parallel. Instead of using real BRBs, a 1000 kN force-controlled actuator was used to simulate the brace axial force on the gusset plate. The nominal strength of the BRB in test was assumed to be 500 kN.

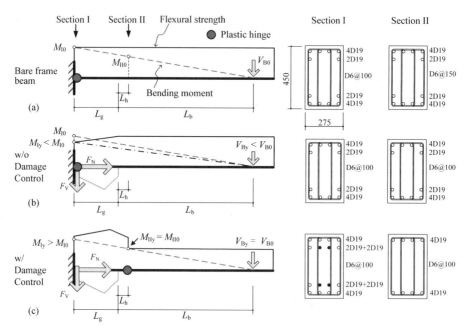

Figure 7.5.7 Control of beam plastic hinge relocation: (a) Bare beam, (b) braced beam without damage control and (c) braced beam with damage control

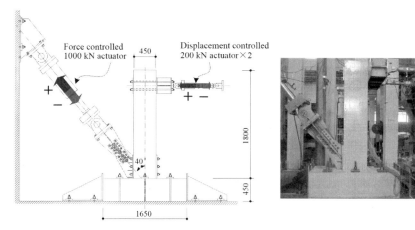

Figure 7.5.8 Cyclic loading test setup of unconstrained gusset connection

The combination of two types of connection details and two sets of beam reinforcement leads to four specimens of braced beams. A bare beam was also included as the control specimen. Therefore, a total of five specimens were tested by the above setup (Table 7.5.1). Cyclic static loading was performed with gradually increased story drift amplitudes. The hysteresis of the BRB was assumed to be elastic-perfectly plastic during the loading.

In Figure 7.5.9 and 7.5.10, the damage to the RC beams are summarized in terms of apparent cracks and strain distributions of the longitudinal rebars. The beam in Specimen No.1 is an ordinary cantilever RC beam which yielded at the fixed end. Cracks wider than 0.2 mm on the beam surface clearly indicated a plastic hinge at the fixed end, while some of them were wide spread along the beam.

Table 7.5.1 Specimen properties

Specimen	No.1 (Bare)	No.2	No.3	No.4	No.5
Connecting method	-	PT	EB	PT	EB
Stud	-	-	24ϕ16	-	24ϕ16
Post-tensioned rod	-	6ϕ21 (C)	-	6ϕ21 (C)	-
Post-tensioning force (kN)	-	1489.6	-	1466.5	-
Damage control	-	No	No	Yes	Yes
Concrete compressive strength (MPa)*	70.7	70.7	70.0	70.7	71.4
Concrete elastic modulus (MPa)*	42648	42648	39333	42648	36996

* obtained by compression tests on 150 by 300-mm concrete cylinders.

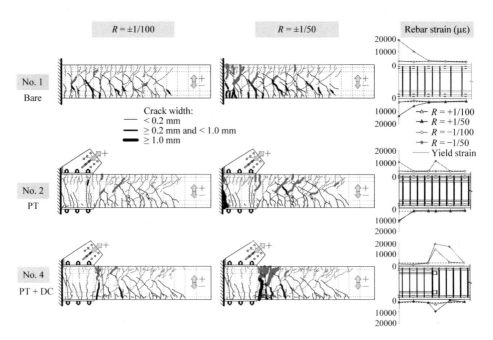

Figure 7.5.9 Effects of RC beam hinge relocation

For Specimen No.2 and No.3, the beams also yielded at the fixed end during the positive loading. During negative loading, however, they yielded at both the fixed end and the section immediately outside the gusset plate. Major cracks of Specimen No.3 (EB) spread widely into the gusset plate region while those of No.2 (PT) were much constrained near the beam-to-column interface because the concrete underneath the gusset plate is confined by the pre-stressed rods.

For Specimen No.4 and No.5 in which the beam reinforcement is adjusted for damage control, the longitudinal rebars only yielded at sections outside the gusset plate region and major cracks also concentrated there, indicating that the plastic hinges of the beams were successfully moved outside the connection region. Because of the pre-stress of the concrete, the cracks within the connection region in Specimen No.4 (PT+DC) were much less than those in No.5 (EB+DC) and were almost perpendicular to the beam axis.

These results confirmed that the design of local damage control at RC beam end was effective in moving potential plastic hinges to outside the connection region. A significant benefit of doing so is to prevent BRBs from dislocating from the rest of the structure in case the beam fails in extreme earthquake events.

Figure 7.5.10 Cracks on RC beams with unconstrained gusset plates

7.5.3 Continuously buckling restrained braced RC frames

The 'continuously buckling restrained braced frame' (CBRBF) system provides a system-level approach for better connecting BRBs to concrete members [7.5.25]. As illustrated in Figure 7.5.11, BRBs in the system are arranged in a zigzag layout and those in neighboring stories share the same gusset plate so that they run continuously along the height of the structure. Instead of fitting into the corners of beams and columns, shared gusset plates are attached to the sides of beam-column joints so that the 'frame action' in conventional corner gusset connections is avoided, making it much easier to determine the capacity demands for connections. This is made possible by eliminating beams in the braced span, which are zero-force members if the braced span is considered as a planar cantilevered truss (Figure 7.5.12). In the truss analogy, the removal of vertical zero-force web members has no effect on forces of other members and makes the truss into a 'Warren truss,' which has long been received as an efficient structural system for bridges. It can be equally efficient as a lateral system for building structures when erected vertically, as in the CBRBF system.

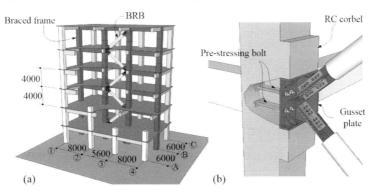

Figure 7.5.11 RC frame with BRBs in zigzag configuration: (a) structural layout and BRB configuration and (b) details of BRB connection [7.5.25]

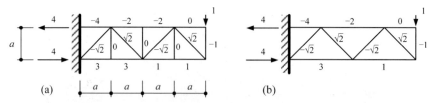

Figure 7.5.12 Truss analogy for a concentrically braced frame: (a) with vertical web members and (b) without vertical web members (Warren truss)

While other connection details may also be available, it is recommended to anchor gusset plates by post-tensioning bolts embedded in beam-column joints along with pairs of RC corbels that jut out from columns on both the top and bottom ends of gusset plates (Figure 7.5.11(b)). The horizontal (i.e., the embedded bolts) and the vertical (i.e., RC corbels) resistances of the connection are essentially independent of each other, so both the bolts and the corbels are under relatively simple load conditions. Therefore, their behavior becomes easier to predict and control.

To validate the proposed connection detail, cyclic loading test on 1/2-scale subassemblies of CBRBF system was conducted. The subassemblage, which is colored in red in Figure 7.5.11(a), is separated from the rest of the architype structure by assuming that the inflection points of both the beam and the column are located at the mid-length, and its 1/2-scale models were taken as the test specimens. The RC part of a specimen consisted of a column extending half the story height above and below the joint, and a half-span beam framing into it.

The subassembly specimens were rotated 90 degrees and were loaded by the test setup shown in Figure 7.5.13, which can accomplish necessary boundary conditions that are equivalent to those when the un-rotated subassemblies were loaded laterally.

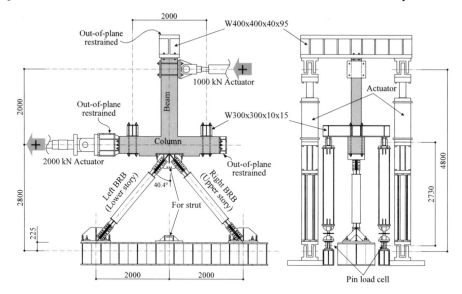

Figure 7.5.13 Test setup for RC frame subassemblage with BRBs in zigzag configuration

Cyclic loading with increasing story drift amplitudes was conducted for each specimen. Figure 7.5.14 shows the cracks of the RC part of a specimen during positive and negative loading at 1/50 story drift ratio. The flexural-shear cracks of the column appeared only in the lower half of the column during positive loading (Figure 7.5.14(a)) and only in the upper half of the column during negative loading (Figure 7.5.14(b)). In other words, the column segment underneath the active corbel was free of flexural cracking. This suggests that the column underneath the active corbel was subject to much less moment than the other half.

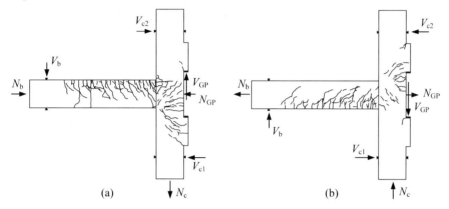

Figure 7.5.14 Cracks on RC parts in a subassemblage specimen at: (a) +1/50 and (b) -1/50 story drift ratio

Although obvious rotations at the ends of the BRBs was observed in the subassemblage test, all BRBs exhibited stable hysteresis practically the same as that in a uniaxial component test, which was carried out on a 750kN BRB before the subassemblage test (Figure 7.5.15).

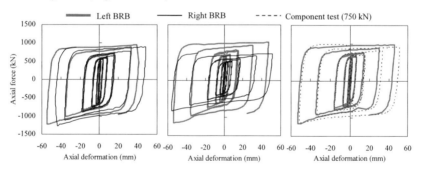

Figure 7.5.15 BRB hysteresis

The effect of employing buckling restrained braces in RC frames is demonstrated through a case study of a 36-story RC building as shown in Figure 7.5.16. Two different BRB configurations are adopted to enhance the seismic resistance of the bare frame. In one configuration, conventional single diagonal BRBs are installed in the middle span of each story of the building, while in the other configuration, the afore-mentioned continuous buckling restrained braced frame (CBRBF) is adopted, in which the RC beams in the braced span are replaced by steel link beams with pins on both ends. The cross sections of the RC columns in the braced span are enlarged and the rebars are increased. In addition, every BRB in the CBRBF configuration spans over two stories. The fundamental periods of the two braced frames are both 2.77 s, while that of the bare frame is 2.92 s. Full details of the structural systems can be found in [7.5.26].

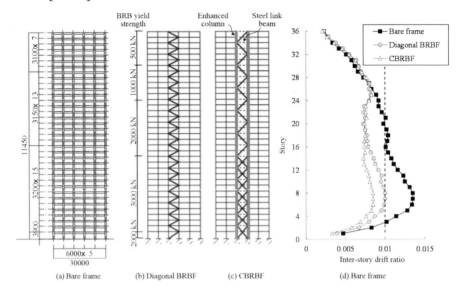

Figure 7.5.16 Structural configurations of a 36-story RC building of (a) bare frame; (b) diagonal BRBF and (c) CBRBF and (d) their seismic response under simulated Hachinohe record at PGV=75 cm/s.

Nonlinear time history analysis of the three structural systems is conducted on MIDAS Gen Ver. 830 (MIDAS Information Technology Co., LTD., 2012). Modified Takeda model is used for the RC columns and beams. Tangent stiffness-proportional damping is adopted with a damping ratio of 0.03. The BRBs are modeled by truss elements with elasto-perfectly plastic hysteresis. Six ground motion records are used as the earthquake input and are normalized to PGV=50 and 75 cm/s, respectively, to define two intensity levels. The maximum story drifts of the three systems under the simulated Hachinohe record of PGV=75 cm/s are depicted in Figure 7.5.16(d).

Although the periods of the three systems are similar, the braced frames sustained much smaller maximum inter-story drift. In addition, the maximum inter-story drift of the CBRBF is even smaller than that of the diagonal BRBF. This reduction is consistent with the higher energy dissipation efficiency of the BRBs in CBRBF. The accumulated energy dissipations of the BRB at the 23rd story of the diagonal BRBF and the CBRBF are compared in Figure 7.5.17. For CBRBF, half of the energy dissipation of the BRB that spans over the 23rd and the 24th stories is depicted.

The energy dissipated by the BRB in the CBRBF system is almost 5 times that of the counterpart BRB in the conventional diagonal BRBF system at the end of the ground shaking. This difference is primarily attributed to two factors. First, because a BRB in the CBRBF spans over two stories, its axial deformation for a given story drift is expected to be two times that of a BRB in the conventional diagonal BRBF, while the former BRB is only about 20% longer than the latter one. As a result, the plastic strain in the BRBs that span over two stories is much larger. In addition, the braced span in the CBRBF is expected to deform more because of the RC beams are eliminated. This also helps increase the plastic strain in the BRBs.

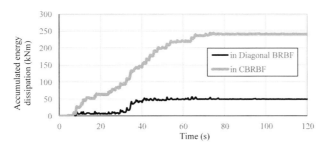

Figure 7.5.17 Accumulated energy dissipation of BRB at 23rd story (PGV=75 cm/s)

The BRBF system is supposed to vibrate primarily in its first mode and higher modes would not have significant influence on the maximum lateral drift. However, higher modes may significantly influence the internal forces in the system, and in turn may impair the BRB force balance at the local connection. This is evident from the results of nonlinear time history analysis on a 12-story RC frame with buckling restrained braces in zigzag configuration as shown in Figure 7.5.18(a) [7.5.27]. The BRB-to-concrete connection was modelled by specifically proposed nonlinear spring models as shown in Figure 7.5.18(b). The analysis results show that there is significant horizontal force although it is supposed to be negligible if the system deforms in its first mode. By comparing the time history results during 2 s to 5 s of the inter-story drift at the 7th floor and that of the forces in the BRB connection at the same floor, it is shown that the peak story drifts, as indicated by hollow circles in the figure, take place when the vertical force is at its maximum and the horizontal force is very small. In other words, there is a phase difference between the peak story drift and peak horizontal force.

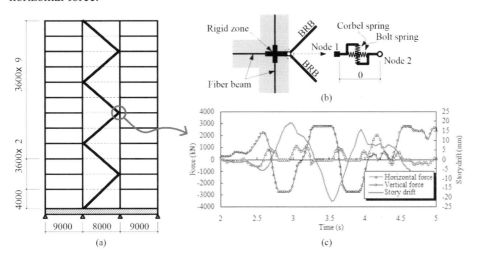

Figure 7.5.18 (a) Architype building for analysis, (b) modeling of BRB connection and (c) force time history at BRB connection

Figure 7.5.19 depicts the 1st and 2nd modal forces of the upper BRB connecting to the 7th floor. The modal forces obtained by the nonlinear (NL) dynamic analysis is compared with that obtained by linear elastic (LE) analysis. The 1st mode BRB force is suppressed by yielding while the 2nd mode force in nonlinear analysis remains comparable to that in linear elastic analysis. The maximum force of the 2nd mode is only 16% of that of the 1st mode in the linear elastic analysis, while this ratio grows up to 87% in nonlinear analysis. In the 2nd mode, neighboring BRBs in some stories may deform in the same direction, i.e., both in tension or in compression. This may lead to significant horizontal force demand for the bolt connection (Figure 7.5.19). Such effects of higher modes on both the magnitudes and distribution of internal forces have been observed and reported in previous research for either slender shear walls [7.5.28] or moment resisting frames even if the first mode dominates the vibration [7.5.29].

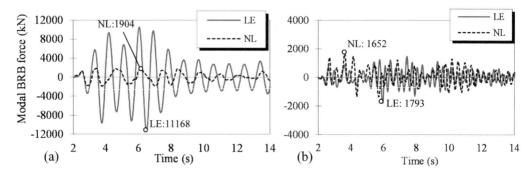

Figure 7.5.19 Modal decomposition of the axial force of the upper BRB connecting to the 7th floor under the JMA Kobe-NS: (a) 1st mode and (b) 2nd mode.

7.5.4 Double-K braced RC frames with BRBs

The double-K bracing as shown in Figure 7.5.20 provides a solution to eliminate the aforementioned detrimental higher mode effect [7.5.30]. Similar to those in zigzag configurations, the BRBs in a double-K configuration share gusset plates. The two neighboring braces are always acting in opposite directions, that is, one in tension and the other in compression. This mechanism is not influenced by higher mode vibration because it takes place within a single story. Ideally, when BRBs of the same properties are used in a single span, there will be little unbalanced tension force on the gusset plate. As a result, much less studs or post-installed anchors would be required to transfer the brace axial force to the concrete. Some unbalanced compression force may rise from the higher compression strength of BRBs.

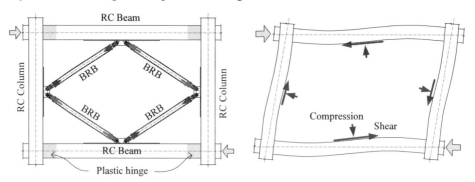

Figure 7.5.20 RC frames braced by BRBs in double-K configuration

In double-K bracing, the gusset connections at the mid-length of the beams and columns are free of the detrimental 'frame action', and are thus easier to proportion. In addition, the gusset connections are away from the potential 'plastic hinges' at the

RC beam ends, and therefore the inelastic behavior (e.g., concrete cracking, rebar yielding) would not interact with the gusset connections in an unintended manner. For quick construction, the four BRBs and their gusset plates in a single span can be prefabricated as an integrated energy-dissipating unit ready to be shipped to the site for on-site installation.

Three 1/2-scaled RC frame subassemblies were subjected to cyclic loading with increasing lateral drift amplitudes to assess the seismic damage to RC frames and the cyclic performance of BRBs in double-K configuration. Two of the specimens were braced by BRBs, whereas the other one was a bare frame counterpart for comparison. To simulate the behavior of a middle story in a multi-story building, the RC part in each subassembly consists of two beams framing into two columns. Four identical BRBs were installed in a double-K configuration in each braced specimen. The BRBs were bolted to the gusset plates, which were anchored to the RC beams or columns by either embedded stud group or post-installed chemical anchor for the two braced specimens.

The specimens were mounted on two mechanical pins that were firmly fastened on the strong floor (Figure 7.5.21). Two horizontal actuators of 1000 kN capacity were employed to load the specimens. The upper actuator was displacement-controlled to impose the desired inter-story drift ratio (IDR) on the specimen, while the lower actuator was force-controlled to fully counteract the upper actuator so that the bottom mechanical pins were waived from excessive shear.

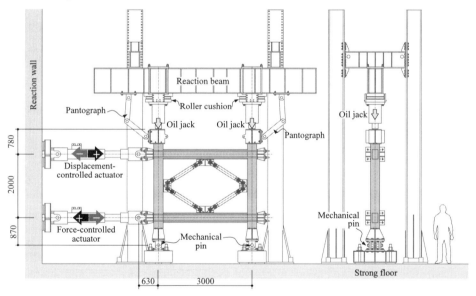

Figure 7.5.21 Test setup for RC frames braced by BRBs in double-K configuration [0]

Figure 7.5.22 compares the concrete cracking of the bare frame specimen and a braced specimen. Regardless of the existence of the BRBs, the crack pattern (both the distribution and widths) of the braced specimen was similar to that of the bare frame specimen. As intended, most damage was concentrated in the beam ends, where major cracks developed and slight concrete spalling was observed at the final stage of the loading. In the braced specimen, cracks were first observed on the beams, and no cracks were found on the columns until the second load cycle of IDR = 1/100. At IDR = 1/100, a few cracks at the beam ends grew to wider than 0.2 mm. These cracks continued to open and some of them became wider than 1.0 mm at IDR = 1/50. Cracks on the columns were distributed at the beam-to-column joints and regions close to the joints. The column crack widths were considerably smaller than those on the beams.

This shows that the BRBs and their gusset connections in the double-K configuration would not deteriorate the seismic performance of the RC frame. The similar levels of damage should not be interpreted in a way that the BRBs bring no benefit to reduce the structural damage because such a similarity is observed at the same story drift. The maximum story drift of an RC frame equipped with BRBs would be much less than that of a bare frame because of the additional stiffness and energy dissipation provided by the braces. In such cases, the damage to the RC frame braced by BRBs is expected to be much less than that to a bare frame.

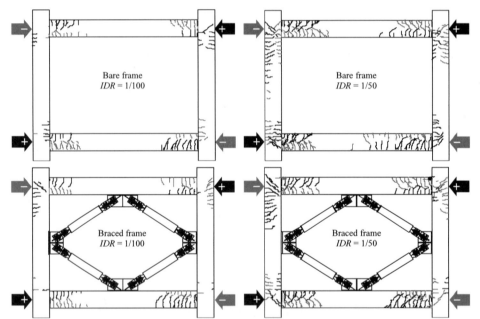

Figure 7.5.22 Cracks on RC frames with or without BRBs

7.5.5 Summary

The results of both experimental tests and numerical simulations show that BRBs would yield at much smaller lateral drift than RC frames do and therefore are efficient in dissipating earthquake energy to protect the RC frames. However, the interaction between BRBs and concrete members may impair the performance of BRB-RC systems and even may impose safety issues if brace connections were not properly designed. Innovative approaches of applying BRBs in RC frames are introduced in this section to address the connection issue in the component-level (i.e., unconstrained gusset connection), subassembly-level (i.e., double-K braced frame with BRBs) and system-level (i.e., CBRBF system). All these approaches provide effective control of the local damage around BRB connections by reducing complicated and often detrimental interaction between BRBs and concrete members.

References

[7.5.1] Kukita S, Haginoya M, Miyagawa K, Kinoshita R, Fujisawa K, Fujinaga T et al.: Experimental Study on Seismic Retrofit for Existing R/C Building by using CHS Bracing. *Summaries of Technical Papers of AIJ Annual Meeting*, 2000, C-2, Structure IV:377-382. (*in Japanese*)

[7.5.2] Brown AP, Aiken ID, Jafarzadeh FJ: Buckling Restrained Braces Provide the Key to the Seismic Retrofit of the Wallace F. Bennett Federal Building. *Modern Steel Construction*, 2001.

[7.5.3] Di Sarno L and Manfredi G: Seismic retrofitting with buckling restrained braces: Application to an existing non-ductile RC framed building. *Soil Dynamics and Earthquake Engineering*, 2010; **30**(11):1279-1297.

[7.5.4] Oviedo AJA, Midorikawa M and Asari T: Earthquake response of ten-story story-drift-controlled reinforced concrete frames with hysteretic dampers. *Engineering Structures*, 2010; **32**(6):1735-1758.

[7.5.5] Di Sarno L and Manfredi G: Experimental tests on full-scale RC unretrofitted frame and retrofitted with buckling restrained braces. *Earthquake Engineering and Structural Dynamics*, 2012; **41**(2):315-333

[7.5.6] Priestley MJN, Calvi GM, Kowalsky MJ: Displacement-based seismic design of structures. *IUSS Press, Pavia, Italy*, 2007;223-224.

[7.5.7] Ishimura M, Sadasue K, Miyauchi Y, Yokoyama T, Fujii T and Minami K: Seismic Performance Evaluation for Retrofitting Steel Brace of Existing RC Buildings with Low-Strength Concrete. *Proc. of 15th World Conference on Earthquake Engineering, Lisbon, Portugal*, 2012.

[7.5.8] Harayama K, Kawamoto T, Inai E and Matsukane Y: An experimental study of a seismic retrofitting method with framed steel brace systems partially and concentrically jointed with anchors. *Proc. of 15th World Conference on Earthquake Engineering, Lisbon, Portugal*, 2012.

[7.5.9] Ogawa Y, Isoda K, Kitamura Y, et al.: Experimental study on the structural properties of high strength reinforced concrete frames with brace dampers. *Summaries of Technical Papers of AIJ Annual Meeting*, 2004;1227-1230. (*in Japanese*)

[7.5.10] Gu LZ, Gao XY, Xu JW, et al.: Research on seismic performance of BRB concrete frames. *Journal of Building Structures*, 2011; **32**(7):101-111. (*in Chinese*)

[7.5.11] GJBT-1092: National building standard design drawing for passive controlled building structures. *China Institute of Building Standard Design & Research*, 2009. (*in Chinese*)

[7.5.12] Benavent-Climent A, Oliver-Saiz E, Donaire-Avila J: New connection between reinforced concrete building frames and concentric braces: Shaking table tests. *Engineering Structures*, 2015; **96**(1):7-21.

[7.5.13] Ichikawa Y, Okayasu T, Nakamura H, Yamada S, Wada A: Experimental study on joint of seismic retrofitting brace for steel structure using shear-key plate adhered to concrete slab. *AIJ J. Struct. Constr. Eng.*, 2005; **596**:133-40. (*in Japanese*)

[7.5.14] Kishiki S, Yamada S, Wada A: Experimental evaluation of structural behavior of gusset plate connection in BRB frame system. *Proc. of 14th World Conference on Earthquake Engineering, Beijing, China*, 2008.

[7.5.15] Tsai KC, Hsiao PC, Wang KJ, Weng TT, Lin ML, Lin KC, Chen CH, Lai JW; Lin SL: Pseudo-dynamic tests of a full-scale CFT/BRB frame - Part I: Specimen design, experiment and analysis. *Earthquake Engineering and Structural Dynamics*, 2008; **37**(7):1081-1098.

[7.5.16] Chou CC, Liu JH, Pham DH: Steel buckling-restrained braced frames with single and dual corner gusset connections: seismic tests and analyses. *Earthquake Engineering and Structural Dynamics*, 2012; **41**(7):1137-1156.

[7.5.17] Maheri MR, Ghaffarzadeh H: Connection overstrength in steel-braced RC frames. *Engineering Structures*, 2008; **30**(7):1938-1948.

[7.5.18] Sabelli R, Mahin S, Chang C: Seismic demands on steel braced frame buildings with buckling-restrained braces. *Engineering Structures*, 2003; **25**(5):655-666.

[7.5.19] Ariyaratana C, Fahnestock LA: Evaluation of buckling-restrained braced frame seismic performance considering reserve strength. *Engineering Structures*, 2011; **33**(1):77-89.

[7.5.20] Lin PC, Tsai KC, Wu AC and Chuang MC: Seismic design and test of gusset connections for buckling-restrained braced frames. *Earthquake Engineering and Structural Dynamics*, 2014; **43**(4):565-587.

[7.5.21] Ishii T, Mukai T, Kitamura H, Shimizu T, Fujisawa K and Ishida Y. Seismic Retrofit for Existing R/C Building Using Energy Dissipative Braces. *13th World Conference on Earthquake Engineering*, 2004.

[7.5.22] Berman JW and Bruneau M: Cyclic testing of a buckling restrained braced frame with unconstrained gusset connections. *ASCE Journal of Structural Engineering*, 2009; **135**(12):1499-1510.

[7.5.23] Qu Z, Kishiki S, Maida Y, Sakata H: Subassemblage cyclic loading tests of buckling restrained braced RC frames with unconstrained gusset connections. *ASCE Journal of Structural Engineering*, 2016; **142**(2):04015128.

[7.5.24] Jones SL, Fry GT and Engelhardt MD: Experimental evaluation of cyclically loaded reduced beam section moment connections. *ASCE Journal of Structural Engineering*, 2002; **128**(4):441-451.

[7.5.25] Qu Z, Kishiki S, Sakata H, Wada A, Maida Y: Subassemblage cyclic loading test of RC frame with buckling restrained braces in zigzag configuration. *Earthquake Engineering and Structural Dynamics*, 2013; **42**(7):1087-1102.

[7.5.26] Maida Y, Maegawa T, Demizu T, Hamada M, Qu Z, Kishiki S, Sakata H, Wada A: Seismic response control of super high-rise RC buildings utilizing buckling restrained braces and the design of brace connections. *AIJ J. Struct. Constr. Eng.*, 2015; **80**(710):647-657. (*in Japanese*)

[7.5.27] Qu Z, Kishiki S, Maida Y, Sakata H., Wada A: Seismic responses of reinforced concrete frames with buckling restrained braces in zigzag configuration. *Engineering Structures*, 2015; **105**:12-21.

[7.5.28] Panagiotou M, Restrepo JI: Dual-plastic hinge design concept for reducing higher-mode effects on high-rise cantilever wall buildings. *Earthquake Engineering and Structural Dynamics*, 2009; **38**(12):1359-1380.

[7.5.29] Maniatakis C, Psycharis IN, Spyrakos CC: Effect of higher modes on the seismic response and design of moment-resisting RC frame structures. *Engineering Structures*, 2013; **56**:417-430.

[7.5.30] Qu Z, Xie JJ, Wang T, Kishiki S: Cyclic loading test of double K-braced reinforced concrete frame subassemblies with buckling restrained braces. *Engineering Structures,* 2017; **139**:1-14.

7.6 APPLICATIONS FOR TRUSS AND SPATIAL STRUCTURES

7.6.1. Seismic design concept for spatial structures

Spatial structures can be defined as those which achieve an architectural function through the structural geometric form covering the large space, typically including shell, cable or lattice structures. These are 'spatial structures' and the seismic design strategy is rarely directly prescribed by design codes. If narrowed in scope to lattice and certain truss structures, these are lightweight, highly redundant and stiff, with low inherent damping. While conventionally designed to remain elastic or nominally ductile, in recent years response-control techniques have been applied to control non-structural damage or as a reaction to observed damage.

Two key challenges arise when applying BRBs to spatial structures: 1) these are often so light that the required core size is extremely small, and 2) it can be a challenge to find attachment positions with sufficient relative displacements to be efficient. Fabrication tolerances become increasingly challenging to control for thin or small core cross sections, although low yield point steels such as LY100 or LY225 may be a good alternative. Determining the brace location depends on the structural topology.

Response control techniques can be classified into two categories: isolation and distributed damping. Isolation lengthens the fundamental periods to a lower energy portion of the response spectrum by inserting rubber or other soft bearings. This can be effective for most spatial structures given their short fixed base period, but bearings must be carefully selected considering the lightweight and longspan nature. Distributed damping involves inserting dampers into the main frame between points of large differential displacements [7.6.1], [7.6.2]. It can be a challenge to locate efficient damper positions given the large in-plane stiffness and the inherent redundancy may require an impractical number of dampers. Never-the-less, a number of effective response control techniques have been developed for domes, truss structures, and cable structures [7.6.2]-[7.6.4]. This section categorizes these recent developments and introduces applications for BRBs in metal spatial structures, including design examples from recently realized projects.

7.6.2 Types of spatial structure applications

a) Truss structures

Truss structures are commonly used in towers, industrial facilities and long span roofs. These are usually composed of slender axial members with the collapse mechanism determined by member buckling or connection fracture. Due to the low available ductility, elastic design is prevalent, with predictably poor performance in large earthquakes where the design capacity is exceeded. For these structures it is often possible to strategically select a few truss members to replace with dampers, as depicted in Figures 7.6.1 and 7.6.2 [7.6.2]. Similar concepts are described in [7.6.5]-[7.6.7].

Figure 7.6.1(a) shows a conventional truss with the capacity determined by buckling of the column or brace members. A basic strategy to improve the seismic response is shown in Figure 7.6.1(b), where critical members are replaced with BRBs, improving the collapse mechanism, increasing the energy dissipation capacity, and protecting the remaining compression members with BRB's force-limiting function.

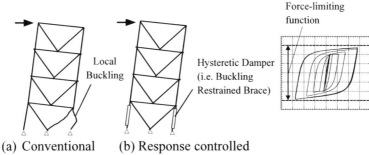

(a) Conventional   (b) Response controlled
Figure 7.6.1 Response control for truss structures

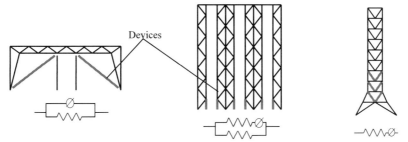

(T-1) Parallel layout   (T-2) Series layout (chord)   (T-3) Series layout (diagonal)
Figure 7.6.2 Device layout types for response-controlled truss structures

Several layouts can typically be use, as shown in Figure 7.6.2. In (T-1), the devices are installed parallel to the main frame, while in (T-2), each chord member is replaced by a corresponding device. (T-3) also involves replacing members, but in this case the diagonals. In general, the following methods can be used to select where to place the energy dissipation devices [7.6.2].

1) For truss structures with low stiffness, energy dissipation members are installed such that they connect points with the largest relative displacements.
2) For truss structures with high stiffness, identify the buckling and yield sequence through push-over analysis and replace critical members with energy dissipation devices.

The effectiveness of above concepts can be also confirmed in a more rigorous manner using optimization techniques [7.6.8].

b) Latticed roof structures
The seismic response of lattice domes or shells is unique, with anti-symmetric vertical vibrations amplified by horizontal excitation. This coupled acceleration response can be roughly modeled as a combination of the horizontal and vertical distributions, as shown in Figure 7.6.3 [7.6.9], [7.6.10]. However, the amplification of both components is driven not only by the horizontal input, but also by the dynamic characteristics of the supporting sub-structure.

Several effective response control strategies are available, as indicated in Figure 7.6.4. In (R-1), energy dissipation devices are installed in the roof plane. As the relative in-plane displacements are small, these bracing elements generally have a limited effect. Similarly, devices such as tuned mass dampers (TMD) have been investigated to control the out-of-plane response, but generally the effects are also limited. Such systems have been investigated in [7.6.11]-[7.6.13]. A promising approach is intermediate isolation at the roof level (R-2), which is effective in reducing both horizontal and vertical responses. A moderate number of examples of this system have been realized and such systems have been studied in [7.6.14]-[7.6.16]. Compared with multistory buildings, the roof is relatively light and the space necessary for device deformation is often insufficient. Therefore, the effective natural period of the roof tends to be less than that of base-isolated multistory buildings

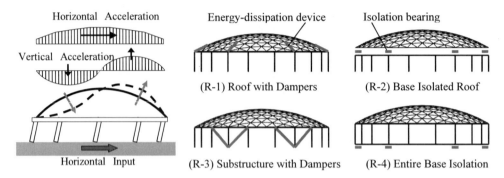

Figure 7.6.3 Seismic response of raised roof

Figure 7.6.4 Device layout for response-controlled roof structures

An effective strategy in which BRBs can be applied is shown in (R-3), where the devices are installed in the substructure. This strategy is widely used for stadiums and gymnasiums and design proceeds much in the same manner as conventional buildings. A final strategy (R-4) is to isolate the entire structure; this has also been applied to numerous multistory buildings with roofs, as described in the following section.

7.6.3 Realized structures

Examples of response controlled spatial structures are listed in Table 7.6.1, which has been extracted from [7.6.2]. Evidently, device layouts from each of the above categories have been applied in practice, with BRBs used for all but the isolation options.

a) Truss structures

Figure 7.6.5 shows a gymnasium for a high school in Japan [7.6.17] as an example of a truss structure using hysteretic dampers in a parallel layout, as indicated in Figure 7.6.2 (T-1). The roof structure comprises a system truss with clear spans of 32x38m. Four BRBs with 180kN yield strengths (LY225) are attached in the transverse direction, with a pair installed at each end of the frame. Time history analysis was used to confirm that all truss members other than the BRBs remained elastic under a Level-2 earthquake (A_{max}= 500 cm/s^2). The response reduction ratio due to the dampers was estimated as 72-7.6% in story drift and by 27-30% in its base shear.

Table 7.6.1 List of Realized Project [7.6.2]

No.	Project Name	Site	Year	Type	Devices
1	Soma High School Gymasium	Tochigi, Japan	2003	T-1	BRB
2	Communication Tower Retrofit	Aichi, Japan	2005	T-3	BRB
3	Safeco Field Stadium	Seattle, USA	1999	T-2	Fluid
4	Kyoto Aqua Arena	Kyoto, Japan	2002	R-2	Laminated Rubber
5	Saitama Super Arena	Saitama, Japan	2000	R-2	Laminated Rubber
6	Yamaguchi Kirara Dome	Yamaguchi, Japan	2001	R-2	Laminated Rubber
7	Ataturk Int. Airport Terminal	Istanbul, Turkey	2000	R-2	Friction Pendulum
8	Seahawks Football Stadium	Seattle, USA	2002	R-2	Friction Pendulum
9	Shanghai Int. F1 Circuit	Shanghai, China	2004	R-2	Pot-type Friction
10	Toyota Stadium	Aichi, Japan	2001	R-3	BRB
11	San Francisco Int. Airport Terminal	SF, USA	2000	R-4	Friction Pendulum
12	Suqian City Gymnasium	Jyangsu, China	2002	R-4	Laminated Rubber
13	Guangzhou Gymnasium	Guangzou, China	2003	R-2	Friction Pendulum
14	Ningbo Int. Conv. & Exh. Center	Ningbo, China	2003	R-2	Slide+FP
15	Shimokita Dome	Aomori, Japan	2005	R-1	BRB
16	Peking University Gymnasium	Beijing, China	2006	R-2	Friction Pendulum
17	Wukesong Indoor Stadium	Wukesong, China	2006	R-2	Slide and Spring
18	Fujian Stadium	Fujian, China	2007	R-2	Laminated Rubber

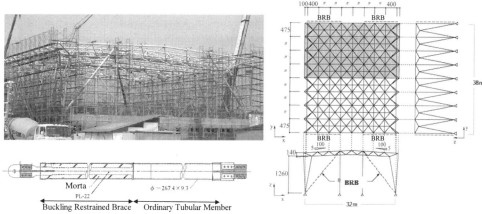

Figure 7.6.5 BRB connected with a CHS member (Soma Gymnasium)

A second example using BRBs was a retrofit program of communication towers that had been constructed in Japan in the 1970's, shown in Figure 7.6.6. These towers are frequently constructed on building roofs, and risk collapse during severe earthquakes due to amplification through the supporting structures. Prior to retrofit, the cumulative post-buckling deformation capacities of the tubular members was investigated with cyclic loading tests of full scale representations of the frames [7.6.7]. As shown in Figure 7.6.7 (a), the tubular braces undergo local buckling and fracture soon thereafter due to plastic strain concentration. During the moderate 2007 Chuetsu-Oki Earthquake, numerous fractures were observed at nuclear power plant towers located near the epicenter (Figure 7.6.7 (b)).

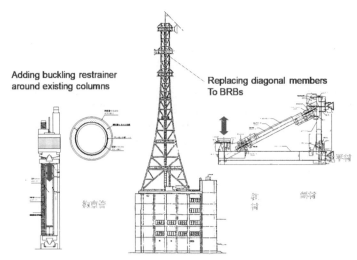

Figure 7.6.6 Seismic retrofit of tower structures with BRBs

(a) Fracture of tubular members after buckling

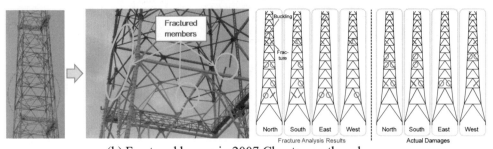

(b) Fractured braces in 2007 Chuetsu earthquake

Figure 7.6.7 Collapse mechanism

Two retrofit strategies were proposed for a towers in Mie Prefecture, Japan. The first concept (center, Figure 7.6.8) consisted of reinforcing the critical members with restrainers, effectively transforming these sections into tube-in-tube BRBs. The restrainers would be installed by welding two partial length semi-circular halves and injecting grout. However, the high yield strength of the new BRBs resulted in other unreinforced member becoming critical, buckling even under the 50 year earthquake demand. The second strategy that was ultimately adopted (right, Figure 7.6.8) involved replacing the critical members with lower yield strength BRBs, which then act as energy dissipation members. As shown in Figure 7.6.9, the second option proved most effective in reducing accelerations throughout the height. This also happened to result in the lower construction cost, and on average it took three workers two weeks to install 40

BRBs. The generic retrofit was applied to 50 towers, with a retrofitted tower shown in Figure 7.6.10.

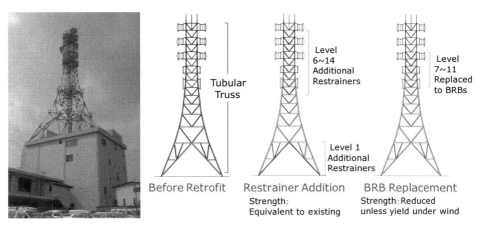

Figure 7.6.8 Retrofitted communication tower and retrofit options

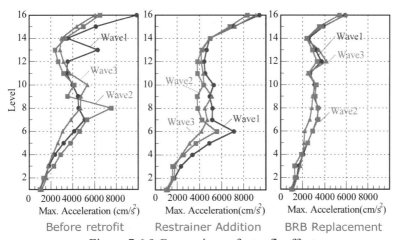

Figure 7.6.9 Comparison of retrofit effects

Figure 7.6.10 Seismic retrofit of tower with BRB

b) Roof structures

BRBs have also been applied as response control devices for roof structures, with the devices most commonly located in the substructure (R-3 from Figure 7.6.4). A number of stadiums with long span roofs have employed this concept, with the Toyota stadium (Figure 7.6.11) a typical example.

Figure 7.6.11 Toyota Stadium

Of the four response control layouts from Figure 7.6.4, only a few structures have employed in-plane dampers (R-1). One exception is the Symokita Dome as shown in Figure 7.6.12 [7.6.18]. In this structures BRBs are inserted in both the roof and supporting structure. Time history analysis indicates that the in-plane roof dampers reduced response in the horizontal and vertical accelerations by 17% and 1%, respectively. The substructure dampers had a greater response reduction effect, estimated as 26% and 17% for the horizontal and vertical accelerations, respectively.

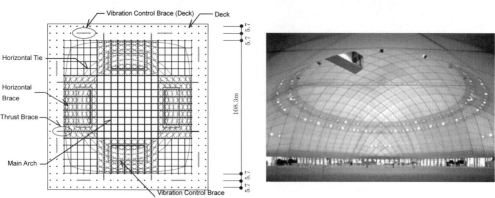

Figure 7.6.12 Shimokita Dome

During the East Japan Great Earthquake in 2011 and Kumamoto Earthquake in 2016, numerous gymnasiums and auditoriums experienced damage, preventing these spaces from being used in the emergency response and recover efforts. Observed damage (Figures 7.6.13 and 7.6.14) included buckling and fracture of roof brace members, spalling at the roof-to-wall connections, ceiling collapses, and damage to walls associated with out-of-plane response. Much of this damage was attributed to the large excitation of the roofs. Studies [7.6.19] have indicated that installing supplementary energy dissipation devices in the substructures (R-3 type retrofit) would be an effective means to reduce the roof acceleration and deformation, protecting the non-structural components.

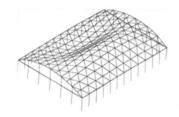

Principal vibration mode

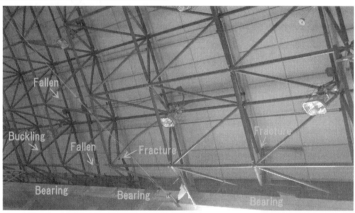

Figure 7.6.13 Damaged truss roof in Kumatoto Earthquake 2016 and their typical vibration mode

Figure 7.6.14 Damaged ceiling in school gymnasia in Tohoku Earthquake 2011

Figure 7.6.15 shows a typical gymnasium in Ibaraki Prefecture in Japan with a steel lattice roof that was damaged during the 2011 Tohoku earthquake and then afterwards retrofitted with BRBs. The original vertical bracing members were designed in the 1970's for a low base shear, and all were severely buckled or fractured. Though somewhat effective in limiting acceleration demands in the roof, the fractured braces meant that the gymnasium was not available to shelter refugees in the critical post-disaster months.

Figure7.6.15 Damaged gymnasium in Tsukuba by Tohoku Earthquake 2011

A damage-tolerant retrofit strategy was selected to replace the 24 original braces with 8 BRBs, arranged as shown in Figure 7.6.16. As indicated by Figure 7.6.17 [7.6.19], stiffening the supporting structure would have increased the acceleration response in both the horizontal and vertical directions, introducing the potential for damage to the acceleration sensitive ceilings and suspended services. With energy dissipating devices, the roof accelerations are slightly improved as in Figure 7.6.17 and the substructure is protected, enabling this facility to be used as an emergency shelter in future events.

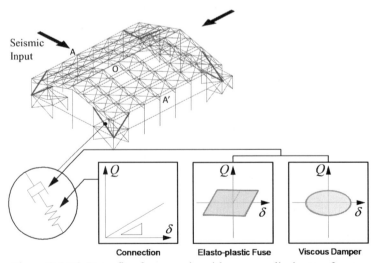

Figure7.6.16 Retrofit of gymnasia with energy-dissipaton fuses

Chapter 7. Applications for BRBF 199

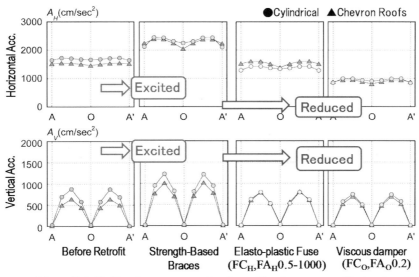

Figure7.6.17 Roof response reduction effect by energy-dissipation fuses

The BRBs were arranged as shown in Figure 7.6.18 and installed by welding gusset plates to the existing frames with shear-force transfer beams anchored to the RC floor beams, as shown in Figure 7.6.19. The retrofit design work was carried out in May 2012, and construction took place between September and December 2012, with each BRB installed in one day, including site welding and fixture.

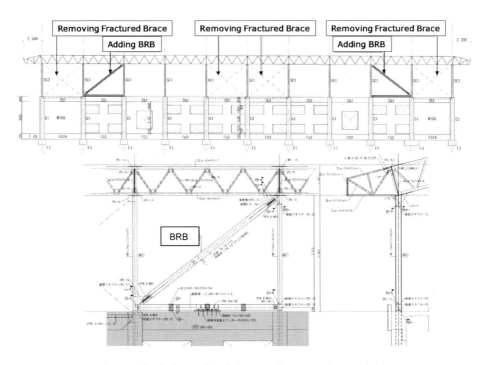

Figure7.6.18 Retrofit of damaged gymnasium with BRBs

Figure7.6.19 Installation of BRBs into damaged gymnasium

A second example of this type of retrofit is shown in Figure 7.6.20. This single story gymnasium is located near the border of Fukushima and Ibaragi Prefectures in Japan, with the structure consisting of a steel cylindrical shell roof with vertical braces along the longitudinal direction. Although not damaged during the 2011 earthquake, a seismic retrofit was planned because the shear strength of the original angle braces is expected to be insufficient for future events.

The initial retrofit concept called for additional angle braces, but as these yield at 0.13% drift and have a low ductility capacity, the strength of the existing moment frame could not be utilized as it is not fully developed until 2% drift (left, Figure 7.6.20). This would require the braces to resist nearly the full base shear, and so it was proposed to replace the large number required with 4 BRBs. As these are effective through 3% drift, the structure could be treated as a dual system with the base shear resisted by the combined strength of the BRBs and existing moment frame (right part of Figure 7.6.20).

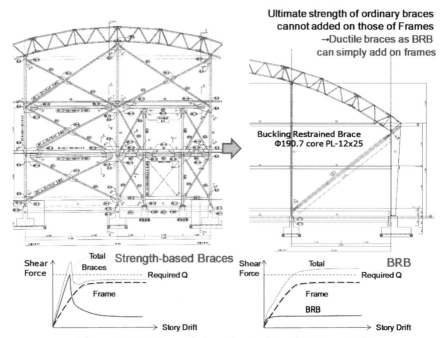

Figure7.6.20 Strength-based retrofit and BRB retrofit

Figure7.6.21 BRB retrofit in a junior high-school

Construction photos are shown in Figure 7.6.21. Given the lightweight roof, low yield strength BRBs with only 100kN yield strength and 190mm circular restrainers were used. Given the lengths required and to improve stiffness, the BRBs were connected in series to non-buckling circular braces. Similar to the previous example, gusset plates were welded to the existing frames, and the BRBs attached with bolted connections and friction bolts.

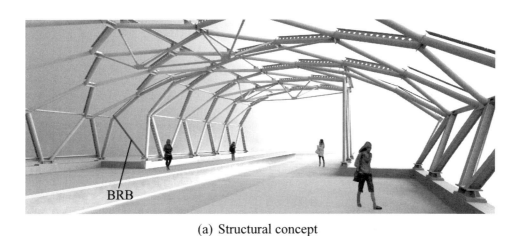

(a) Structural concept

(b) Station roof overview (c) Attached BRB

Figure7.6.22 BRB for railway station roof (Tokyu-Midorigaoka)

BRB are also applicable to control the response of railway station structures. Figure 7.6.22 shows the small BRB attached to the membrane roof for Tokyu Midorigaoka station in Tokyo. The roof structure is soft in transverse direction, and there ware a risk for amplified response caused by supporting RC structure. Therefore, two set of small BRBs with 114mm diameter (Ny=140kN) were attached to add stiffness and hysteretic damping to keep the maximum story drift within 1/300 against Level-2 earthquake.

7.6.3 Applications to bridge structures

Bridge applications have also been increasing in recent years. In Japan BRBs are frequently used to retrofit steel arch bridges, as shown in Figure 7.6.23 [7.6.20]. The diagonals of arch and vertical trusses are replaced by BRBs, improving the buckling strength and ductility against transverse directions. This method has been applied many steel arch bridges in Japan after Hanshin Great Earthquake 2011 (Figure 7.6.24). Researchers in the US have explored using BRBs in highway bridges. One proposal is to install vertical braces at the RC piers to improve the transverse response or to use BRB as horizontal members at the expansion joints acting in both the transverse and longitudinal directions, with the later scheme depicted in Figure 7.6.25 [7.6.21].

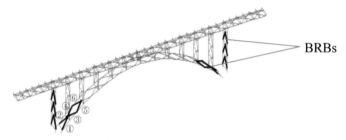

Figure 7.6.23 Seismic retrofit of steel arch bridge with BRBs [7.6.20]

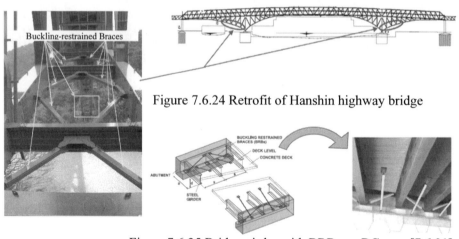

Figure 7.6.24 Retrofit of Hanshin highway bridge

Figure 7.6.25 Bridge girder with BRBs on RC peer [7.6.21]

References

[7.6.1] Giuliani GC: Up To Date Dynamic Control of Structures, *IASS 2004 Symposium Montpelier,* 2004.

[7.6.2] Takeuchi T, Xue SD, Nakazawa S, Kato S: Recent Applications of Response Control Techniques to Metal Spatial Structures, *Journal of the Int. Assoc. for Shell and Spatial Structures*, 2012; **53**(2), n.172:99-110.

[7.6.3] Takeuchi T, Ogawa T, Kumagai T: State-of-Art Views on Response Control Technologies on Metal Space Structures, *IASS 2009 Symposium, Valencia,* 2009.

[7.6.4] Xue SD, Takeuchi T, Kato S: Review and New Development of Seismic Isolation Technology for Spatial Structures, *IASS 2010 Symposium, Shanghai,* 2010.

[7.6.5] Kato S, Atumi F, Shimaoka S, Nakazawa S, Ueki T: Reduction of Structural Material and Increase of Seismic Performance Based on Additional Use of Hysteresis Dampers Applied to the Feet of Columns of Gable Trusses, *IASS Symposium 2003, Taipei*, 2003.

[7.6.6] Takeuchi T, Suzuki K: Performance-Based Design for Truss Frame Structures using Energy Dissipation Devices, *Steel Structures in Seismic Area (STESSA)* ,Naples, 2003:55.

[7.6.7] Yamada K, Ishihara K: Application of the Damage Control Design to an Arch, *IASS Symposium 2005, Bucharest*, 2005.

[7.6.8] Takeuchi T, Kinouchi Y, Matsui R, Ogawa T: Optimal Arrangement of Energy- Dissipating Members for Seismic Retrofitting of Truss Structures *American Journal of Engineering and Applied Sciences*, 2015; **8**(4):455-464 DOI: 10.3844/ ajeassp.2015.455.464.

[7.6.9] Kato S, Nakazawa S: Seismic Design Method to Reduce the Responses of Single Layer Reticular Domes by Means of Substructure under Severe Earthquake Motions, *IASS 2001 Symposium Nagoya*, 2001; TP077.

[7.6.10] Takeuchi T, Ogawa T, Kumagai T: Seismic Response Evaluation of Lattice Shell Roofs using Amplification Factors, Journal of the Int. Assoc. for Shell and Spatial Structures, 2007; **48**(3):197-210.

[7.6.11] Kasai K, Motoyui S, Ooki Y: Viscoelastic Damper Modeling and its Application to Dynamic Analysis of Viscoelastically Dampered Space Frames, *IASS Symposium 2001, Nagoya*, 2001; TP119.

[7.6.12] Yigang Z, Guangzi R: A Practical Method on Seismic Response Controlled Double Layer Cylindrical Latticed Shell with Variable Stiffness Members, *IASS Symposium 2001*, Nagoya, 2001; TP122.

[7.6.13] Xue ST, Qin L, Yamada M, Otani S: Vertical Vibration Control for Large Space Arch subjected to Horizontal Earthquake Wave, *IASS Symposium 2001, Nagoya*, 2001; TP123.

[7.6.14] Uchukoshi M, Kato S, Nakazawa S, Mukaiyama T: How to Realize a Super Large Dome under Severest Earthquake? A Dome with Seismic Isolation System, *IASS Symposium 2001, Nagoya*, 2001; TP115.

[7.6.15] Matsui T, Qiao F, Moribe Y, Sugiyama E, Esaka Y: Response of Seismically Isolated Large Span Domes to Fluctuating Wind Loads, *IASS Symposium 2001, Nagoya*, 2001; TP120.

[7.6.16] Shingu K, Niki T: A Study on Base Isolated Shell, *IASS Symposium 2001, Nagoya*, 2001; TP117.

[7.6.17] Takeuchi T, Ogawa T, Suzuki T, Kumagai T, Yamagata C: A Basic Study on Damage-Controlled Design Concept for Truss Frame Structures, *AIJ, J. of Struct. Eng.*, 2005; **51B**:31-37. (*in Japanese*)

[7.6.18] Hosozawa O, Mizutani T: Structural Design of Simokita Dome, *IASS 2005 Symposium Bucharest*, 2005:707.

[7.6.19] Takeuchi T: Retrofit of Damaged Gymnasia and Towers according to Response Control Concept, *Proceedings of 10th International Conference on Urban Earthquake Engineering (Tokyo)*, 2013:17-24.

[7.6.20] Usami T, Lu Z, Ge H: A seismic upgrading method for steel arch bridges using Buckling-restrained Braces, *Earthquake Engineering and Structural Dynamics*, 2005; **34**(4-5, 10-25):471-496.

[7.6.21] Celik O, Bruneau M: Skewed Slab-on-Girder Steel Bridge Superstructures with Bidirectional-Ductile End Diaphragms, *ASCE Journal of Bridge Engineering*, 2011; **16**(2):207-218

7.7 SPINE FRAME CONCEPTS

7.7.1. Self-centering, rocking, and spine concepts

One of the relatively recent application of BRBs is as part of a Rocking or Spine Frame, alternatively known as a "Strong-back system", or "Mast Frame." When BRBs are used as the sole lateral force resisting system, the low post-yield stiffness may result in damage or residual drift concentrating at one level, even if the capacities are relatively well balanced over the height of the structure [7.7.1], as observed in Great Hanshin Earthquake in 1995 (Figure 7.7.1). Spine frames address this deficiency by providing a stiff, continuous vertical member. As the base of the spine is pinned, it functions to redistribute and smooth out the story drift from one level to another and is not expected to develop flexural hinges. Performance can be further improved by borrowing design concepts from self-centering systems and rocking frames.

Self-centering systems aim to limit residual drifts to negligible values by introducing a supplementary restoring force. Examples of self-centering systems include: (1) moment resisting frames with post-tensioned (PT) beam-to-column rocking connections [7.7.2]. (2) Braced frames with self-centering braces fabricated with super-elastic pre-tensioned strands [7.7.3, 7.7.4]. (3) Rocking walls with restoring force provided envelope frames, PT elements, or gravity [7.7.5~23].

Rocking action has long been recognized to reduce dynamic demands and was observed by Housner as early as 1963 [7.7.8]. Clough and Hucklebridge [7.7.9] conducted some of the earliest rocking frame tests and compared them with the conventional pin-base frame. It was found that the member force of the rocking frame was lower than that of the conventional frame. Priestley et al. [7.7.10] developed a simple method to evaluate the rocking response of structures by a displacement response spectrum using the equivalent damping of the rocking system. Midorikawa et al. [7.7.5, 7.7.11] conducted shaking table tests of a half-scale three-story rocking frame after installing yielding plates at the bottoms of columns to dissipate energy.

Numerous researchers and practitioners have proposed spine frame systems featuring various combinations of damper, rocking and/or restoring components. Taga et al [7.7.15] distributed BRBs along the vertical elastic spine composed of strong braced frame, named as "Dual spine". Qu, Wada et al. [7.7.16] used a similar concept at the connections of columns in the middle story of a slender, tall frame (Figure 7.7.2). Tremblay et al. [7.7.7]

Figure 7.7.1 Midstory collapse in Great Hanshin Earthquake

Figure 7.7.2 Retrofit with RC Spine Wall [7.7.16]

proposed a braced steel frame with viscous dampers vertically equipped between the column bases and the foundations. Janhunen, Tipping, Mar et al. [7.7.17] employed a pivoting spine concept in the seismic retrofitting of a steel building in the U.S. A concrete wall acts as the core of the rocking to redistribute the lateral forces and displacements without adding significant strength. Gunay et al. [7.7.18] investigated the seismic performance of a brittle reinforced concrete frame, which was retrofitted with rocking infill walls, and proved its efficacy in reducing soft story failure risks.

Eatherton, Deierlein, Hajjar et al. [7.7.19~23] studied an uplifting rocking frame system with PT strands that provide self-centering resistance. Steel butterfly-shaped fuses and BRBs were employed as replaceable energy dissipation members.

Ikenaga et al. [7.7.12] developed a column base consisting of PT bars and steel plate dampers. Takamatsu et al. [7.7.13] proposed a column base with anchor bolts that dissipate energy by elongation. Takeuchi et al. [7.7.14] used buckling-restraint columns (BRCs) at the bases of truss frames to concentrate major damage into BRCs and prevent collapses caused by the buckling of members in the main structure.

7.7.2. Dual spine system

The first concept is the Dual Spine proposed by Taga et al. [7.7.15] in 1998 and shown in Figure 7.7.3. This system consists of a stiff elastic braced spine with a pinned base, BRBs distributed adjacent to the spine and an elastic "envelope" moment frame. The elastic spine distributes the ductility demand, engaging the BRBs in shear action as the building displaces laterally in bending action. Restoring force is provided by the moment frame. This system was applied to the 23-story MT building in Osaka (Figure 7.7.4) and compared favorably against a conventional BRB scheme, both in terms of base shear and story drift distribution, as indicated in Figure 7.7.5. A similar concept was proposed by Lai, Mahin et al [7.7.24], coined the "strong-back system," and has been implemented in a low rise structure in California [7.7.25].

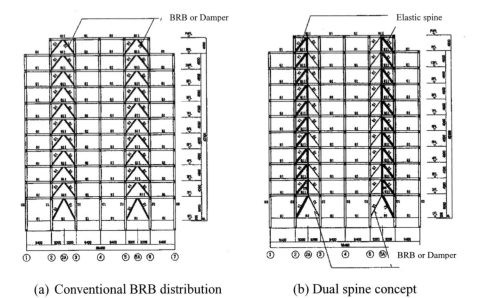

(a) Conventional BRB distribution   (b) Dual spine concept

Figure 7.7.3 Concept of Dual spine system [7.7.15]

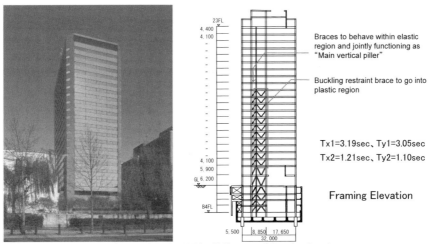

Figure 7.7.4 MT building and its dual spine

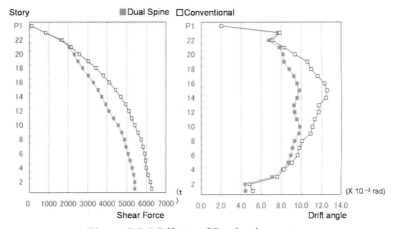

Figure 7.7.5 Effects of Dual spine system

7.7.3. Controlled rocking system

A second system places a BRB vertically at the base of a steel rocking frame, with restoring force provided by PT strands, an envelope moment frame or gravity. Energy dissipation is provided by the BRB, and any soft stories in the moment frame are protected by the rocking frame, which acts as the spine element. The first system with PT strands (Figure 7.7.6) was studied by Deierlein G., Ma X., Eatherton M., Hajjar J. et al [7.7.19-23], and produces a flag-shaped hysteretic loop, characteristic of self-centering systems. In this case overturning resistance is provided by a combination of the elastic restoring action provided by the prestressed PT strands and the energy dissipating fuses. The initial overturning resistance, MOT is a function of the initial prestress in the steel tendons and the yield strength of the fuse. During rocking, the PT strands load and unload elastically, while the steel fuse yields and dissipates energy through hysteresis (Figure 7.7.7). The relative contribution of the post-tensioning tendons and fuse to the overturning resistance dictates the tradeoff between the self-centering ability and energy dissipation in the system. The performance of this system was confirmed by large shaking table tests at E-Defense in 2009 (Figure 7.7.8) [7.7.23].

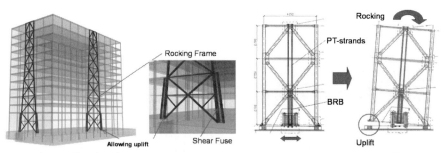

Figure 7.7.6 Controlled (uplifting) rocking system

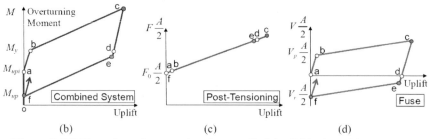

Figure 7.7.7 Flag-shape hysteresis of controlled (uplifting) rocking system

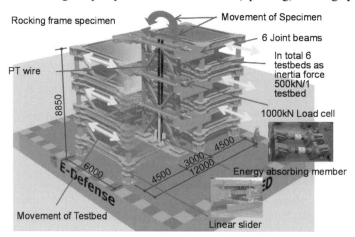

Figure 7.7.8 Shaking table test of controlled rocking system [7.7.23]

7.7.4. Non-uplifting hinged spine frame systems

An alternative rocking frame concept arranges BRBs as the first story column elements, coined buckling restrained columns (BRCs). This creates a non-uplifting system, avoiding the need for complicated uplift details. Similar to the previous concept, the rocking frame acts as a spine to avoid damage at soft stories, while restoring force is then provided either by an envelope moment frame or gravity. This system was introduced earlier in Figure 7.6.1 of Section 7.6, and was implemented in a 5-story laboratory building at Tokyo Institute of Technology, completed in 2014 and shown in Figures 7.7.9-7.7.11.

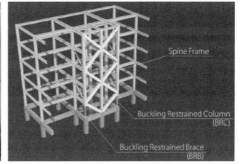

Figure 7.7.9 Material Research Building   Figure 7.7.10 Structural System

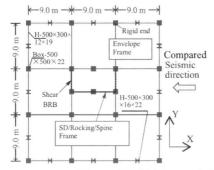

Figure 7.7.11 Plan and the base of NL spine frame

7.7.5. Comparison of spine frame systems

The relative benefits and performance of the two rocking frame systems, as compared to a conventional BRBF following the Damage Tolerant Structure concept are illustrated by the design study conducted for the Material Research Building (Figures 7.7.9 to 7.7.11). The typical hysteresis of each system is shown in Figure 7.7.9, expressed by overturning moment (M_{OT}) and roof drift ratio (RDR). The conventional BRB frame arranged as a shear damper system (SD) (Figure 7.7.12 (a)) can perform

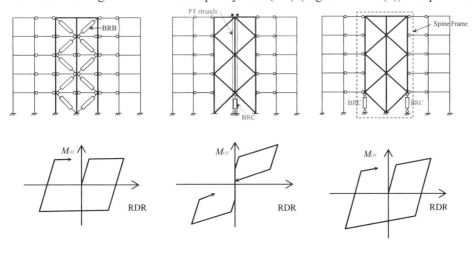

(a) Conventional BRBF (SD)   (b) Lift-up Rocking Frame (LU)   (c) Non-uplifting Spine Frame (NL)

Figure 7.7.12 Concept and hysteretic curves of the three structural systems

well when the Damage Tolerance Design concept is applied, keeping the main frame elastic. However, if the elastic frame stiffness is insufficient or too many plastic hinges form, damage concentration at weak stories and residual deformations are expected, similar when BRBs comprise the sole lateral force resisting system. The uplifting (LU) and non-uplifting (NL) rocking frame concepts are shown in Figures 7.7.12(b) and (c), respectively.

a) Building models

The structure shown in Figures 7.7.9 to 7.7.11 was redesigned with each of the concepts: conventional BRBF (SD), lift up rocking frame (LU), and non-uplifitng rocking frame (NL). Details are in Ref.[7.7.26]. In this building the first story is slightly taller at 4.2m than the others (4m), and the rocking frame is positioned in the middle of a 27m 3x3 bay frame, but acts only in the X direction.

The moment and spine frame member sizes are listed in Table 7.7.1. BRBs in the conventional SD model were sized proportional to the equivalent static lateral force distribution (Ai distribution) and are summarized in Table 7.7.2 and 7.7.3. All models were designed for the same overturning yield moment ($M_{OT} = 46000$kNm) as the SD model.

Table7.7.1 Dimensions, gravity load, and mass distribution of the models

	Story height (m)	Span of beam (m)	Gravity load (kN/m^2)	Mass (kN/m^2)
Roof	-	4.5	11.3	10.6
Second–fifth stories	4.0	4.5	7.75	6.65
First story	4.2	-	-	-
Total	20.2	27	30500	27000

Table 7.7.2 Sizes and materials of typical members

Structural members	Size (mm)	Material	M_p (kN·m)
Beams	H-500 × 300 × 12 × 19	SN400B	870
Columns in MRF	Box-500 × 500 × 19	SN490B	2360
Columns in BRBF/RF	Box-550 × 550 × 25	SN490B	3700
Braces in RF	H-600 × 550 × 25 × 25	SN490B	3374

Table 7.7.3 Cross-sectional areas and yielding forces of BRBs in SD model

Story	Area, A_{BRBi} (mm^2)	Yield force, F_{y_BRBi} (kN)
5	4300	970
4	5900	1330
3	7100	1600
2	8000	1800
1	8700	1960

Restoring force in the LU model primarily consists of the PT strand prestress and gravity, with elastic force in the PT strands and envelope moment frame conservatively neglected. Gravity load per column is $G_{rf}/2 = 1700$kN and the rocking frame lever arm $b_{rf}/2 = 4.5$m. BRCs were selected with a yield force of F_y=4500kN and hence 139cm^2 core area (SN490B), and PT strands were selected with an 8300mm^2 area (16 x 28ϕ), and 1860kN prestress (11% of tensile strength). The sum of prestress and gravity load is 5250kN, exceeding the BRC yield force and ensuring self centering.

$$M_{OT} = (G_{rf} + F_{PT} + F_y^{BRC}) \cdot \frac{b_{rf}}{2} \tag{7.7.1}$$

Restoring force in the NL model is purely from the envelope moment frame, as gravity load is locked into the model prior to installing the BRCs and no PT strands are present. The braces and center column are rigidly connected to the foundation and plastic hinges activate at large rocking drift. The BRCs are located along the lines of the side columns to maximize their energy dissipation performance. The yielding force of the BRCs was selected by determining the same initial yielding overturning resistance of the spine frame as that of the LU model. Equation (7.7.2) expresses the initial yielding overturning moment of the spine frame of the NL model.

$$M_{OT} = F_y^{BRC} b_{rf} \tag{7.7.2}$$

where M_{OT} is the overturning moment of the spine frame; F_y^{BRC} is the yielding axial force of the BRC on one side; b_{rf} is the width of the spine frame. The cross-sectional area and yielding force of the BRCs are 13900 mm^2 and 4500 kN, respectively.

The braced frames are connected to the outer moment frames through pin-ended beams. These beams are designed with sufficient stiffness to transmit horizontal force without extensive axial deformation, but they do not restrain the vertical displacement of the rocking frames.

Three-dimensional models were developed in OpenSEES, with framing element modelled with fiber sections and the BRCs as equivalent truss elements [7.7.27]. Second-order effects (Global PΔ effects) were included in the nonlinear transformation of the columns and brace elements. Pushover analysis (Figure 7.7.13) indicates that all three models yield at the same overturning moment of 46000kNm. The increased strain hardening ratio of the LU model is due to the elastic PT strands.

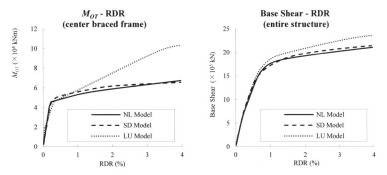

Figure 7.7.13 Pushover analysis results of the three models

b) Seismic performance of several spine systems

A suite of 4 records spectrally matched to the Level 2 design spectrum and one artificial wave (BCJ-L2) were used for comparison. These are shown in the frequency domain in Figure 7.7.14, along with the 3rd and 6th mode periods, which correspond to the translational modes of the rocking frame.

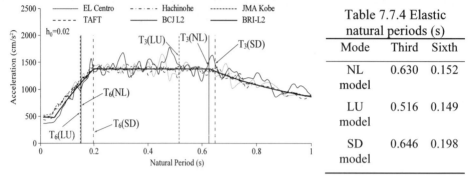

Figure 7.7.14 Acceleration spectra of normalized input ground motions ($h_0 = 0.02$)

Table 7.7.4 Elastic natural periods (s)

Mode	Third	Sixth
NL model	0.630	0.152
LU model	0.516	0.149
SD model	0.646	0.198

A typical hysteresis of the overturning moment (M_{OT}) by roof drift is shown in Figure 7.7.15, confirming the characteristic self-centering flag-shaped behavior of the LU model. In each model the peak story drift occurred at the same time (Figure 7.7.16), and at the 2nd story (Figure 7.7.17). However, while the SD model had a strong tendency to concentrate deformation in the second story, the spine frame models (LU and NL) ensure a more uniform distribution. This is clearly shown in Figure 7.7.18,

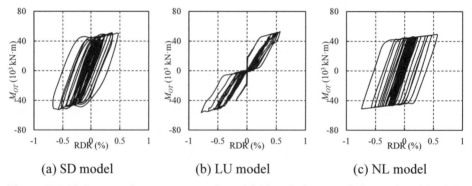

(a) SD model   (b) LU model   (c) NL model

Figure 7.7.15 Overturning moment and roof drift ratio hysteresis loops (Hachinohe)

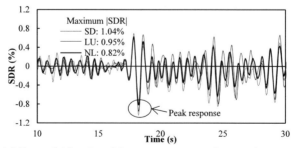

Figure 7.7.16 Story drift - time history response of second story (Hachinohe)

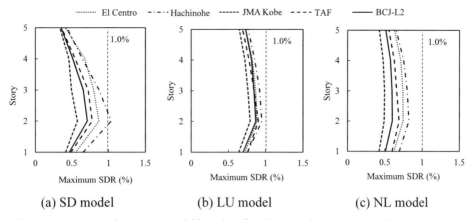

Figure 7.7.17 Maximum story drift ratio of each story in SD, LU, and NL models

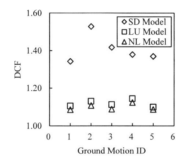

Figure 7.7.18 Drift concentration factors of SD, LU, and NL models
(Ground motion ID: 1. El Centro; 2. Hachinohe; 3. JMA Kobe; 4. TAFT; 5. BCJ-L2;)

where the story drift concentration (DCF) is defined as the ratio of peak story drift (SDR) to roof drift (RDR) [7.7.16]. While both spine frame models performed much better than the convention BRBF (SD), the NL model exhibited both the smallest SDR and DCF.

The benefit of controlling the DCF is also apparent in the residual drift (ReSDR), as shown in Figure 7.7.19. While all three models resulted in acceptable performance, the drift concentration of the non-spine frame model (SD) resulted in significantly

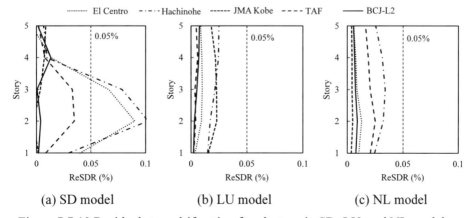

Figure 7.7.19 Residual story drift ratio of each story in SD, LU, and NL models

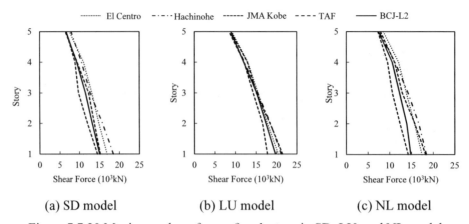

Figure 7.7.20 Maximum shear force of each story in SD, LU, and NL models

greater residual drift for some records. Between the two spin frames, the PT strands in the LU model resulted in full recentering for most records, while the NL model only partially recentered. Figure 7.7.20 shows the peak shear forces. Generally the LU model experience larger shears, while the SD and NL models performed similarly. In all cases the moment frame remained elastic.

As a final comparison, the robustness of the frames was assessed using incremental dynamic analysis (IDA) [7.7.29]. A particular concern was the behavior of the LU frame if the PT strands were to yield. Peak ground acceleration was selected as the intensity measure (IM), and peak story drift the damage measure (DM), with ground motion scaled until SDR reached or 10% or collapse was detected.

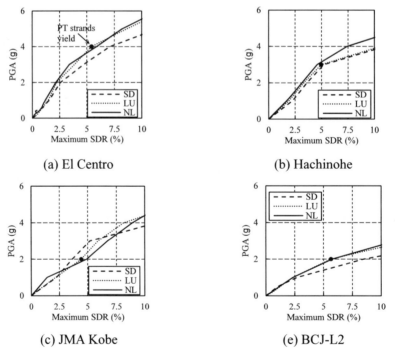

Figure 7.7.21 IDA curves of SD, LU, and NL models

IDA curves for each model are shown in Figure 7.7.21, with the conventional SD frame generally experiencing greater peak story drift at all intensities, in agreement with previous observations. For this structure, the PT strands do not yield until peak story drift is approximately 5%. Yielding of the PT strand did not significantly increase the rate of softening relative to the NL model for most records, with Hachinohe being the sole exception. In general, spine frames improve the robustness of the system.

c) Seismic performance with single-story irregular configuration

Vertically structural irregularities are frequently introduced by architectural requirements, and the presence of variations of strength, stiffness, or mass can significantly degrade the seismic behavior [7.7.29, 7.7.30]. While spine frame have been shown to improve drift concentration, each of the models was modified by degrading the stiffness and strength of all moment frame columns in a single story. Peak story drift (SDR) and concentration factors (DCF) are shown in Figures 7.7.22 and 7.7.23, respectively, with columns reduced to 320mm square box sections at the first, and then second story.

The effect was far more pronounced in the SD model, with the average DCFs increasing from 1.4 (Figure 7.7.17) to 1.6 and 2.0 for the soft first and second stories, respectively. Even with the irregularities, the spine frames maintained a relatively uniform drift distribution and controlled the DCF.

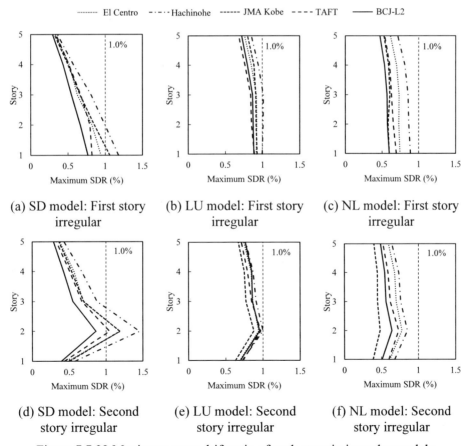

Figure 7.7.22 Maximum story drift ratio of each story in irregular models

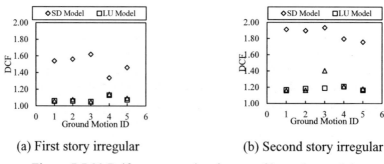

(a) First story irregular (b) Second story irregular

Figure 7.7.23 Drift concentration factors of irregular models

A similar trend is observed in the residual drifts (Figure 7.7.24), which were negligible for the LU mode, small for the NL model and significantly increased (up to 0.25%) for the SD model. For the second-story irregular models, the maximum ReSDR of the SD model was also approximately 0.25% and those of the LU and NL models were even smaller than those of the first-story irregular models.

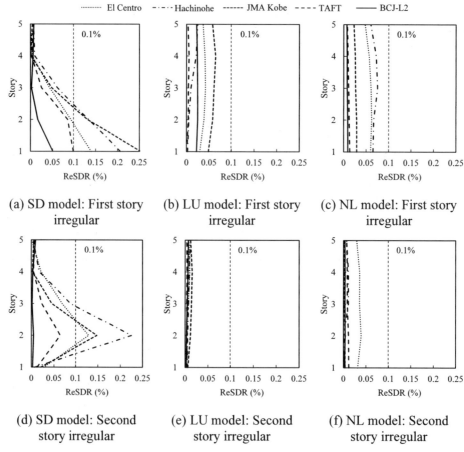

(a) SD model: First story irregular (b) LU model: First story irregular (c) NL model: First story irregular

(d) SD model: Second story irregular (e) LU model: Second story irregular (f) NL model: Second story irregular

Figure 7.7.24 Residual story drift ratio of each story in irregular models

The IDA curves of the soft 1st story models had an interesting result (Figure 7.7.25). As only a single compressive brace is effective at the 1st story of the LU spine frame, if this member buckles the strength is expected to rapidly degrade. In this model the

Chapter 7. Applications for BRBF 217

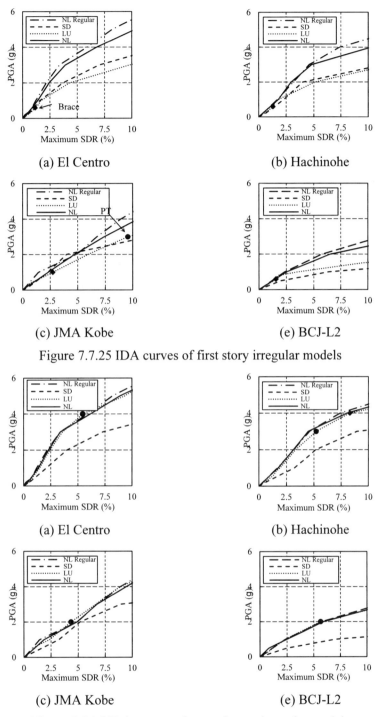

Figure 7.7.25 IDA curves of first story irregular models

Figure 7.7.26 IDA curves of second story irregular models

brace buckled at 0.6 ~ 1.0g, with the subsequent softening tracking closely to the SD model. Without the envelope moment frame, it would be vital that the 1st story brace be designed to remain elastic in order to avoid collapse.

Both the SD and NL frames have matching tension and compression braces at each floor, and so do not suffer the same issue. IDA curves for the soft 2nd story (Figure 7.7.26) were virtually identical to the previous for the spine frame models, while the SD model exhibited increased softening.

7.7.6 Application Examples

Several other recent projects have applied BRBs as fuses connecting multiple components of the lateral force resisting system. Figure 7.7.27 shows the retrofit of existing steel frame building in SF, USA with an RC spine frame and short BRBs connected horizontally near the base [7.7.17].

Figure 7.7.27 680 Folsom Street, SF, US [7.7.17]

A similar concept has also been applied to a 3 story RC structure, utilizing horizontal BRBs as fuses linking stiff RC shear walls to a flexible RC moment frame [7.7.31]. The 8 horizontal BRBs (1100kN each) are installed below the roof and 3rd floor, limiting the core demand while allowing the full capacity of the moment frame to develop. The combined system utilizes the strength of both the cores and moment frame, while concentrating damage in the replaceable BRBs and respecting the architectural intent for an open, unobstructed façade (Figure 7.7.28).

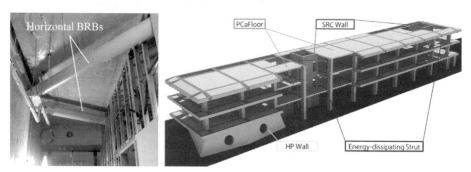

Figure 7.7.28 Earth Life Science Institute, Tokyo Tech [7.7.31]

Recently, the Damped Outrigger concept has become increasingly common to control wind and/or seismic demands in tall buildings [7.7.32, 7.7.33]. Figure 7.7.29 shows Wilshire Grand Tower, a 335m, 73-story building in LA, USA [7.7.34]. BRBs are used as outrigger dampers, with up to 10000kN capacity achieved by installing 4 in parallel.

Figure 7.7.29 Wilshire Grand Tower, LA, US [7.7.34]

References

[7.7.1] Uriz P, Mahin S: Toward earthquake-resistant design of concentrically braced steel-frame structures, *PEER Report*, 2008/09

[7.7.2] Garlock M, Sause R, Ricles J: Behavior and design of posttensioned steel frame systems, *Journal of Structural Engineering*, ASCE, Vol. 133(3), 389-399, 2007

[7.7.3] Miller D, Fahnestock L, Eatherton M: Development and experimental validation of a nickel-titanium shape memory alloy self-centering buckling-restrained brace, *Engineering Structures*, Vol. 40, 288-298, 2012

[7.7.4] Christopoulos C, Tremblay R, Kim H.J, Lacerte M: Self-centering energy dissipative bracing system for the seismic resistance of structures: *development and validation*, Vol. 134, 96-107, 2008

[7.7.5] Midorigawa M, Azuhata T, Ishihara T, Matsuba Y, Matsushima Y, Wada A: Earthquake response reduction of buildings by rocking structural system, *Smart Structures and Materials 2002: Smart Systems for Bridges, Structures, and Highways, Proceedings of SPIE*, Vol. 4696, 265-272, 2002

[7.7.6] Wada A, Yamada S, Fukuta O, Tanigawa M: Passive controlled slender structures having special devices at column connections, *7th International Seminar on Seismic Isolation, Passive Energy Dissipation and Active Control of Vibrations of Structures*, Assisi, Italy, 2001.10

[7.7.7] Tremblay R, Poirier L.P, Bouaanani N, Leclerc M, Rene V, Fronteddu L, Rivest S: Innovative viscously damped rocking braced steel frames, *Proceedings of 14th World Conference on Earthquake Engineering*, 2008

[7.7.8] Housner G: The behavior of inverted pendulum structures during earthquakes, *Bulletin of the Seismological Society of America*, Vol. 53(2), 403-417, 1963

[7.7.9] Clough R, Huckelbridge A: Preliminary experimental study of seismic uplift of a steel frame, *Earthquake Engineering Research Center (EERC) Report*, No.

UCB/EERC-77/22, August, 1977

[7.7.10] Priestley M, Evison R, Carr A: Seismic response of structures free to rock on their foundations, *Bulletin of the New Zealand National Society for Earthquake Engineering*, Vol. 11(3), 141-150, 1978

[7.7.11] Midorikawa M, Azuhata T, Ishihara T, Wada A: Shaking table tests on seismic response of steel braced frames with column uplift, *Journal of Earthquake Engineering and Structural Dynamics*, Vol.35, 17.77-1785, 2006

[7.7.12] Ikenaga M, Nagae T, Nakashima M, and Suita K: Development of Column Bases Having Self-Centering and Damping Capability" *Proceedings of the Fifth International Conference on Behaviour of Steel Structures in Seismic Areas STESSA 2006*, Yokohama, Japan, August 14-17, 2006, Taylor and Francis, London, U.K.

[7.7.13] Takamatsu T, Tamai H, Yamanishi T, Matsuo A: Rehabilitation of steel structure by means of wedge device, The 14th World Conference on Earthquake Engineering, 2008

[7.7.14] Takeuchi T, Suzuki K: Performance-based design for truss-frame structures using energy dissipation devices, STESSA, 2003

[7.7.15] Taga K, Koto M, Tokuda Y, Tsuruta J, Wada A: Hints on how to design passive control structure whose damper efficiency is enhanced, and practicality of this structure, *Proc. Passive Control Symposium 2004*, 105-112, Tokyo Tech, 2004.11

[7.7.16] Qu Z, Wada A, Motoyui S, Sakata H, Kishiki S: Pin-supported walls for enhancing the seismic performance of building structures. *Earthquake Engineering and Structural Dynamics* 2012; 41:2075-2091

[7.7.17] Janhunen B, Tipping S, Wolfe J, Mar T: Seismic Retrofit of a 1960s steel moment-frame highrise using a pivoting spine, *SEAOC 2013* Convention Proceedings

[7.7.18] Günay S, Korolyk M, Mar D, Mosalam K, Rodgers J: Infill Walls as a Spine to Enhance the Seismic Performance of Non-Ductile Reinforced Concrete Frames. *Improving the Seismic Performance of Existing Buildings and Other Structures*: 1093-1104, 2009

[7.7.19] Eatherton M., Hajjar J., Ma X., Krawinkler H., Deierlein G: Seismic Design and Behavior of Steel Frames with Controlled Rocking—Part I: Concepts and Quasi-Static Subassembly Testing. *ASCE Structures Congress 2010*, 1523-1533, 2010

[7.7.20] Eatherton M, Hajjar J: Residual drifts of self-centering systems including effects of ambient building resistance, *Earthquake Spectra*, Vol. 27 (3), 719-774, 2011

[7.7.21] Ma X., Eatherton M., Hajjar J., Krawinkler H., Deierlein G: Seismic Design and Behavior of Steel Frames with Controlled Rocking—Part II: Large Scale Shake Table Testing and System Collapse Analysis. Structures Congress 2010: 1534-1543, 2010

[7.7.22] Deierlein G, Ma X, Eatherton M, Hajjar J, Krawinkler H, Takeuchi T, Kasai K, Midorikawa M: Earthquake resilient steel braced frames with controlled rocking and energy dissipating fuses. *EUROSTEEL*, 2011

[7.7.23] Takeuchi T, Midorikawa M, Kasai K, Deierlein G, Ma X, Hajjar J, Hikino T. Shaking table test of controlled rocking frames using multipurpose test bed,

EUROSTEEL, 2011

[7.7.24] Lai J, Mahin S: Strongback system: A way to reduce damage concentration in steel-braced frames, *Journal of Structural Engineering*, Vol. 141(9), 2014

[7.7.25] Panian L, Bucci N, Janhunen B: BRBM Frames: An improved approach to seismic resistant design using buckling restrained braces, *2nd ATC Conference on Improving the Seismic Performance of Existing Buildings and Other Structures*, 2015.

[7.7.26] Takeuchi T, Chen X, Matsui R: Seismic performance of controlled spine frames with energy-dissipating members, *Journal of Constructional Steel Research*, Vol.115, 51-65, 2015.11

[7.7.27] Mazzoni S, McKenna F, Scott M, Fenves G: Open system for earthquake engineering simulations user command-language manual, September 2006.

[7.7.28] Vamvatsikos D, Cornell C: Incremental dynamic analysis, Journal of *Earthquake Engineering and Structural Dynamics*, Vol.31(3), 491-514, 2002

[7.7.29] Al-Ali A, Krawinkler H: Effects of vertical irregularities on seismic behavior of building structures, *Report No. 130, The John A. Blume Earthquake Engineering Center*, Department of Civil and Environmental Engineering, Stanford University, Stanford, U.S.A.

[7.7.30] Chintanapakdee C, Chopra A: Seismic response of vertically irregular frames: response history and modal pushover analyses, *Journal of Structural Engineering, ASCE*, Vol. 130, No. 8, pp. 1177-1185.

[7.7.31] Takeuchi T, Hiroshige K, Maehara K, Shibata M, Tsukamoto Y, Nousaku F: Structural design of low-rise building connecting core walls and soft frames with energy dissipation fuses. *AIJ Journal of Technology and Design*, Vol.22, Issue 51, 2016, pp.549-554. (in Japanese)

[7.7.32] Smith R, Willford M: The damped outrigger concept for tall buildings, *The Structural Design of Tall and Special Buildings*, Vol.16, 2007, pp.501-217.

[7.7.33] Huang B, Takeuchi T: Dynamic Response Evaluation of Damped-Outrigger Systems with Various Heights, *Earthquake Spectra*, 2017.

[7.7.34] Joseph LM, Gulec C, Schwaiger K, Justin M: Wilshire Grand: Outrigger Designs and Details for a Highly Seismic Site, *International Journal of High-Rise Buildings*, Vol.5, Issue 1, 2016, pp.1-12

Appendix

CHAPTER CONTENTS

A.1 TYPICAL BRB DETAILS

A.2 ROTATIONAL SPRING AT CONNECTIONS

A.3 BRB BUCKLING CAPACITY

A.4 Pδ MOMENT DISTRIBUTION AT CONNECTION ZONE

A.1 TYPICAL BRB DETAILS

Member List of Typical BRB

Bolted Plate (−) Type

The casing tube and plate sizes/grade shown below are examples only and actual sizes/grade may vary. Contact the BRB manufacturer for actual applications. Any unauthorized copy, reproduction, and use of this information are prohibited.

Member ID	Yield Force Ny (kN)	Yield Force Ny (kips)	Casing Tube (STK400)	Type	Core Plate Material	Ac (cm²)	t (mm)	WC (mm)	W2 (mm)	In the case of α=1.50 Allowable Buckling Length ℓb in (2.1.13) (m)
UB225-050-1	504	113	φ−216.3x4.5	−	LYP225 (σy=225 N/mm²)	22.4	16	140	185	6.42
UB225-075-1	748	168	φ−216.3x4.5			33.3	19	175	188	5.27
UB225-100-1	1020	229	φ−267.4x6.0			45.3	22	206	230	7.15
UB225-125-1	1249	281	φ−267.4x6.0			55.5	25	222	222	6.46
UB225-150-1	1498	337	φ−267.4x6.0			66.6	32	208	242	5.90
UB225-175-1	1750	393	φ−318.5x6.0			77.8	32	243	273	7.13
UB225-200-1	2002	450	φ−355.6x6.4			89.0	32	278	315	8.13
UB225-225-1	2246	505	φ−355.6x6.4			99.8	32	312	312	7.68
UB225-250-1	2495	561	φ−355.6x6.4			110.9	36	308	317	7.29
UB225-300-1	3006	676	φ−406.4x6.4			133.6	40	334	337	8.14
UB400-054-1	541	122	φ−216.3x4.5	−	SN400B (σy=235 N/mm²)	23.0	16	144	185	6.46
UB400-072-1	723	163	φ−216.3x4.5			30.8	19	162	188	5.59
UB400-090-2	902	203	φ−267.4x6.0			38.4	19	202	223	7.93
UB400-108-3	1085	244	φ−318.5x6.0			46.2	19	243	273	9.45
UB400-144-3	1442	324	φ−355.6x6.4			61.4	22	279	309	10.00
UB490-075-1	749	168	φ−216.3x4.5	−	SN490B (σy=325 N/mm²)	23.0	16	144	200	5.50
UB490-100-1	1000	225	φ−216.3x4.5			30.8	19	162	188	4.75
UB490-125-2	1260	283	φ−267.4x6.0			38.8	19	204	223	6.71
UB490-150-2	1507	339	φ−318.5x6.0			46.4	19	244	273	8.02
UB490-175-2	1759	395	φ−318.5x6.0			54.1	22	246	273	7.42
UB490-200-3	2002	450	φ−355.6x6.4			61.6	22	280	309	8.49
UB490-250-3	2503	563	φ−406.4x6.4			77.0	22	350	359	9.31

ELEVATION VIEW

PLAN VIEW

Section A

Appendix 225

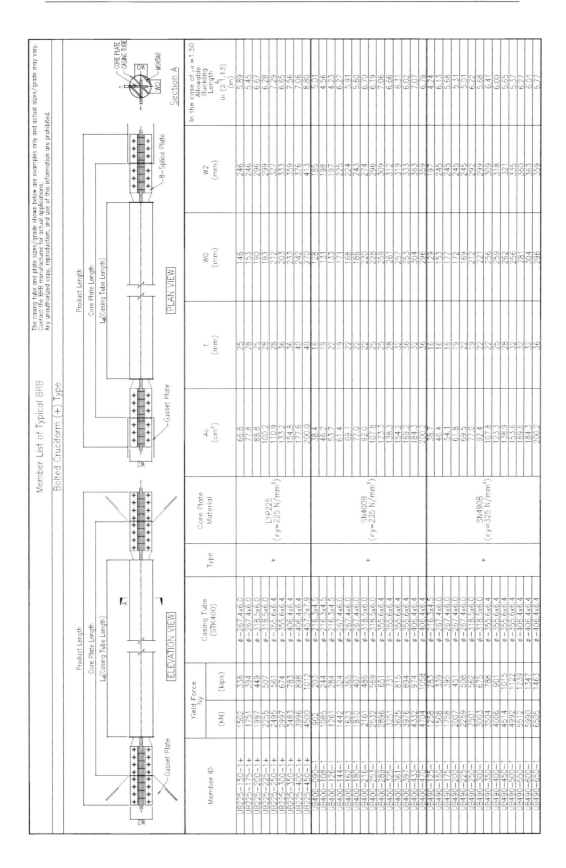

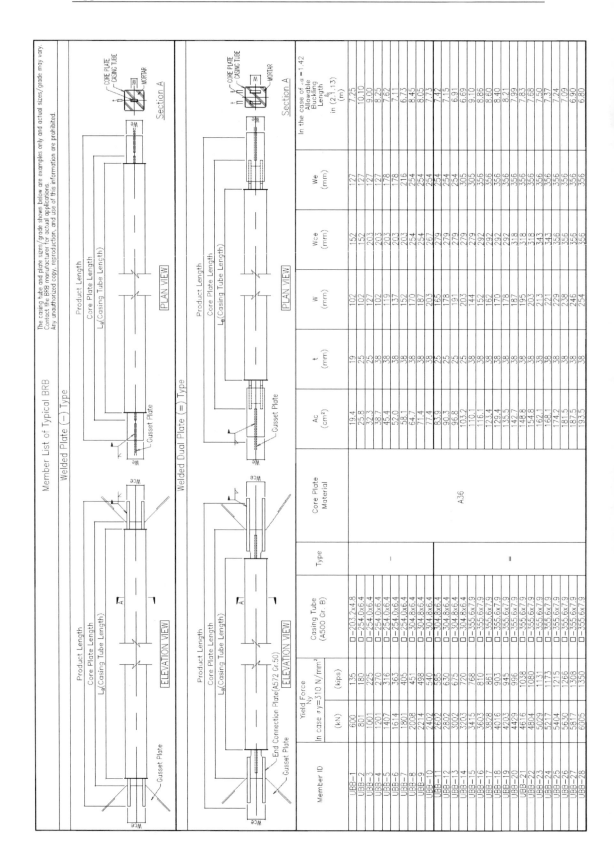

Member List of Typical BRB

Pinned Plate (–) Type

The casing tube and plate sizes/grade shown below are examples only and actual sizes/grade may vary.
Contact the BRB manufacturer for actual applications.
Any unauthorized copy, reproduction, and use of this information are prohibited.

Member ID	Yield Force N_y (In case σ_y=310 N/mm²)		Casing Tube (A53 Gr. B / API 5LB)	Core Plate Material	A_c (cm²)	t (mm)	W (mm)	W_t (mm)	W_2 (mm)	R_{d1} (mm)	L_{dp} (mm)	L_{ed} (mm)	Gusset Reinforcement (A572 Gr. 50) t_{gr} (mm)	Pin (A434 Gr. BD) d_p (mm)	In the case of a=1.42 Allowable Buckling Length l_b in (2.1.13) (m)
	(kN)	(kips)													
UBB-P3	600	135	φ-219.1×6.4	A36	19.4	19	102	152	89	127	76	102	10	50	7.20
UBB-P4	801	180	φ-219.1×6.4		25.8	25	102	165	108	133	79	105	10	56	6.25
UBB-P5	1001	225	φ-273.1×6.4		32.3	25	127	178	121	159	95	121	16	63	7.84
UBB-P6	1201	270	φ-273.1×6.4		38.7	25	152	206	121	184	114	140	16	69	7.16
UBB-P7	1407	316	φ-273.1×6.4		45.2	38	119	184	127	203	140	165	19	72	6.61
UBB-P8	1614	363	φ-323.9×6.4		51.6	38	137	197	140	203	165	191	19	82	8.00
UBB-P9	1801	405	φ-323.9×6.4		58.1	38	152	206	140	229	152	178	16	94	7.59
UBB-P10	2008	451	φ-323.9×6.4		64.5	38	170	225	146	241	165	191	19	94	7.19
UBB-P11	2214	498	φ-323.9×6.4		71.0	38	187	248	159	235	178	203	19	101	6.84
UBB-P12	2402	540	φ-323.9×6.4		77.4	38	203	270	171	248	197	222	25	101	7.58
UBB-P13	2608	586	φ-355.6×6.4		83.9	38	221	292	178	279	197	222	25	114	7.27
UBB-P14	2815	633	φ-355.6×6.4		90.3	38	238	314	178	286	197	222	25	114	7.00
UBB-P15	3021	679	φ-406.4×6.4		96.8	44	219	292	178	305	216	241	25	114	8.28
UBB-P16	3218	724	φ-406.4×6.4		103.2	44	233	311	191	305	229	254	25	126	8.02
UBB-P17	3415	768	φ-406.4×6.4		109.7	44	248	330	191	305	241	267	32	126	7.79
UBB-P18	3612	812	φ-406.4×6.4		116.1	44	262	346	203	378	267	292	32	126	7.57
UBB-P19	3809	856	φ-457.2×9.5		122.6	44	276	362	203	330	279	292	32	126	10.70
UBB-P20	4006	901	φ-457.2×9.5		129.0	44	291	381	203	356	305	305	32	139	10.40
UBB-P21	4203	945	φ-457.2×9.5		135.5	44	305	406	216	356	305	330	32	139	10.19

ELEVATION VIEW PLAN VIEW Section A

A.2 ROTATIONAL SPRING AT CONNECTIONS

The gusset rotational stiffness and strength is required for out-of-plane stability in Chapter 4. Kinoshita *et al.* [A2.1] proposed a simple method to determine the out-of-plane flexural stiffness and yield moment of stiffened gusset plates, assuming fixity at the beam/column flanges and stiffeners. This method is based on Rigid Body Spring Model (RBSM) of a quadrilateral plate proposed by Kawai [A2.2].

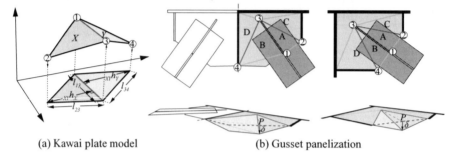

(a) Kawai plate model   (b) Gusset panelization

Figure A2.1 Model for gusset out-of-plane stiffness [A2.2]

For the quadrilateral plate with stiff edges shown in Figure A2.1(a), stiffness terms K_{11} and K_{22} correspond to the deflection from a coincident out-of-plane load at points 1 and 2, for Poisson's ratio v, modulus E and plate thickness t.

$$k_{XY} = \frac{2l_{13}}{{}_{XY}h_X + {}_{XY}h_Y} \cdot \frac{Et_g^3}{12(1-v^2)} \tag{A2.1}$$

$$K_{22} = \frac{k_{XY}}{{}_{XY}h_X^2}, \qquad K_{11} = k_{XY}\left(\frac{\sqrt{l_{23}^2 - {}_{XY}h_X^2}}{l_{13\,XY}h_X} + \frac{\sqrt{l_{34}^2 - {}_{XY}h_Y^2}}{l_{13\,XY}h_Y}\right)^2 \tag{A2.2}$$

Kinoshita applied these panel stiffness terms to the idealised gussets shown in Figure b), such that the out-of-plane rotational stiffness K_{Rg} may be calculated as:

$$K_{Rg} = l_{13}^2 \frac{P}{\delta} = l_{13}^2 \left(K_{AB} + K_{AC} + K_{BD}\right) \tag{A2.3}$$

where, $K_{AB} = \dfrac{2l_{13}}{{}_{AB}h_A + {}_{AB}h_B} \cdot \dfrac{Et_g^3}{12(1-v^2)} \cdot \left(\dfrac{\sqrt{l_{23}^2 - {}_{AB}h_A^2}}{l_{13}\cdot{}_{AB}h_A} + \dfrac{\sqrt{l_{34}^2 - {}_{AB}h_B^2}}{l_{13}\cdot{}_{AB}h_B}\right)^2$,

$$K_{AC} = \frac{2l_{23}}{{}_{AC}h_A + {}_{AC}h_C} \cdot \frac{Et_g^3}{12(1-v^2)} \cdot \frac{1}{{}_{AC}h_A^2}, \quad K_{BD} = \frac{2l_{34}}{{}_{BD}h_B + {}_{BD}h_D} \cdot \frac{Et_g^3}{12(1-v^2)} \cdot \frac{1}{{}_{BD}h_B^2} \tag{A2.4}$$

This can be further simplified by defining the internal angles θ_A and θ_B, panel aspect ratios AR_{AB}, AR_{AC}, and AR_{BD}, and plate stiffness D.

$$D = \frac{E t_g^3}{12(1-v^2)}, \quad |\cot\theta_A| = \frac{\sqrt{l_{23}^2 - {}_{AB}h_A^2}}{{}_{AB}h_A}, \quad |\cot\theta_B| = \frac{\sqrt{l_{34}^2 - {}_{AB}h_B^2}}{{}_{AB}h_B} \tag{A2.5}$$

$$AR_{AB} = \frac{l_{13}}{{}_{AB}h_A + {}_{AB}h_B}, \quad AR_{AC} = \frac{l_{23}}{{}_{AC}h_A + {}_{AC}h_C}, \quad AR_{BD} = \frac{l_{34}}{{}_{BD}h_B + {}_{BD}h_D} \tag{A2.6}$$

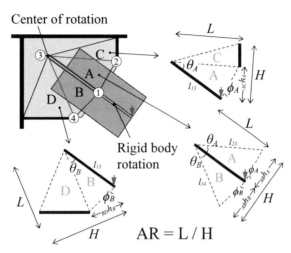

Figure A2.2 Simplified Kinoshita's Method

Substituting these into Equation A2.4 and assuming that each panel thickness is equal to t_g, the gusset rotational stiffness reduces to a compact equation that can be determined from simple geometric relationships:

$$K_{Rg} = DB_g = D \cdot 2\left(AR_{AB}\left(|\cot\theta_A| + |\cot\theta_B|\right)^2 + AR_{AC}\csc^2\theta_A + AR_{BD}\csc^2\theta_B \right) \tag{A2.7}$$

The yield moment under pure flexure is then given by:

$$M_y^g = \frac{t_g^2 f_y}{6} \cdot \frac{l_{13}}{l_{13}+l_j} \cdot l_{13} \left(\frac{\sqrt{l_{23}^2 - {}_{AB}h_A^2}}{{}_{AB}h_A} + \frac{\sqrt{l_{34}^2 - {}_{AB}h_B^2}}{{}_{AB}h_B} + \frac{l_{23}}{{}_{AC}h_A} + \frac{l_{34}}{{}_{BD}h_B} \right) \tag{A2.8}$$

While Kinoshita included the splice plate (acting non-compositely) when determining the panel thickness K_{AB}, this may conservatively be neglected. This method should be applied with caution to irregular gusset geometries resulting in panels with extreme aspect ratio. Refer to [A2.1, A2.2] for further details.

Furthermore, stiffeners are assumed effectively rigid and must be sensibly proportioned for both strength and stiffness. This can be achieved by ensuring the stiffness and yield moment exceeds that of the gusset plate itself:

$$M_y^{g,Stiffener} = \frac{\xi L_0}{h_v} \cdot \frac{B_s^2 t_s f_y}{6}, \frac{\xi L_0}{h_h} \cdot \frac{B_s^2 t_s f_y}{6} \tag{A2.9}$$

The rotational spring stiffness of the gusset plate, K_{Rg2}', and upper beam, K_{Rb}, in Chapter 4, Table 4.4.1 were obtained directly by experiments prior to specimen loading as shown in Figure A2.3. This includes the gusset plate deformation, the torsional stiffness of the main beam, the torsional stiffness given by rigidly connected secondary beams perpendicular to the main beam, the bending stiffness of the other BRB in tension, and the bending deformation of the main beam section along weak axis.

Also, an evaluation method for calculation of torsional stiffness of the main beam is proposed as follows in reference [A2.3], whose validity is confirmed by FEM analyses.

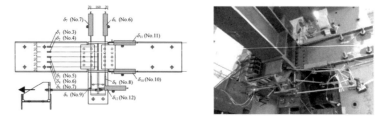

Figure A2.3 Experimental evaluation of rotational spring stiffness

The rotational springs of upper beams K_{Rb} can be derived as follows.

$$K_{Rb} = K_{RbT} + K_{RbSB} \tag{A2.10}$$

where, K_{RbT} is the torsional stiffness of the main beam the BRB is attached on, and K_{RbSB} is the torsional stiffness provided by the rigidly connected secondary beams perpendicular to the main beam. Equation (A2.11) neglects the bending stiffness of the other BRB in tension and the floor slab, and assumes that the main beam rotates in torsion as a rigid body. Assuming the beam has both torsion and warping end restraints, K_{RbT} can be estimated by the following equation.

$$K_{RbT} = \frac{GJv}{vl_G/2 - \tanh vl_G/2}, \quad v = \sqrt{\frac{GJ}{E\Gamma}} \tag{A2.11}$$

Where, l_G is the half length of attached main beam as shown in Figure A2.4, and GJ and $E\Gamma$ are Saint-Venant's torsional stiffness and bending torsional stiffness of the main beam, respectively.

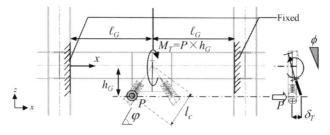

Figure A2.4 Rotational spring of attached beam

K_{RbSB} can be estimated by the following equation.

$$K_{RbSB} = \frac{3EI_{SB}}{l_{SB}}\left(\frac{l_c}{h_{SB}}\right)^2 \quad (A2.12)$$

where, l_{SB} is the length of secondary beam, EI_{SB} is bending stiffness of secondary beam, and h_{SB} is the vertical distance from the restrainer end to the center of the secondary beam as shown in Figure A2.5. l_c is the connection length along the brace from the center of the main beam as in Figure A2.4.

The above estimation formula can be used where the BRB connection point is placed at the center of the main beam, is detailed with stiffeners, and the vertical deflection of the other end of secondary beam is restrained. When a concrete floor slab is attached on the main beam, the above method gives conservative values. The method is also valid for situations requiring a large void adjacent to the main beam.

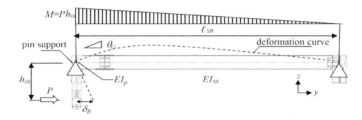

Figure A2.5 Effect of out-of-plane secondary beam

References

[A2.1] Kinoshita T, Koetaka Y, Inoue K, Iitani K. Out-of-plane stiffness and yield strength of cruciform connection for buckling-restrained brace. *AIJ J. of Struct. Constr. Eng.,* 2008; **73**(632):1865-1873. (*in Japanese*)

[A2.2] Kawai T, Kondou K. Collapse load analysis of bending plates by a new discrete model. *Journal of the Society of Naval Architects of Japan* 1977; **142**: 190-196. (in Japanese)

[A2.3] Ohyama S, Takeuchi T, et al. Stability assessment of buckling restrained braces taking connections into account, (part 15: calculation methods of rotational stiffness of brace connections in chevron configuration). *Summaries of technical papers of Annual Meeting Architectural Institute of Japan,* 2015; C-1, Structure III:1095–1096 *(in Japanese)*.

A.3 BRB BUCKLING CAPACITY

BRBs are generally not prismatic or flexurally continuous. An idealized model was proposed by (Takeuchi et al. 2014, 2016), where connection zone at each end and restrainer are modelled as prismatic elements with spring fixity at all four joints. This model will be retained for the following study.

Elastic Buckling Capacity

The elastic buckling capacity of a BRB can be derived using one of several methods, including:

- Differential equation method (Timoshenko and Gere 1963)
- Strain Energy method (Timoshenko and Gere 1963)
- Stability functions (Horne and Merchant 1965)
- Eigenanlysis in finite element software

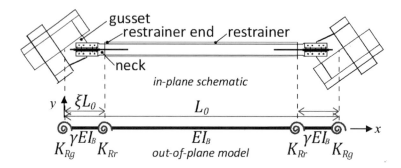

Figure A3.1 Simplified BRB stability model

In this analysis, the differential equation method will be used to extend the derivations presented in (Matsui et al. 2010). This method utilizes the general displacement function given by Equation (A3.1) and solves for α given the respective boundary conditions for the assumed mode shape using stability model as shown in A3.1. Instead of directly solving the unknowns $_iC_j$, the non-trivial solution requires that the determinate be equal to zero, with the modal buckling load the values of α satisfying this criteria.

$$y_i = {_iC_1}\sin\alpha x + {_iC_2}\cos\alpha x + {_iC_3}x + {_iC_4} \tag{A3.1}$$

$$\text{Where } \alpha = \sqrt{\frac{N}{EI_B}}$$

Generally this method results in transcendental equations, which must then be solved numerically, either by applying the Newton-Raphson method or by incrementally increasing N until the Equations (A3.4), or (A3.6) is satisfied. In the following, the process of deriving Equations (A3.4) and (A3.6) is introduced.

Note that when solving numerically, tangent functions should be avoided to prevent round-off errors.

1. Single Diagonal Symmetric Mode

The connection stiffness and length at each end is assumed to be the same. The following simplifying notion is used in the following derivations: (I_B, γ_J are described as I, γ)

$$S_1 = \sin \frac{\alpha}{\sqrt{\gamma}} \xi L_0; \quad C_1 = \cos \frac{\alpha}{\sqrt{\gamma}} \xi L_0$$

$$S_2 = \sin \alpha \xi L_0; \quad C_2 = \cos \alpha \xi L_0$$

$$S_3 = \sin \alpha \tfrac{L_0}{2}; \quad C_3 = \cos \alpha \tfrac{L_0}{2}$$

$$S_4 = \sin \alpha L_0 \left(\tfrac{1}{2} - \xi\right); \quad C_4 = \cos \alpha L_0 \left(\tfrac{1}{2} - \xi\right)$$

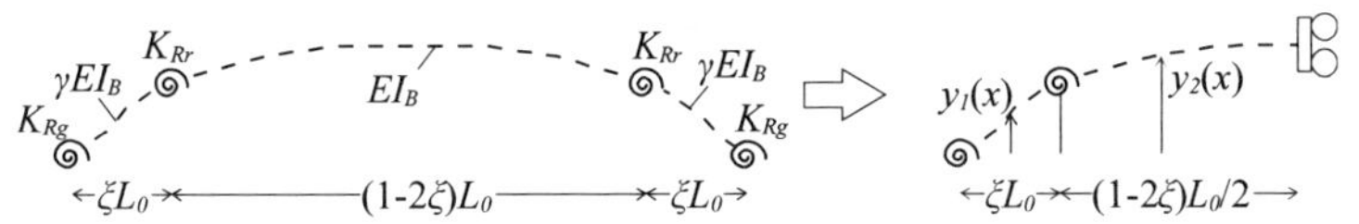

Figure A3.2 Symmetric mode shape

The lateral displacement along the connection and restrainer segments are given by:

$$y_1 = {}_1 C_1 \sin \frac{\alpha}{\sqrt{\gamma}} x + {}_1 C_2 \cos \frac{\alpha}{\sqrt{\gamma}} x + {}_1 C_3 x + {}_1 C_4$$

$$y_2 = {}_2 C_1 \sin \alpha x + {}_2 C_2 \cos \alpha x + {}_2 C_3 x + {}_2 C_4$$

Support, continuity and symmetry boundary conditions give:

Type	Condition	Displacement Equation
Boundary conditions at $x = 0$		
1: Displacement	$y_1 = 0$	${}_1 C_2 + {}_1 C_4 = 0$
2: Moment	$\gamma EI_B \frac{d^2 y_1}{dx^2} = K_{Rg} \frac{dy_1}{dx}$	$\frac{K_{Rg}\alpha}{\sqrt{\gamma}} {}_1 C_1 + \alpha^2 EI_r {}_1 C_2 + K_{Rg} {}_1 C_3 = 0$
Continuity conditions at $x = \xi L_0$		
3: Displacement	$y_1 = y_2$	$S_1 {}_1 C_1 + C_1 {}_1 C_2 + \xi L_0 {}_1 C_3 + {}_1 C_4$ $-S_2 {}_2 C_1 - C_2 {}_2 C_2 - \xi L_0 {}_2 C_3 - {}_2 C_4 = 0$
4: Shear	$N \frac{dy_1}{dx} + \gamma EI_B \frac{d^3 y_1}{dx^3} = N \frac{dy_2}{dx} + EI_B \frac{d^3 y_2}{dx^3}$	${}_1 C_3 - {}_2 C_3 = 0$
5: Moment	$-\gamma EI_B \frac{d^2 y_1}{dx^2} = K_{Rr}\left(\frac{dy_1}{dx} - \frac{dy_2}{dx}\right)$	$\left(\alpha^2 EI_B S_1 - \frac{K_{Rr}\alpha}{\sqrt{\gamma}} C_1\right) {}_1 C_1 + \left(\alpha^2 EI_B C_1 + \frac{K_{Rr}\alpha}{\sqrt{\gamma}} S_1\right) {}_1 C_2$ $-K_{Rr} {}_1 C_3 + K_{Rr}\alpha C_2 {}_2 C_1 - K_{Rr}\alpha S_2 {}_2 C_2 + K_{Rr} {}_2 C_3 = 0$
6: Moment	$-EI_B \frac{d^2 y_2}{dx^2} = K_{Rr}\left(\frac{dy_1}{dx} - \frac{dy_2}{dx}\right)$	$-\frac{K_{Rr}\alpha}{\sqrt{\gamma}} C_1 {}_1 C_1 + \frac{K_{Rr}\alpha}{\sqrt{\gamma}} S_1 {}_1 C_2$ $-K_{Rr} {}_1 C_3 + \left(\alpha^2 EI_B S_2 + K_{Rr}\alpha C_2\right) {}_2 C_1$ $+\left(\alpha^2 EI_B C_2 - K_{Rr}\alpha S_2\right) {}_2 C_2 + K_{Rr} {}_2 C_3 = 0$
Symmetry conditions at $x = L_0/2$		
7: Rotation	$\frac{dy_2}{dx} = 0$	$\alpha C_3 {}_2 C_1 - \alpha S_3 {}_2 C_2 + {}_2 C_3 = 0$
8: Shear	$EI_B \frac{d^3 y_2}{dx^3} = 0$	$-C_3 {}_2 C_1 + S_3 {}_2 C_2 = 0$

234   Appendix

These simultaneous equations are assembled in matrix form and the following row operations applied, where [i] represents equation i from the above table:

From (4)+(7)+α(8), $_1C_3$=0

From (7)+α(8), $_2C_3$=0

2': For $_1C_3$=0, (2) becomes $\frac{K_{Rg}}{\sqrt{\gamma}}\,_1C_1 + \alpha EI_B\,_1C_2 = 0$

3': From -(3)+(5)-(6)+(1), $_1C_2$+$_2C_4$=0

4': From (5)-K_{Rr}(4),

$$\left(\alpha EI_B S_1 - \frac{K_{Rr}}{\sqrt{\gamma}}C_1\right)_1 C_1 + \left(\alpha EI_B C_1 + \frac{K_{Rr}}{\sqrt{\gamma}}S_1\right)_1 C_2 + K_{Rr}C_2\,_2C_1 - K_{Rr}S_2\,_2C_2 = 0$$

5': From (5)-(6), $-S_1\,_1C_1 - C_1\,_1C_2 + S_2\,_2C_1 + C_2\,_2C_2 = 0$

6': From (8), $-C_3\,_2C_1 + S_3\,_2C_2 = 0$

The matrix simplifies to:

$$
\left\{
\begin{matrix}
0 & 1 & 1 & 0 & 0 & 0 \\
\frac{K_{Rg}}{\sqrt{\gamma}} & \alpha EI_B & 0 & 0 & 0 & 0 \\
0 & 1 & 0 & 0 & 0 & 1 \\
\alpha EI_B S_1 - \frac{K_{Rr}}{\sqrt{\gamma}}C_1 & \alpha EI_B C_1 + \frac{K_{Rr}}{\sqrt{\gamma}}S_1 & 0 & K_{Rr}C_2 & -K_{Rr}S_2 & 0 \\
-S_1 & -C_1 & 0 & S_2 & C_2 & 0 \\
0 & 0 & 0 & -C_3 & S_3 & 0
\end{matrix}
\right\}
\left\{
\begin{matrix}
_1C_1 \\ _1C_2 \\ _1C_4 \\ _2C_1 \\ _2C_2 \\ _2C_4
\end{matrix}
\right\} = \{0\}
\qquad (A3.3)
$$

For a non-trivial result, the determinate must equal zero. Through static condensation this can be solved analytically, resulting in:

$$\alpha^2 (EI_B)^2 S_1 C_4 + \alpha EI_B \left(K_{Rr} S_1 S_4 - \frac{K_{Rg} + K_{Rr}}{\sqrt{\gamma_J}} C_1 C_4 \right) - K_{Rg} K_{Rr} \left(\frac{1}{\gamma_J} S_1 C_4 + \frac{1}{\sqrt{\gamma_J}} C_1 S_4 \right) = 0 \quad (A3.4)$$

To determine the critical elastic buckling load of the symmetric mode, solve for the lowest value of α satisfying Equation (A3.4).

Appendix   235

2. Single Diagonal Anti-symmetric Mode

Just as for the symmetric mode, the connection stiffness and length at each end is assumed to be the same. However, the mode shape is forced into an anti-symmetric pattern.

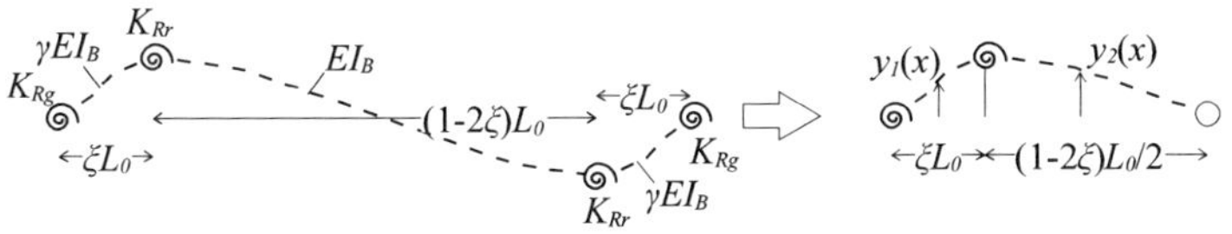

Figure A3.1 Anti-symmetric mode shape

The displacement equations, and support and continuity boundary conditions are unchanged, but the symmetry condition is modified:

Type	Condition	Displacement Equation
Boundary conditions at $x = 0$		
1: Displacement	$y_1 = 0$	$_1C_2 + {_1}C_4 = 0$
2: Moment	$\gamma EI_B \frac{d^2 y_1}{dx^2} = K_{Rg}\frac{dy_1}{dx}$	$\frac{K_{Rg}\alpha}{\sqrt{\gamma}} {_1}C_1 + \alpha^2 EI_B {_1}C_2 + K_{Rg} {_1}C_3 = 0$
Continuity conditions at $x = \xi L_0$		
3: Displacement	$y_1 = y_2$	$S_1 {_1}C_1 + C_1 {_1}C_2 + \xi L_0 {_1}C_3 + {_1}C_4$ $-S_2 {_2}C_1 - C_2 {_2}C_2 - \xi L_0 {_2}C_3 - {_2}C_4 = 0$
4: Shear	$N\frac{dy_1}{dx} + \gamma EI_B\frac{d^3 y_1}{dx^3} = N\frac{dy_2}{dx} + EI_B\frac{d^3 y_2}{dx^3}$	$_1C_3 - {_2}C_3 = 0$
5: Moment	$-\gamma EI_B\frac{d^2 y_1}{dx^2} = K_{Rr}\left(\frac{dy_1}{dx} - \frac{dy_2}{dx}\right)$	$\left(\alpha^2 EI_B S_1 - \frac{K_{Rr}\alpha}{\sqrt{\gamma}}C_1\right){_1}C_1 + \left(\alpha^2 EI_B C_1 + \frac{K_{Rr}\alpha}{\sqrt{\gamma}}S_1\right){_1}C_2$ $-K_{Rr} {_1}C_3 + K_{Rr}\alpha C_2 {_2}C_1 - K_{Rr}\alpha S_2 {_2}C_2 + K_{Rr} {_2}C_3 = 0$
6: Moment	$-EI_B\frac{d^2 y_2}{dx^2} = K_{Rr}\left(\frac{dy_1}{dx} - \frac{dy_2}{dx}\right)$	$-\frac{K_{Rr}\alpha}{\sqrt{\gamma}}C_1 {_1}C_1 + \frac{K_{Rr}\alpha}{\sqrt{\gamma}}S_1 {_1}C_2$ $-K_{Rr} {_1}C_3 + \left(\alpha^2 EI_B S_2 + K_{Rr}\alpha C_2\right){_2}C_1$ $+\left(\alpha^2 EI_B C_2 - K_{Rr}\alpha S_2\right){_2}C_2 + K_{Rr} {_2}C_3 = 0$
Symmetry conditions at $x = L_0/2$		
7: Displacement	$y_2 = 0$	$S_3 {_2}C_1 + C_3 {_2}C_2 + \frac{L_0}{2} {_2}C_3 + {_2}C_4 = 0$
8: Moment	$EI_B\frac{d^2 y_2}{dx^2} = 0$	$-S_3 {_2}C_1 - C_3 {_2}C_2 = 0$

These simultaneous equations can be solved by assembling in matrix formulation and applying the following row operations.

2': From $[(2)-K_{Rg}(4)]L_0-2(7')$, $\frac{K_{Rg}\alpha}{\sqrt{\gamma}}L_0 {_1}C_1 + \left(\alpha^2 EI_B L_0 + 2K_{Rg}\right){_1}C_2 = 0$

3': From $-(3)+(5)-(6)+(1)$, $_1C_2 + {_2}C_4 = 0$

5': From $(5)-K_{Rr}(4)$,

$$\left(\alpha EI_B S_1 - \frac{K_{Rr}}{\sqrt{\gamma}}C_1\right){_1}C_1 + \left(\alpha EI_B C_1 + \frac{K_{Rr}}{\sqrt{\gamma}}S_1\right){_1}C_2 + K_{Rr}C_2 {_2}C_1 - K_{Rr}S_2 {_2}C_2 = 0$$

6': From $(5)-(6)$, $-S_1 {_1}C_1 - C_1 {_1}C_2 + S_2 {_2}C_1 + C_2 {_2}C_2 = 0$

7': From $(7)+(8)-(3')$, $-_1C_2 + \frac{L_0}{2} {_2}C_3 = 0$

Appendix

The matrix simplifies to:

$$
\begin{bmatrix}
0 & 1 & 0 & 1 & 0 & 0 & 0 & 0 \\
\frac{K_{Rr}\alpha}{\sqrt{\gamma}}L_0 & \alpha^2 EI_B L_0 + 2K_{Rg} & 0 & 0 & 0 & 0 & 0 & 0 \\
0 & 1 & 0 & 0 & 0 & 0 & 0 & 1 \\
0 & 0 & 1 & 0 & 0 & 0 & -1 & 0 \\
\alpha EI_B S_1 - \frac{K_{Rr}}{\sqrt{\gamma}}C_1 & \alpha EI_B C_1 + \frac{K_{Rr}}{\sqrt{\gamma}}S_1 & 0 & 0 & K_{Rr}C_2 & -K_{Rr}S_2 & 0 & 0 \\
-S_1 & -C_1 & 0 & 0 & S_2 & C_2 & 0 & 0 \\
0 & -1 & 0 & 0 & 0 & 0 & \frac{L_0}{2} & 0 \\
0 & 0 & 0 & 0 & -S_3 & -C_3 & 0 & 0
\end{bmatrix}
\begin{Bmatrix}
{}_1C_1 \\ {}_1C_2 \\ {}_1C_3 \\ {}_1C_4 \\ {}_2C_1 \\ {}_2C_2 \\ {}_2C_3 \\ {}_2C_4
\end{Bmatrix} = 0
\qquad (A3.5)
$$

For a non-trivial result, the determinate must equal zero. Through static condensation this can be solved analytically, resulting in:

$$
\alpha^3 (EI_B)^2 L_0 S_1 S_4 - \alpha^2 EI_B L_0 \left(K_{Rr} S_1 C_4 + \frac{K_{Rg} + K_{Rr}}{\sqrt{\gamma_J}}C_1 S_4 \right) + 2\alpha EI_B K_{Rg} S_1 S_4
$$

$$
+ \alpha K_{Rg} K_{Rr} L_0 \left(\frac{1}{\sqrt{\gamma_J}}C_1 C_4 - \frac{1}{\gamma_J}S_1 S_4 \right) - 2K_{Rg} K_{Rr} \left(S_1 C_4 + \frac{1}{\sqrt{\gamma_J}}C_1 S_4 \right) = 0
\qquad (A3.6)
$$

To determine the critical elastic buckling load of the anti-symmetric mode, solve for the lowest value of α satisfying Equation (A3.6).

A.4 Pδ MOMENT DISTRIBUTION AT CONNECTION ZONE

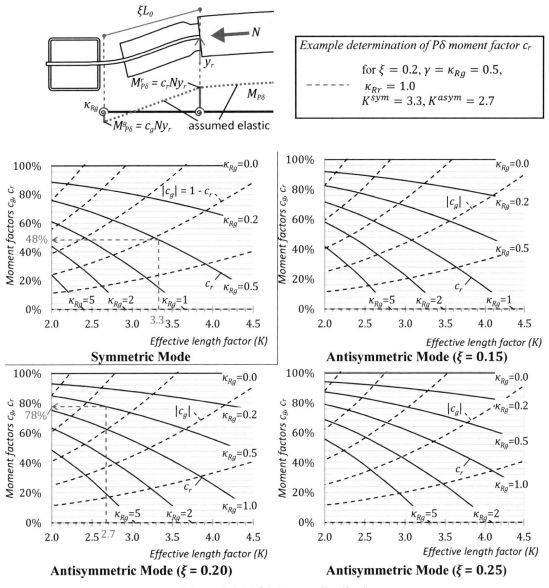

Figure A4.1 Pδ Moment distribution

NAME INDEX

Aiken I	5
Akiyama H	93, 97
Berman J	50, 83
Bruneau M	50, 54, 83, 202
Celik OC	169, 202
Clark P	5
Chou CC	50, 83, 173
Christopulos A	50
Cofin LF	88
Connor J	124
Deierlein G	207
Eatherton M	207
Fahnestock L	83
Fujimoto M	3
Fujishita K	169
Gu LZ	173
Hajjar JF	33, 44, 207
Hasegawa H	91
Hikino T	50, 55
Inoue K	28, 50, 54
Ishii T	175
Iwata M	4, 6, 29, 124, 147
Kajiwara K	50
Kasai K	83, 134, 135
Kato B	93
Kawai H	124
Kishiki S	173
Kimura I	5
Kimura K	3
Kinoshita T	228
Ko E	5
Koetaka Y	29, 50, 54
Lin PC	26, 29, 83
Maeda Y	88, 103
Mahin S	206
Matsui R	50, 58, 64, 101
Manson SS	88
Menegotto M	22, 103
Midorikawa M	29, 205
Motizuki S	3
Murai M	6, 29
Muto K	125
Muir L	83
Nakagomi T	88
Nakashima M	13
Nakamura H	54, 103
Newmark NM	134

Nishimoto K	26, 44, 108
Okazaki T	55
Okamoto Y	29
Ozaki H	61
Palmer K	50, 83
Pinto PE	22,103
Priestley MJN	172
Qu Z	179, 184, 205
Rousenblueth E	134
Sabelli E	177
Saeki E	3, 49
Sakata H	179, 184, 205
Sitler B	86
Sutcu F	157, 169
Suzuki K	89
Takeda T	3, 158
Takeuchi T	4, 26, 50, 61, 147, 190, 206
Taga K	206
Tavernelli JF	88
Tsai KC	26, 50, 54, 173
Usami T	202
Uriz P	50, 82
Wada A	3, 4, 13, 103, 108, 124, 205
Wakabayashi M	3
Walters M	50
Watanabe A	3, 124
Wigle VR	50, 83
Wu AC	26
Yamada S	89
Yoshida F	29

SUBJECT INDEX

Absorbed energy	98, 134, 159
Bridge structure	202
Buckling-restrained brace	2
Chevron configuration	70, 81, 114
Clearance between core and restrainer	13, 17, 101
Connection	48, 52, 83, 224, 228
Core plate	2, 7, 12, 27, 44, 103
Cumulative deformation	88, 117
Cumulative dissipated energy	97
Cyclic loading test	33, 65, 74, 91, 112
Damage tolerant concept	5, 124
Damped outrigger	218
Debonding gap	17, 101
Damper distributions	139, 142, 163
Earthquake engineering	v, 124
Elastic buckling capacity	79, 232
Equivalent damping ratio	138, 161
Global instability	49
Great Hanshin Earthquake 1995	205
Great Tohoku Earthquake 2011	119
Gymnasium	197
History of development	3
Hysteresis model	23
Inclined test	113
In-frame test	114
Inspection	120
Initial imperfections	13, 57, 113
In-plane deformation	81
Isotropic hardening	21
Kinematic hardening	21
Local buckling	2, 26
Local bulging	26
Loading protocol	114
Low-cycle fatigue	88
Manson-Coffin coefficients	88
Miner's rule	90
Mortar Strength	43
One-way configuration	57, 81
Out-of-plane deformation	49, 57, 113
Overstrength factor	18
Performance test	112
Rain flow method	89
Reinforced concrete	172
Residual deformation	168, 213, 216
Response evaluation	133, 157
Restrainer	12
Rotational spring at connection	51, 57, 72, 78, 228

Seismic retrofit	147, 157
Single brace test	112
Steel material	18
Stiffness of BRB	19, 133, 138, 162
Rocking frame	205, 207
Roof structure	191, 196
Self-centering	205, 212
Spine frame	205
Truss structure	190, 192
Uniaxial test	112
Yield line theory	30, 228